YOUR MOST COMPREHENSIVE AND REVEALING INDIVIDUAL FORECAST

SUPER HOROSCOPE

SCORPIO 1998

October 23 – November 22

B

BERKLEY BOOKS, NEW YORK

The publishers regret that they cannot answer
individual letters requesting personal horoscope information.

1998 SUPER HOROSCOPE SCORPIO

PRINTING HISTORY
BERKLEY TRADE EDITION / AUGUST 1997

ISBN: 0-425-15893-4

PRINTED IN THE UNITED STATES OF AMERICA

10 9 8 7 6 5 4 3 2 1

CONTENTS

THE CUSP-BORN SCORPIO

Are you *really* a Scorpio? If your birthday falls during the third to fourth week of October, at the beginning of Scorpio, will you still retain the traits of Libra, the sign of the Zodiac before Scorpio? And what if you were born late in November—are you more Sagittarius than Scorpio? Many people born at the edge, or cusp, of a sign have difficulty determining exactly what sign they are. If you are one of these people, here's how you can figure it out, once and for all.

Consult the cusp table on the facing page, then locate the year of your birth. The table will tell you the precise days on which the Sun entered and left your sign for the year of your birth. In that way you can determine if you are a true Scorpio—or whether you are a Libra or Sagittarius—according to the variations in cusp dates from year to year (see also page 17).

If you were born at the beginning or end of Scorpio, yours is a lifetime reflecting a process of subtle transformation. Your life on Earth will symbolize a significant change in consciousness, for you are either about to enter a whole new way of living or are leaving one behind.

If you were born at the beginning of Scorpio, you may want to read the horoscope book for Libra as well as Scorpio, for Libra holds the keys to much of the complexity of your spirit and reflects many of your hidden weaknesses, secret sides, and unspoken wishes.

You have a keen way of making someone feel needed and desired, whether you care deeply or not. Sex is a strong directive in your life and you could turn your talents toward superficiality in relationships, merely winning people over with your sexual magnetism and sheer magic. You can love with an almost fatal obsession, a bigger-than-both-of-you type thing, where you will blind your eyes to facts to keep the peace in a relationship—then suddenly declare war.

No one in the whole Zodiac is as turned on to the passions of life as you. You can survive any crisis, for deep in your spirit lie the seeds of immortality and you know it. Above all you are the symbol that life goes on—the personification of awakening desire and passion.

If you were born at the end of Scorpio, you may want to read the horoscope book for Sagittarius as well as Scorpio. You are the symbol of the human mind awakening to its higher capabilities. What you are leaving behind is greed, blind desire, and shallow lust, as you awaken to your own ability to learn, create, understand.

You want to travel, see new places, see how people live, figure yourself out, acquire knowledge—yet you are often not quite ready to take the plunge. When you shift your behavior patterns significantly and permanently, new worlds open up and you turn on to immortality and the infinite possibilities of your own mind.

THE CUSPS OF SCORPIO

DATES SUN ENTERS SCORPIO (LEAVES LIBRA)

October 23 every year from 1900 to 2000, except for the following:

October 22	October 24			
1992	1902	1911	1923	1943
96	03	14	27	47
	06	15	31	51
	07	18	35	55
	10	19	39	59

DATES SUN LEAVES SCORPIO (ENTERS SAGITTARIUS)

November 22 every year from 1900 to 2000, except for the following:

November 21		November 23		
1976	1992	1902	1915	1931
80	93	03	19	35
84	96	07	23	39
88		10	27	43
		11		

THE ASCENDANT: SCORPIO RISING

Could you be a "double" Scorpio? That is, could you have Scorpio as your Rising sign as well as your Sun sign? The tables on pages 8–9 will tell you Scorpios what your Rising sign happens to be. Just find the hour of your birth, then find the day of your birth, and you will see which sign of the Zodiac is your Ascendant, as the Rising sign is called. The Ascendant is called that because it is the sign rising on the eastern horizon at the time of your birth. For a more detailed discussion of the Rising sign and the twelve houses of the Zodiac, see pages 17–20.

The Ascendant, or Rising sign, is placed on the 1st house in a horoscope, of which there are twelve houses. The 1st house represents your response to the environment—your unique response. Call it identity, personality, ego, self-image, facade, come-on, body-mind-spirit—whatever term best conveys to you the meaning of the you that acts and reacts in the world. It is a you that is always changing, discovering a new you. Your identity started with birth and early environment, over which you had little conscious control, and continues to experience, to adjust, to express itself. The 1st house also represents how others see you. Has anyone ever guessed your sign to be your Rising sign? People may respond to that personality, that facade, that body type governed by your Rising sign.

Your Ascendant, or Rising sign, modifies your basic Sun sign personality, and it affects the way you act out the daily predictions for your Sun sign. If your Rising sign is indeed Scorpio, what follows is a description of its effects on your horoscope. If your Rising sign is not Scorpio, but some other sign of the Zodiac, you may wish to read the horoscope book for that sign as well.

With Scorpio on your Ascendant, that is, in the 1st house, the planets rising in the 1st house are Mars and Pluto, the rulers of Scorpio. You have here the tremendous energy of Mars and the implacable avenging power of Pluto, which together make you a tower of forcefulness in whatever you choose to do. Mars accentuates action; Pluto signifies spiritual development. These tendencies combined for Scorpio, an emotional, fixed sign, could make you a bold crusader for truth, a relentless foe of injustice. On the other hand, this placement could make you bitter, sarcastic, vengeful, and incapable of controlling destructive impulses toward the self as well as society.

There may be dramatic extremes in the conduct of your life. You will relentlessly pursue a goal, be consumed by it, seemingly drop it, then move on to a new sphere of endeavor and influence. Pluto, the planet of transformation, emphasizes beginnings and endings in a continuum of development. The marked variations in your lifestyle may be an expression of that cycle of change. Your capacity to learn from experience is immense, for it is a learning informed by your whole being, not just the intellect. You sense all of reality. The lessons you learn from your experience enable you to rise to great positions during a lifetime.

Control is a byword for Scorpio Rising. Whether it is control over the self, control over others, or control through others, you have a deep-seated need to dominate. You are a great strategist when it comes to gaining social control. Among your arsenal of weapons are such contradictory traits as subtlety, intensity, self-ishness, self-sacrifice, ruthlessness, possessiveness, aloofness, impulsiveness, determination. Closely linked to your need for control is your love of power. You have enough passion and endurance to attain power, as well as to use it to change the environment in accord with your inner dictates.

As much as you like to dominate, you hate being dominated. You will go to great lengths to escape being trapped in a chafing relationship or situation. People often see you as perverse and self-seeking, ready for flight or fight. You also hate to lose, whether your conquest is a lover, an argument, or a cause. Your anger and jealousy are well known. You get deeply involved, though your social manner is not very personal. You have a penchant for solitude and secretiveness, which make people think you are introverted and shy—until they get to know you.

Your potential for inner growth and external change is almost unlimited. A constantly developing spiritual component imposes itself on your personality and, through it, on the world. You can be in touch, so to speak, with the more mysterious forces of the universe. Your energy and drive are rooted in the psychosexual nature of humankind, which is indeed a basic, pervasive organizer of all human effort and thought. On an operational level, your initiative and inventiveness give you a practical side that often obscures the depths of your being.

Stamina and transformation are two key words for Scorpio Rising. You can change situations for good or bad, for greedy, selfish motives, or for an enlightened mode of survival and struggle.

RISING SIGNS FOR SCORPIO

Hour of Birth*	Day of Birth		
	October 23–27	October 28–31	November 1–5
Midnight	Leo	Leo	Leo
1 AM	Leo	Leo; Virgo 10/30	Virgo
2 AM	Virgo	Virgo	Virgo
3 AM	Virgo	Virgo	Virgo; Libra 11/5
4 AM	Libra	Libra	Libra
5 AM	Libra	Libra	Libra
6 AM	Libra	Libra; Scorpio 10/30	Scorpio
7 AM	Scorpio	Scorpio	Scorpio
8 AM	Scorpio	Scorpio	Scorpio
9 AM	Sagittarius	Sagittarius	Sagittarius
10 AM	Sagittarius	Sagittarius	Sagittarius
11 AM	Sagittarius	Capricorn	Capricorn
Noon	Capricorn	Capricorn	Capricorn
1 PM	Capricorn; Aquarius 10/26	Aquarius	Aquarius
2 PM	Aquarius	Aquarius	Pisces
3 PM	Pisces	Pisces	Pisces; Aries 11/5
4 PM	Aries	Aries	Aries
5 PM	Aries; Taurus 10/26	Taurus	Taurus
6 PM	Taurus	Taurus	Gemini
7 PM	Gemini	Gemini	Gemini
8 PM	Gemini	Gemini	Cancer
9 PM	Cancer	Cancer	Cancer
10 PM	Cancer	Cancer	Cancer
11 PM	Leo	Leo	Leo

*Hour of birth given here is for Standard Time in any time zone. If your hour of birth was recorded in Daylight Saving Time, subtract one hour from it and consult that hour in the table above. For example, if you were born at 7 AM D.S.T., see 6 AM above.

Hour of Birth	Day of Birth		
	November 6–11	November 12–16	November 17–23
Midnight	Leo	Leo; Virgo 11/15	Virgo
1 AM	Virgo	Virgo	Virgo
2 AM	Virgo	Virgo	Virgo; Libra 11/21
3 AM	Libra	Libra	Libra
4 AM	Libra	Libra	Libra
5 AM	Libra	Libra; Scorpio 11/14	Scorpio
6 AM	Scorpio	Scorpio	Scorpio
7 AM	Scorpio	Scorpio	Scorpio; Sagittarius 11/21
8 AM	Sagittarius	Sagittarius	Sagittarius
9 AM	Sagittarius	Sagittarius	Sagittarius
10 AM	Sagittarius	Capricorn	Capricorn
11 AM	Capricorn	Capricorn	Capricorn
Noon	Capricorn; Aquarius 11/10	Aquarius	Aquarius
1 PM	Aquarius	Aquarius	Pisces
2 PM	Pisces	Pisces	Pisces; Aries 11/21
3 PM	Aries	Aries	Aries
4 PM	Aries	Taurus	Taurus
5 PM	Taurus	Taurus	Gemini
6 PM	Gemini	Gemini	Gemini
7 PM	Gemini	Gemini; Cancer 11/16	Cancer
8 PM	Cancer	Cancer	Cancer
9 PM	Cancer	Cancer	Cancer; Leo 11/22
10 PM	Leo	Leo	Leo
11 PM	Leo	Leo	Leo

THE PLACE OF ASTROLOGY IN TODAY'S WORLD

Does astrology have a place in the fast-moving, ultra-scientific world we live in today? Can it be justified in a sophisticated society whose outriders are already preparing to step off the moon into the deep space of the planets themselves? Or is it just a hangover of ancient superstition, a psychological dummy for neurotics and dreamers of every historical age?

These are the kind of questions that any inquiring person can be expected to ask when they approach a subject like astrology which goes beyond, but never excludes, the materialistic side of life.

The simple, single answer is that astrology works. It works for many millions of people in the western world alone. In the United States there are 10 million followers and in Europe, an estimated 25 million. America has more than 4000 practicing astrologers, Europe nearly three times as many. Even down-under Australia has its hundreds of thousands of adherents. In the eastern countries, astrology has enormous followings, again, because it has been proved to work. In India, for example, brides and grooms for centuries have been chosen on the basis of their astrological compatibility.

Astrology today is more vital than ever before, more practicable because all over the world the media devotes much space and time to it, more valid because science itself is confirming the precepts of astrological knowledge with every new exciting step. The ordinary person who daily applies astrology intelligently does not have to wonder whether it is true nor believe in it blindly. He can see it working for himself. And, if he can use it—and this book is designed to help the reader to do just that—he can make living a far richer experience, and become a more developed personality and a better person.

Astrology and Relationships

Astrology is the science of relationships. It is not just a study of planetary influences on man and his environment. It is the study of man himself.

We are at the center of our personal universe, of all our relationships. And our happiness or sadness depends on how we act, how we relate to the people and things that surround us. The emotions that we generate have a distinct effect—for better or worse—on the world around us. Our friends and our enemies will confirm this. Just look in the mirror the next time you are angry. In other words, each of us is a kind of sun or planet or star radiating our feelings on the environment around us. Our influence on our personal universe, whether loving, helpful, or destructive, varies with our changing moods, expressed through our individual character.

Our personal "radiations" are potent in the way they affect our moods and our ability to control them. But we usually are able to throw off our emotion in some sort of action—we have a good cry, walk it off, or tell someone our troubles—before it can build up too far and make us physically ill. Astrology helps us to understand the universal forces working on us, and through this understanding, we can become more properly adjusted to our surroundings so that we find ourselves coping where others may flounder.

The Challenge of Love

The challenge of love lies in recognizing the difference between infatuation, emotion, sex, and, sometimes, the intentional deceit of the other person. Mankind, with its record of broken marriages, despair, and disillusionment, is obviously not very good at making these distinctions.

Can astrology help?

Yes. In the same way that advance knowledge can usually help in any human situation. And there is probably no situation as human, as poignant, as pathetic and universal, as the failure of man's love.

Love, of course, is not just between man and woman. It involves love of children, parents, home, and friends. But the big problems usually involve the choice of partner.

Astrology has established degrees of compatibility that exist between people born under the various signs of the Zodiac. Because people are individuals, there are numerous variations and modifications. So the astrologer, when approached on mate and marriage matters, makes allowances for them. But the fact remains that some groups of people are suited for each other and some are not, and astrology has expressed this in terms of characteristics we all can study and use as a personal guide.

No matter how much enjoyment and pleasure we find in the different aspects of each other's character, if it is not an overall compatibility, the chances of our finding fulfillment or enduring happiness in each other are pretty hopeless. And astrology can help us to find someone compatible.

Astrology and Science

Closely related to our emotions is the "other side" of our personal universe, our physical welfare. Our body, of course, is largely influenced by things around us over which we have very little control. The phone rings, we hear it. The train runs late. We snag our stocking or cut our face shaving. Our body is under a constant bombardment of events that influence our daily lives to varying degrees.

The question that arises from all this is, what makes each of us act so that we have to involve other people and keep the ball of activity and evolution rolling? This is the question that both science and astrology are involved with. The scientists have attacked it from different angles: anthropology, the study of human evolution as body, mind and response to environment; anatomy, the study of bodily structure; psychology, the science of the human mind; and so on. These studies have produced very impressive classifications and valuable information, but because the approach to the problem is fragmented, so is the result. They remain "branches" of science. Science generally studies effects. It keeps turning up wonderful answers but no lasting solutions. Astrology, on the other hand, approaches the question from the broader viewpoint. Astrology began its inquiry with the totality of human experience and saw it as an effect. It then looked to find the cause, or at least the prime movers, and during thousands of years of observation of man and his *universal* environment came up with the extraordinary principle of planetary influence—or astrology, which, from the Greek, means the science of the stars.

Modern science, as we shall see, has confirmed much of astrology's foundations—most of it unintentionally, some of it reluctantly, but still, indisputably.

It is not difficult to imagine that there must be a connection between outer space and Earth. Even today, scientists are not too sure how our Earth was created, but it is generally agreed that it is only a tiny part of the universe. And as a part of the universe, people on Earth see and feel the influence of heavenly bodies in almost every aspect of our existence. There is no doubt that the Sun has the greatest influence on life on this planet. Without it there would be no life, for without it there would be no warmth, no division into day and night, no cycles of time or season at all. This is clear and easy to see. The influence of the Moon, on the other hand, is more subtle, though no less definite.

There are many ways in which the influence of the Moon manifests itself here on Earth, both on human and animal life. It is a well-known fact, for instance, that the large movements of water on our planet—that is the ebb and flow of the tides—are caused by the Moon's gravitational pull. Since this is so, it follows that these water movements do not occur only in the oceans, but that all bodies of water are affected, even down to the tiniest puddle.

The human body, too, which consists of about 70 percent water, falls within the scope of this lunar influence. For example the menstrual cycle of most women corresponds to the 28-day lunar month; the period of pregnancy in humans is 273 days, or equal to nine lunar months. Similarly, many illnesses reach a crisis at the change of the Moon, and statistics in many countries have shown that the crime rate is highest at the time of the Full Moon. Even human sexual desire has been associated with the phases of the Moon. But it is in the movement of the tides that we get the clearest demonstration of planetary influence, which leads to the irresistible correspondence between the so-called metaphysical and the physical.

Tide tables are prepared years in advance by calculating the future positions of the Moon. Science has known for a long time that the Moon is the main cause of tidal action. But only in the last few years has it begun to realize the possible extent of this influence on mankind. To begin with, the ocean tides do not rise and fall as we might imagine from our personal observations of them. The Moon as it orbits around Earth sets up a circular wave of attraction which pulls the oceans of the world after it, broadly in an east to west direction. This influence is like a phantom wave crest, a loop of power stretching from pole to pole which passes over and around the Earth like an invisible shadow. It travels with equal effect across the land masses and, as scientists were recently amazed to observe, caused oysters placed in the dark in the middle of the United States where there is no sea to open their shells to receive the nonexistent tide. If the land-locked oysters react to this invisible signal, what effect does it have on us who not so long ago in evolutionary time came out of the sea and still have its salt in our blood and sweat?

Less well known is the fact that the Moon is also the primary force behind the circulation of blood in human beings and animals, and the movement of sap in trees and plants. Agriculturists have established that the Moon has a distinct influence on crops, which explains why for centuries people have planted according to Moon cycles. The habits of many animals, too, are directed by the movement of the Moon. Migratory birds, for instance, depart only at or near the time of the Full Moon. And certain sea creatures, eels in particular, move only in accordance with certain phases of the Moon.

Know Thyself—Why?

In today's fast-changing world, everyone still longs to know what the future holds. It is the one thing that everyone has in common: rich and poor, famous and infamous, all are deeply concerned about tomorrow.

But the key to the future, as every historian knows, lies in the past. This is as true of individual people as it is of nations. You cannot understand your future without first understanding your past, which is simply another way of saying that you must first of all know yourself.

The motto "know thyself" seems obvious enough nowadays, but it was originally put forward as the foundation of wisdom by the ancient Greek philosophers. It was then adopted by the "mystery religions" of the ancient Middle East, Greece, Rome, and is still used in all genuine schools of mind training or mystical discipline, both in those of the East, based on yoga, and those of the West. So it is universally accepted now, and has been through the ages.

But how do you go about discovering what sort of person you are? The first step is usually classification into some sort of system of types. Astrology did this long before the birth of Christ. Psychology has also done it. So has modern medicine, in its way.

One system classifies people according to the source of the impulses they respond to most readily: the muscles, leading to direct bodily action; the digestive organs, resulting in emotion; or the brain and nerves, giving rise to thinking. Another such system says that character is determined by the endocrine glands, and gives us such labels as "pituitary," "thyroid," and "hyperthyroid" types. These different systems are neither contradictory nor mutually exclusive. In fact, they are very often different ways of saying the same thing.

Very popular, useful classifications were devised by Carl Jung, the eminent disciple of Freud. Jung observed among the different faculties of the mind, four which have a predominant influence on character. These four faculties exist in all of us without exception, but not in perfect balance. So when we say, for instance, that someone is a "thinking type," it means that in any situation he or she tries to be rational. Emotion, which may be the opposite of thinking, will be his or her weakest function. This thinking type can be sensible and reasonable, or calculating and unsympathetic. The emotional type, on the other hand, can often be recognized by exaggerated language—everything is either marvelous or terrible—and in extreme cases they even invent dramas and quarrels out of nothing just to make life more interesting.

The other two faculties are intuition and physical sensation. The sensation type does not only care for food and drink, nice clothes and furniture; he or she is also interested in all forms of physical experience. Many scientists are sensation types as are athletes and nature-lovers. Like sensation, intuition is a form of perception and we all possess it. But it works through that part of the mind which is not under conscious control—consequently it sees meanings and connections which are not obvious to thought or emotion. Inventors and original thinkers are always intuitive, but so, too, are superstitious people who see meanings where none exist.

Thus, sensation tells us what is going on in the world, feeling (that is, emotion) tells us how important it is to ourselves, thinking enables us to interpret it and work out what we should do about it, and intuition tells us what it means to ourselves and others. All four faculties are essential, and all are present in every one of us. But some people are guided chiefly by one, others by another. In addition, Jung also observed a division of the human personality into the extrovert and the introvert, which cuts across these four types.

A disadvantage of all these systems of classification is that one cannot tell very easily where to place oneself. Some people are reluctant to admit that they act to please their emotions. So they deceive themselves for years by trying to belong to whichever type they think is the "best." Of course, there is no best; each has its faults and each has its good points.

The advantage of the signs of the Zodiac is that they simplify classification. Not only that, but your date of birth is personal—it is unarguably yours. What better way to know yourself than by going back as far as possible to the very moment of your birth? And this is precisely what your horoscope is all about, as we shall see in the next section.

WHAT IS A HOROSCOPE?

If you had been able to take a picture of the skies at the moment of your birth, that photograph would be your horoscope. Lacking such a snapshot, it is still possible to recreate the picture—and this is at the basis of the astrologer's art. In other words, your horoscope is a representation of the skies with the planets in the exact positions they occupied at the time you were born.

The year of birth tells an astrologer the positions of the distant, slow-moving planets Jupiter, Saturn, Uranus, Neptune, and Pluto. The month of birth indicates the Sun sign, or birth sign as it is commonly called, as well as indicating the positions of the rapidly moving planets Venus, Mercury, and Mars. The day and time of birth will locate the position of our Moon. And the moment—the exact hour and minute—of birth determines the houses through what is called the Ascendant, or Rising sign.

With this information the astrologer consults various tables to calculate the specific positions of the Sun, Moon, and other planets relative to your birthplace at the moment you were born. Then he or she locates them by means of the Zodiac.

The Zodiac

The Zodiac is a band of stars (constellations) in the skies, centered on the Sun's apparent path around the Earth, and is divided into twelve equal segments, or signs. What we are actually dividing up is the Earth's path around the Sun. But from our point of view here on Earth, it seems as if the Sun is making a great circle around our planet in the sky, so we say it is the Sun's apparent path. This twelvefold division, the Zodiac, is a reference system for the astrologer. At any given moment the planets—and in astrology both the Sun and Moon are considered to be planets—can all be located at a specific point along this path.

Now where in all this are you, the subject of the horoscope? Your character is largely determined by the sign the Sun is in. So that is where the astrologer looks first in your horoscope, at your Sun sign.

The Sun Sign and the Cusp

There are twelve signs in the Zodiac, and the Sun spends approximately one month in each sign. But because of the motion of the Earth around the Sun—the Sun's apparent motion—the dates when the Sun enters and leaves each sign may change from year to year. Some people born near the cusp, or edge, of a sign have difficulty determining which is their Sun sign. But in this book a Table of Cusps is provided for the years 1900 to 2000 (page 5) so you can find out what your true Sun sign is.

Here are the twelve signs of the Zodiac, their ancient zodiacal symbol, and the dates when the Sun enters and leaves each sign for the year 1998. Remember, these dates may change from year to year.

ARIES	Ram	March 20–April 20
TAURUS	Bull	April 20–May 21
GEMINI	Twins	May 21–June 21
CANCER	Crab	June 21–July 22
LEO	Lion	July 22–August 23
VIRGO	Virgin	August 23–September 23
LIBRA	Scales	September 23–October 23
SCORPIO	Scorpion	October 23–November 22
SAGITTARIUS	Archer	November 22–December 21
CAPRICORN	Sea Goat	December 21–January 20
AQUARIUS	Water Bearer	January 20–February 18
PISCES	Fish	February 18–March 20

It is possible to draw significant conclusions and make meaningful predictions based simply on the Sun sign of a person. There are many people who have been amazed at the accuracy of the description of their own character based only on the Sun sign. But an astrologer needs more information than just your Sun sign to interpret the photograph that is your horoscope.

The Rising Sign and the Zodiacal Houses

An astrologer needs the exact time and place of your birth in order to construct and interpret your horoscope. The illustration on the next page shows the flat chart, or natural wheel, an astrologer uses. Note the inner circle of the wheel labeled 1 through 12. These 12 divisions are known as the houses of the Zodiac.

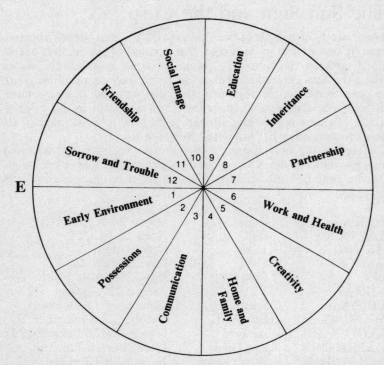

The 1st house always starts from the position marked E, which corresponds to the eastern horizon. The rest of the houses 2 through 12 follow around in a "counterclockwise" direction. The point where each house starts is known as a cusp, or edge.

The cusp, or edge, of the 1st house (point E) is where an astrologer would place your Rising sign, the Ascendant. And, as already noted, the exact time of your birth determines your Rising sign. Let's see how this works.

As the Earth rotates on its axis once every 24 hours, each one of the twelve signs of the Zodiac appears to be "rising" on the horizon, with a new one appearing about every 2 hours. Actually it is the turning of the Earth that exposes each sign to view, but in our astrological work we are discussing apparent motion. This Rising sign marks the Ascendant, and it colors the whole orientation of a horoscope. It indicates the sign governing the 1st house of the chart, and will thus determine which signs will govern all the other houses.

To visualize this idea, imagine two color wheels with twelve divisions superimposed upon each other. For just as the Zodiac is divided into twelve constellations that we identify as the signs, another twelvefold division is used to denote the houses. Now imagine one wheel (the signs) moving slowly while the other wheel (the houses) remains still. This analogy may help you see how the signs keep shifting the "color" of the houses as the Rising sign continues to change every two hours. To simplify things, a Table of Rising Signs has been provided (pages 8–9) for your specific Sun sign.

Once your Rising sign has been placed on the cusp of the 1st house, the signs that govern the rest of the 11 houses can be placed on the chart. In any individual's horoscope the signs do not necessarily correspond with the houses. For example, it could be that a sign covers part of two adjacent houses. It is the interpretation of such variations in an individual's horoscope that marks the professional astrologer.

But to gain a workable understanding of astrology, it is not necessary to go into great detail. In fact, we just need a description of the houses and their meanings, as is shown in the illustration above and in the table below.

THE 12 HOUSES OF THE ZODIAC

1st	Individuality, body appearance, general outlook on life	Personality house
2nd	Finance, possessions, ethical principles, gain or loss	Money house
3rd	Relatives, communication, short journeys, writing, education	Relatives house
4th	Family and home, parental ties, land and property, security	Home house
5th	Pleasure, children, creativity, entertainment, risk	Pleasure house
6th	Health, harvest, hygiene, work and service, employees	Health house
7th	Marriage and divorce, the law, partnerships and alliances	Marriage house
8th	Inheritance, secret deals, sex, death, regeneration	Inheritance house
9th	Travel, sports, study, philosophy and religion	Travel house
10th	Career, social standing, success and honor	Business house
11th	Friendship, social life, hopes and wishes	Friends house
12th	Troubles, illness, secret enemies, hidden agendas	Trouble house

The Planets in the Houses

An astrologer, knowing the exact time and place of your birth, will use tables of planetary motion in order to locate the planets in your horoscope chart. He or she will determine which planet or planets are in which sign and in which house. It is not uncommon, in an individual's horoscope, for there to be two or more planets in the same sign and in the same house.

The characteristics of the planets modify the influence of the Sun according to their natures and strengths.

Sun: Source of life. Basic temperament according to the Sun sign. The conscious will. Human potential.

Moon: Emotions. Moods. Customs. Habits. Changeable. Adaptive. Nurturing.

Mercury: Communication. Intellect. Reasoning power. Curiosity. Short travels.

Venus: Love. Delight. Charm. Harmony. Balance. Art. Beautiful possessions.

Mars: Energy. Initiative. War. Anger. Adventure. Courage. Daring. Impulse.

Jupiter: Luck. Optimism. Generous. Expansive. Opportunities. Protection.

Saturn: Pessimism. Privation. Obstacles. Delay. Hard work. Research. Lasting rewards after long struggle.

Uranus: Fashion. Electricity. Revolution. Independence. Freedom. Sudden changes. Modern science.

Neptune: Sensationalism. Theater. Dreams. Inspiration. Illusion. Deception.

Pluto: Creation and destruction. Total transformation. Lust for power. Strong obsessions.

Superimpose the characteristics of the planets on the functions of the house in which they appear. Express the result through the character of the Sun sign, and you will get the basic idea.

Of course, many other considerations have been taken into account in producing the carefully worked out predictions in this book: the aspects of the planets to each other; their strength according to position and sign; whether they are in a house of exaltation or decline; whether they are natural enemies or not; whether a planet occupies its own sign; the position of a planet in relation to its own house or sign; whether the sign is male or female; whether the sign is a fire, earth, water, or air sign. These are only a few of the colors on the astrologer's pallet which he or she must mix with the inspiration of the artist and the accuracy of the mathematician.

How To Use These Predictions

A person reading the predictions in this book should understand that they are produced from the daily position of the planets for a group of people and are not, of course, individually specialized. To get the full benefit of them our readers should relate the predictions to their own character and circumstances, coordinate them, and draw their own conclusions from them.

If you are a serious observer of your own life, you should find a definite pattern emerging that will be a helpful and reliable guide.

The point is that we always retain our free will. The stars indicate certain directional tendencies but we are not compelled to follow. We can do or not do, and wisdom must make the choice.

We all have our good and bad days. Sometimes they extend into cycles of weeks. It is therefore advisable to study daily predictions in a span ranging from the day before to several days ahead.

Daily predictions should be taken very generally. The word "difficult" does not necessarily indicate a whole day of obstruction or inconvenience. It is a warning to you to be cautious. Your caution will often see you around the difficulty before you are involved. This is the correct use of astrology.

In another section (pages 78–84), detailed information is given about the influence of the Moon as it passes through each of the twelve signs of the Zodiac. There are instructions on how to use the Moon Tables (pages 85–92), which provide Moon Sign Dates throughout the year as well as the Moon's role in health and daily affairs. This information should be used in conjunction with the daily forecasts to give a fuller picture of the astrological trends.

HISTORY OF ASTROLOGY

The origins of astrology have been lost far back in history, but we do know that reference is made to it as far back as the first written records of the human race. It is not hard to see why. Even in primitive times, people must have looked for an explanation for the various happenings in their lives. They must have wanted to know why people were different from one another. And in their search they turned to the regular movements of the Sun, Moon, and stars to see if they could provide an answer.

It is interesting to note that as soon as man learned to use his tools in any type of design, or his mind in any kind of calculation, he turned his attention to the heavens. Ancient cave dwellings reveal dim crescents and circles representative of the Sun and Moon, rulers of day and night. Mesopotamia and the civilization of Chaldea, in itself the foundation of those of Babylonia and Assyria, show a complete picture of astronomical observation and well-developed astrological interpretation.

Humanity has a natural instinct for order. The study of anthropology reveals that primitive people—even as far back as prehistoric times—were striving to achieve a certain order in their lives. They tried to organize the apparent chaos of the universe. They had the desire to attach meaning to things. This demand for order has persisted throughout the history of man. So that observing the regularity of the heavenly bodies made it logical that primitive peoples should turn heavenward in their search for an understanding of the world in which they found themselves so random and alone.

And they did find a significance in the movements of the stars. Shepherds tending their flocks, for instance, observed that when the cluster of stars now known as the constellation Aries was in sight, it was the time of fertility and they associated it with the Ram. And they noticed that the growth of plants and plant life corresponded with different phases of the Moon, so that certain times were favorable for the planting of crops, and other times were not. In this way, there grew up a tradition of seasons and causes connected with the passage of the Sun through the twelve signs of the Zodiac.

Astrology was valued so highly that the king was kept informed of the daily and monthly changes in the heavenly bodies, and the results of astrological studies regarding events of the future. Head astrologers were clearly men of great rank and position, and the office was said to be a hereditary one.

Omens were taken, not only from eclipses and conjunctions of the Moon or Sun with one of the planets, but also from storms and earthquakes. In the eastern civilizations, particularly, the reverence inspired by astrology appears to have remained unbroken since the very earliest days. In ancient China, astrology, astronomy, and religion went hand in hand. The astrologer, who was also an astronomer, was part of the official government service and had his own corner in the Imperial Palace. The duties of the Imperial astrologer, whose office was one of the most important in the land, were clearly defined, as this extract from early records shows:

This exalted gentleman must concern himself with the stars in the heavens, keeping a record of the changes and movements of the Planets, the Sun and the Moon, in order to examine the movements of the terrestrial world with the object of prognosticating good and bad fortune. He divides the territories of the nine regions of the empire in accordance with their dependence on particular celestial bodies. All the fiefs and principalities are connected with the stars and from this their prosperity or misfortune should be ascertained. He makes prognostications according to the twelve years of the Jupiter cycle of good and evil of the terrestrial world. From the colors of the five kinds of clouds, he determines the coming of floods or droughts, abundance or famine. From the twelve winds, he draws conclusions about the state of harmony of heaven and earth, and takes note of good and bad signs that result from their accord or disaccord. In general, he concerns himself with five kinds of phenomena so as to warn the Emperor to come to the aid of the government and to allow for variations in the ceremonies according to their circumstances.

The Chinese were also keen observers of the fixed stars, giving them such unusual names as Ghost Vehicle, Sun of Imperial Concubine, Imperial Prince, Pivot of Heaven, Twinkling Brilliance, Weaving Girl. But, great astrologers though they may have been, the Chinese lacked one aspect of mathematics that the Greeks applied to astrology—deductive geometry. Deductive geometry was the basis of much classical astrology in and after the time of the Greeks, and this explains the different methods of prognostication used in the East and West.

Down through the ages the astrologer's art has depended, not so much on the uncovering of new facts, though this is important, as on the interpretation of the facts already known. This is the essence of the astrologer's skill.

But why should the signs of the Zodiac have any effect at all on the formation of human character? It is easy to see why people thought they did, and even now we constantly use astrological expressions in our everyday speech. The thoughts of "lucky star," "ill-fated," "star-crossed," "mooning around," are interwoven into the very structure of our language.

Wherever the concept of the Zodiac is understood and used, it could well appear to have an influence on the human character. Does this mean, then, that the human race, in whose civilization the idea of the twelve signs of the Zodiac has long been embedded, is divided into only twelve types? Can we honestly believe that it is really as simple as that? If so, there must be pretty wide ranges of variation within each type. And if, to explain the variation, we call in heredity and environment, experiences in early childhood, the thyroid and other glands, and also the four functions of the mind together with extroversion and introversion, then one begins to wonder if the original classification was worth making at all. No sensible person believes that his favorite system explains everything. But even so, he will not find the system much use at all if it does not even save him the trouble of bothering with the others.

In the same way, if we were to put every person under only one sign of the Zodiac, the system becomes too rigid and unlike life. Besides, it was never intended to be used like that. It may be convenient to have only twelve types, but we know that in practice there is every possible gradation between aggressiveness and timidity, or between conscientiousness and laziness. How, then, do we account for this?

A person born under any given Sun sign can be mainly influenced by one or two of the other signs that appear in their individual horoscope. For instance, famous persons born under the sign of Gemini include Henry VIII, whom nothing and no one could have induced to abdicate, and Edward VIII, who did just that. Obviously, then, the sign Gemini does not fully explain the complete character of either of them.

Again, under the opposite sign, Sagittarius, were both Stalin, who was totally consumed with the notion of power, and Charles V, who freely gave up an empire because he preferred to go into a monastery. And we find under Scorpio many uncompromising characters such as Luther, de Gaulle, Indira Gandhi, and Montgomery, but also Petain, a successful commander whose name later became synonymous with collaboration.

A single sign is therefore obviously inadequate to explain the differences between people; it can only explain resemblances, such as the combativeness of the Scorpio group, or the far-reaching devotion of Charles V and Stalin to their respective ideals—the Christian heaven and the Communist utopia.

But very few people have only one sign in their horoscope chart. In addition to the month of birth, the day and, even more, the hour to the nearest minute if possible, ought to be considered. Without this, it is impossible to have an actual horoscope, for the word horoscope literally means "a consideration of the hour."

The month of birth tells you only which sign of the Zodiac was occupied by the Sun. The day and hour tell you what sign was occupied by the Moon. And the minute tells you which sign was rising on the eastern horizon. This is called the Ascendant, and, as some astrologers believe, it is supposed to be the most important thing in the whole horoscope.

The Sun is said to signify one's heart, that is to say, one's deepest desires and inmost nature. This is quite different from the Moon, which signifies one's superficial way of behaving. When the ancient Romans referred to the Emperor Augustus as a Capricorn, they meant that he had the Moon in Capricorn. Or, to take another example, a modern astrologer would call Disraeli a Scorpion because he had Scorpio Rising, but most people would call him Sagittarius because he had the Sun there. The Romans would have called him Leo because his Moon was in Leo.

So if one does not seem to fit one's birth month, it is always worthwhile reading the other signs, for one may have been born at a time when any of them were rising or occupied by the Moon. It also seems to be the case that the influence of the Sun develops as life goes on, so that the month of birth is easier to guess in people over the age of forty. The young are supposed to be influenced mainly by their Ascendant, the Rising sign, which characterizes the body and physical personality as a whole.

It is nonsense to assume that all people born at a certain time will exhibit the same characteristics, or that they will even behave in the same manner. It is quite obvious that, from the very moment of its birth, a child is subject to the effects of its environment, and that this in turn will influence its character and heritage to a decisive extent. Also to be taken into account are education and economic conditions, which play a very important part in the formation of one's character as well.

People have, in general, certain character traits and qualities which, according to their environment, develop in either a positive or a negative manner. Therefore, selfishness (inherent selfishness, that is) might emerge as unselfishness; kindness and consideration as cruelty and lack of consideration toward others. In the same way, a naturally constructive person may, through frustration, become destructive, and so on. The latent characteristics with which people are born can, therefore, through environment and good or bad training, become something that would appear to be its opposite, and so give the lie to the astrologer's description of their character. But this is not the case. The true character is still there, but it is buried deep beneath these external superficialities.

Careful study of the character traits of various signs of the Zodiac are of immeasurable help, and can render beneficial service to the intelligent person. Undoubtedly, the reader will already have discovered that, while he is able to get on very well with some people, he just "cannot stand" others. The causes sometimes seem inexplicable. At times there is intense dislike, at other times immediate sympathy. And there is, too, the phenomenon of love at first sight, which is also apparently inexplicable. People appear to be either sympathetic or unsympathetic toward each other for no apparent reason.

Now if we look at this in the light of the Zodiac, we find that people born under different signs are either compatible or incompatible with each other. In other words, there are good and bad interrelating factors among the various signs. This does not, of course, mean that humanity can be divided into groups of hostile camps. It would be quite wrong to be hostile or indifferent toward people who happen to be born under an incompatible sign. There is no reason why everybody should not, or cannot, learn to control and adjust their feelings and actions, especially after they are aware of the positive qualities of other people by studying their character analyses, among other things.

Every person born under a certain sign has both positive and negative qualities, which are developed more or less according to our free will. Nobody is entirely good or entirely bad, and it is up to each of us to learn to control ourselves on the one hand and at the same time to endeavor to learn about ourselves and others.

It cannot be emphasized often enough that it is free will that determines whether we will make really good use of our talents and abilities. Using our free will, we can either overcome our failings or allow them to rule us. Our free will enables us to exert sufficient willpower to control our failings so that they do not harm ourselves or others.

Astrology can reveal our inclinations and tendencies. Astrology can tell us about ourselves so that we are able to use our free will to overcome our shortcomings. In this way astrology helps us do our best to become needed and valuable members of society as well as helpmates to our family and our friends. Astrology also can save us a great deal of unhappiness and remorse.

Yet it may seem absurd that an ancient philosophy could be a prop to modern men and women. But below the materialistic surface of modern life, there are hidden streams of feeling and thought. Symbology is reappearing as a study worthy of the scholar; the psychosomatic factor in illness has passed from the writings of the crank to those of the specialist; spiritual healing in all its forms is no longer a pious hope but an accepted phenomenon. And it is into this context that we consider astrology, in the sense that it is an analysis of human types.

Astrology and medicine had a long journey together, and only parted company a couple of centuries ago. There still remain in medical language such astrological terms as "saturnine," "choleric," and "mercurial," used in the diagnosis of physical tendencies. The herbalist, for long the handyman of the medical profession, has been dominated by astrology since the days of the Greeks. Certain herbs traditionally respond to certain planetary influences, and diseases must therefore be treated to ensure harmony between the medicine and the disease.

But the stars are expected to foretell and not only to diagnose.

Astrological forecasting has been remarkably accurate, but often it is wide of the mark. The brave person who cares to predict world events takes dangerous chances. Individual forecasting is less clear cut; it can be a help or a disillusionment. Then we come to the nagging question: if it is possible to foreknow, is it right to foretell? This is a point of ethics on which it is hard to pronounce judgment. The doctor faces the same dilemma if he finds that symptoms of a mortal disease are present in his patient and that he can only prognosticate a steady decline. How much to tell an individual in a crisis is a problem that has perplexed many distinguished scholars. Honest and conscientious astrologers in this modern world, where so many people are seeking guidance, face the same problem.

Five hundred years ago it was customary to call in a learned man who was an astrologer who was probably also a doctor and a philosopher. By his knowledge of astrology, his study of planetary influences, he felt himself qualified to guide those in distress. The world has moved forward at a fantastic rate since then, and yet people are still uncertain of themselves. At first sight it seems fantastic in the light of modern thinking that they turn to the most ancient of all studies, and get someone to calculate a horoscope for them. But is it *really* so fantastic if you take a second look? For astrology is concerned with tomorrow, with survival. And in a world such as ours, tomorrow and survival are the keywords for the twenty-first century.

ASTROLOGICAL BRIDGE TO THE 21st CENTURY

As the last decade of the twentieth century comes to a close, planetary aspects for its final years connect you with the future. Major changes completed in 1995 and 1996 give rise to new planetary cycles that form the bridge to the twenty-first century and new horizons. The years 1996 through 1999 and into the year 2000 reveal hidden paths and personal hints for achieving your potential, for making the most of your message from the planets.

All the major planets begin new cycles in the late 1990s. Jupiter, planet of good fortune, transits four zodiacal signs from 1996 through 1999 and goes through a complete cycle in each of the elements earth, air, fire, and water. Jupiter is in Capricorn, then in Aquarius, next in Pisces, and finally in Aries as the century turns. With the dawning of the twenty-first century, each new yearly Jupiter cycle follows the natural progression of the Zodiac, from Aries in 2000, then Taurus in 2001, next Gemini in 2002, and so on through Pisces in 2011. The beneficent planet Jupiter promotes your professional and educational goals while urging informed choice and deliberation. Jupiter sharpens your focus and hones your skills. And while safeguarding good luck, Jupiter can turn unusual risks into achievable aims.

Saturn, planet of reason and responsibility, has begun a new cycle in the spring of 1996 when it entered fiery Aries. Saturn in Aries through March 1999 heightens a longing for independence. Your movements are freed from everyday restrictions, allowing you to travel, to explore, to act on a variety of choices. With Saturn in Aries you get set to blaze a new trail. Saturn enters earthy Taurus in March 1999 for a three-year stay over the turn of the century into the year 2002. Saturn in Taurus inspires industry and affection. Practicality, perseverance, and planning can reverse setbacks and minimize risk. Saturn in Taurus lends beauty, order, and structure to your life. In order to take advantage of opportunity through responsibility, to persevere against adversity, look to beautiful planet Saturn.

Uranus, planet of innovation and surprise, started an important new cycle in January of 1996. At that time Uranus entered its natural home in airy Aquarius. Uranus in Aquarius into the year 2003 has a profound effect on your personality and the lens through which you see the world. A basic change in the way you project yourself is just one impact of Uranus in Aquarius. More significantly, a whole new consciousness is evolving. Winds of change blowing your way emphasize movement and freedom. Uranus in Aquarius poses involvement in the larger community beyond self, family, friends, lovers, associates. Radical ideas and progressive thought signal a journey of liberation. As the century turns, follow Uranus on the path of humanitarianism. While you carve a prestigious niche in public life, while you preach social reform and justice, you will be striving to make the world a better place for all people.

Neptune, planet of vision and mystery, is in earthy Capricorn until late 1998. Neptune in Capricorn excites creativity while restraining fanciful thinking. Wise use of resources helps you build persona and prestige. Then Neptune enters airy Aquarius during November 1998 and is there into the year 2011. Neptune in Aquarius, the sign of the Water Bearer, represents two sides of the coin of wisdom: inspiration and reason. Here Neptune stirs powerful currents bearing a rich and varied harvest, the fertile breeding ground for idealistic aims and practical considerations. Neptune's fine intuition tunes in to your dreams, your imagination, your spirituality. You can never turn your back on the mysteries of life. Uranus and Neptune, the planets of enlightenment and renewed idealism both in the sign of Aquarius, give you glimpses into the future, letting you peek through secret doorways into the twenty-first century.

Pluto, planet of beginnings and endings, has completed one cycle of growth November 1995 in the sign of Scorpio. Pluto in Scorpio marked a long period of experimentation and rejuvenation. Then Pluto entered the fiery sign of Sagittarius on November 10, 1995 and is there into the year 2007. Pluto in Sagittarius during its long stay of twelve years can create significant change. The great power of Pluto in Sagittarius may already be starting its transformation of your character and lifestyle. Pluto in Sagittarius takes you on a new journey of exploration and learning. The awakening you experience on intellectual and artistic levels heralds a new cycle of growth. Uncompromising Pluto, seeker of truth, challenges your identity, persona, and self-expression. Uncovering the real you, Pluto holds the key to understanding and meaningful communication. Pluto in Sagittarius can be the guiding light illuminating the first decade of the twenty-first century. Good luck is riding on the waves of change.

THE SIGNS OF THE ZODIAC

Dominant Characteristics

Aries: March 21–April 20

The Positive Side of Aries

The Aries has many positive points to his character. People born under this first sign of the Zodiac are often quite strong and enthusiastic. On the whole, they are forward-looking people who are not easily discouraged by temporary setbacks. They know what they want out of life and they go out after it. Their personalities are strong. Others are usually quite impressed by the Ram's way of doing things. Quite often they are sources of inspiration for others traveling the same route. Aries men and women have a special zest for life that can be contagious; for others, they are a fine example of how life should be lived.

The Aries person usually has a quick and active mind. He is imaginative and inventive. He enjoys keeping busy and active. He generally gets along well with all kinds of people. He is interested in mankind, as a whole. He likes to be challenged. Some would say he thrives on opposition, for it is when he is set against that he often does his best. Getting over or around obstacles is a challenge he generally enjoys. All in all, Aries is quite positive and young-thinking. He likes to keep abreast of new things that are happening in the world. Aries are often fond of speed. They like things to be done quickly, and this sometimes aggravates their slower colleagues and associates.

The Aries man or woman always seems to remain young. Their whole approach to life is youthful and optimistic. They never say die, no matter what the odds. They may have an occasional setback, but it is not long before they are back on their feet again.

The Negative Side of Aries

Everybody has his less positive qualities—and Aries is no exception. Sometimes the Aries man or woman is not very tactful in communicating with others; in his hurry to get things done he is apt to be a little callous or inconsiderate. Sensitive people are likely to find him somewhat sharp-tongued in some situations. Often in his eagerness to get the show on the road, he misses the mark altogether and cannot achieve his aims.

At times Aries can be too impulsive. He can occasionally be stubborn and refuse to listen to reason. If things do not move quickly enough to suit the Aries man or woman, he or she is apt to become rather nervous or irritable. The uncultivated Aries is not unfamiliar with moments of doubt and fear. He is capable of being destructive if he does not get his way. He can overcome some of his emotional problems by steadily trying to express himself as he really is, but this requires effort.

Taurus: April 21–May 20

The Positive Side of Taurus

The Taurus person is known for his ability to concentrate and for his tenacity. These are perhaps his strongest qualities. The Taurus man or woman generally has very little trouble in getting along with others; it's his nature to be helpful toward people in need. He can always be depended on by his friends, especially those in trouble.

Taurus generally achieves what he wants through his ability to persevere. He never leaves anything unfinished but works on something until it has been completed. People can usually take him at his word; he is honest and forthright in most of his dealings. The Taurus person has a good chance to make a success of his life because of his many positive qualities. The Taurus who aims high seldom falls short of his mark. He learns well by experience. He is thorough and does not believe in shortcuts of any kind. The Bull's thoroughness pays off in the end, for through his deliberateness he learns how to rely on himself and what he has learned. The Taurus person tries to get along with others, as a rule. He is not overly critical and likes people to be themselves. He is a tolerant person and enjoys peace and harmony—especially in his home life.

Taurus is usually cautious in all that he does. He is not a person who believes in taking unnecessary risks. Before adopting any one line of action, he will weigh all of the pros and cons. The Taurus person is steadfast. Once his mind is made up it seldom changes. The person born under this sign usually is a good family person— reliable and loving.

The Negative Side of Taurus

Sometimes the Taurus man or woman is a bit too stubborn. He won't listen to other points of view if his mind is set on something. To others, this can be quite annoying. Taurus also does not like to be told what to do. He becomes rather angry if others think him not too bright. He does not like to be told he is wrong, even when he is. He dislikes being contradicted.

Some people who are born under this sign are very suspicious of others—even of those persons close to them. They find it difficult to trust people fully. They are often afraid of being deceived or taken advantage of. The Bull often finds it difficult to forget or forgive. His love of material things sometimes makes him rather avaricious and petty.

Gemini: May 21–June 20

The Positive Side of Gemini

The person born under this sign of the Heavenly Twins is usually quite bright and quick-witted. Some of them are capable of doing many different things. The Gemini person very often has many different interests. He keeps an open mind and is always anxious to learn new things.

Gemini is often an analytical person. He is a person who enjoys making use of his intellect. He is governed more by his mind than by his emotions. He is a person who is not confined to one view; he can often understand both sides to a problem or question. He knows how to reason, how to make rapid decisions if need be.

He is an adaptable person and can make himself at home almost anywhere. There are all kinds of situations he can adapt to. He is a person who seldom doubts himself; he is sure of his talents and his ability to think and reason. Gemini is generally most satisfied

when he is in a situation where he can make use of his intellect. Never short of imagination, he often has strong talents for invention. He is rather a modern person when it comes to life; Gemini almost always moves along with the times—perhaps that is why he remains so youthful throughout most of his life.

Literature and art appeal to the person born under this sign. Creativity in almost any form will interest and intrigue the Gemini man or woman.

The Gemini is often quite charming. A good talker, he often is the center of attraction at any gathering. People find it easy to like a person born under this sign because he can appear easygoing and usually has a good sense of humor.

The Negative Side of Gemini

Sometimes the Gemini person tries to do too many things at one time—and as a result, winds up finishing nothing. Some Twins are easily distracted and find it rather difficult to concentrate on one thing for too long a time. Sometimes they give in to trifling fancies and find it rather boring to become too serious about any one thing. Some of them are never dependable, no matter what they promise.

Although the Gemini man or woman often appears to be well-versed on many subjects, this is sometimes just a veneer. His knowledge may be only superficial, but because he speaks so well he gives people the impression of erudition. Some Geminis are sharp-tongued and inconsiderate; they think only of themselves and their own pleasure.

Cancer: June 21–July 20

The Positive Side of Cancer

The Moon Child's most positive point is his understanding nature. On the whole, he is a loving and sympathetic person. He would never go out of his way to hurt anyone. The Cancer man or woman is often very kind and tender; they give what they can to others. They hate to see others suffering and will do what they can to help someone in less fortunate circumstances than themselves. They are often very concerned about the world. Their interest in people generally goes beyond that of just their own families and close friends; they have a deep sense of community and respect humanitarian values. The Moon Child means what he says, as a rule; he is honest about his feelings.

The Cancer man or woman is a person who knows the art of patience. When something seems difficult, he is willing to wait until the situation becomes manageable again. He is a person who knows how to bide his time. Cancer knows how to concentrate on one thing at a time. When he has made his mind up he generally sticks with what he does, seeing it through to the end.

Cancer is a person who loves his home. He enjoys being surrounded by familiar things and the people he loves. Of all the signs, Cancer is the most maternal. Even the men born under this sign often have a motherly or protective quality about them. They like to take care of people in their family—to see that they are well loved and well provided for. They are usually loyal and faithful. Family ties mean a lot to the Cancer man or woman. Parents and in-laws are respected and loved. Young Cancer responds very well to adults who show faith in him. The Moon Child has a strong sense of tradition. He is very sensitive to the moods of others.

The Negative Side of Cancer

Sometimes Cancer finds it rather hard to face life. It becomes too much for him. He can be a little timid and retiring, when things don't go too well. When unfortunate things happen, he is apt to just shrug and say, "Whatever will be will be." He can be fatalistic to a fault. The uncultivated Cancer is a bit lazy. He doesn't have very much ambition. Anything that seems a bit difficult he'll gladly leave to others. He may be lacking in initiative. Too sensitive, when he feels he's been injured, he'll crawl back into his shell and nurse his imaginary wounds. The immature Moon Child often is given to crying when the smallest thing goes wrong.

Some Cancers find it difficult to enjoy themselves in environments outside their homes. They make heavy demands on others, and need to be constantly reassured that they are loved. Lacking such reassurance, they may resort to sulking in silence.

Leo: July 21–August 21

The Positive Side of Leo

Often Leos make good leaders. They seem to be good organizers and administrators. Usually they are quite popular with others. Whatever group it is that they belong to, the Leo man or woman is almost sure to be or become the leader. Loyalty, one of the Lion's noblest traits, enables him or her to maintain this leadership position.

Leo is generous most of the time. It is his best characteristic. He or she likes to give gifts and presents. In making others happy, the Leo person becomes happy himself. He likes to splurge when spending money on others. In some instances it may seem that the Lion's generosity knows no boundaries. A hospitable person, the Leo man or woman is very fond of welcoming people to his house and entertaining them. He is never short of company.

Leo has plenty of energy and drive. He enjoys working toward some specific goal. When he applies himself correctly, he gets what he wants most often. The Leo person is almost never unsure of himself. He has plenty of confidence and aplomb. He is a person who is direct in almost everything he does. He has a quick mind and can make a decision in a very short time.

He usually sets a good example for others because of his ambitious manner and positive ways. He knows how to stick to something once he's started. Although Leo may be good at making a joke, he is not superficial or glib. He is a loving person, kind and thoughtful.

There is generally nothing small or petty about the Leo man or woman. He does what he can for those who are deserving. He is a person others can rely upon at all times. He means what he says. An honest person, generally speaking, he is a friend who is valued and sought out.

The Negative Side of Leo

Leo, however, does have his faults. At times, he can be just a bit too arrogant. He thinks that no one deserves a leadership position except him. Only he is capable of doing things well. His opinion of himself is often much too high. Because of his conceit, he is

sometimes rather unpopular with a good many people. Some Leos are too materialistic; they can only think in terms of money and profit.

Some Leos enjoy lording it over others—at home or at their place of business. What is more, they feel they have the right to. Egocentric to an impossible degree, this sort of Leo cares little about how others think or feel. He can be rude and cutting.

Virgo: August 22–September 22

The Positive Side of Virgo

The person born under the sign of Virgo is generally a busy person. He knows how to arrange and organize things. He is a good planner. Above all, he is practical and is not afraid of hard work.

Often called the sign of the Harvester, Virgo knows how to attain what he desires. He sticks with something until it is finished. He never shirks his duties, and can always be depended upon. The Virgo person can be thoroughly trusted at all times.

The man or woman born under this sign tries to do everything to perfection. He doesn't believe in doing anything halfway. He always aims for the top. He is the sort of a person who is always learning and constantly striving to better himself—not because he wants more money or glory, but because it gives him a feeling of accomplishment.

The Virgo man or woman is a very observant person. He is sensitive to how others feel, and can see things below the surface of a situation. He usually puts this talent to constructive use.

It is not difficult for the Virgo to be open and earnest. He believes in putting his cards on the table. He is never secretive or underhanded. He's as good as his word. The Virgo person is generally plainspoken and down to earth. He has no trouble in expressing himself.

The Virgo person likes to keep up to date on new developments in his particular field. Well-informed, generally, he sometimes has a keen interest in the arts or literature. What he knows, he knows well. His ability to use his critical faculties is well-developed and sometimes startles others because of its accuracy.

Virgos adhere to a moderate way of life; they avoid excesses. Virgo is a responsible person and enjoys being of service.

The Negative Side of Virgo

Sometimes a Virgo person is too critical. He thinks that only he can do something the way it should be done. Whatever anyone else does is inferior. He can be rather annoying in the way he quibbles over insignificant details. In telling others how things should be done, he can be rather tactless and mean.

Some Virgos seem rather emotionless and cool. They feel emotional involvement is beneath them. They are sometimes too tidy, too neat. With money they can be rather miserly. Some Virgos try to force their opinions and ideas on others.

Libra: September 23–October 22

The Positive Side of Libra

Libras love harmony. It is one of their most outstanding character traits. They are interested in achieving balance; they admire beauty and grace in things as well as in people. Generally speaking, they are kind and considerate people. Libras are usually very sympathetic. They go out of their way not to hurt another person's feelings. They are outgoing and do what they can to help those in need.

People born under the sign of Libra almost always make good friends. They are loyal and amiable. They enjoy the company of others. Many of them are rather moderate in their views; they believe in keeping an open mind, however, and weighing both sides of an issue fairly before making a decision.

Alert and intelligent, Libra, often known as the Lawgiver, is always fair-minded and tries to put himself in the position of the other person. They are against injustice; quite often they take up for the underdog. In most of their social dealings, they try to be tactful and kind. They dislike discord and bickering, and most Libras strive for peace and harmony in all their relationships.

The Libra man or woman has a keen sense of beauty. They appreciate handsome furnishings and clothes. Many of them are artistically inclined. Their taste is usually impeccable. They know how to use color. Their homes are almost always attractively arranged and inviting. They enjoy entertaining people and see to it that their guests always feel at home and welcome.

Libra gets along with almost everyone. He is well-liked and socially much in demand.

The Negative Side of Libra

Some people born under this sign tend to be rather insincere. So eager are they to achieve harmony in all relationships that they will even go so far as to lie. Many of them are escapists. They find facing the truth an ordeal and prefer living in a world of make-believe.

In a serious argument, some Libras give in rather easily even when they know they are right. Arguing, even about something they believe in, is too unsettling for some of them.

Libras sometimes care too much for material things. They enjoy possessions and luxuries. Some are vain and tend to be jealous.

Scorpio: October 23–November 22

The Positive Side of Scorpio

The Scorpio man or woman generally knows what he or she wants out of life. He is a determined person. He sees something through to the end. Scorpio is quite sincere, and seldom says anything he doesn't mean. When he sets a goal for himself he tries to go about achieving it in a very direct way.

The Scorpion is brave and courageous. They are not afraid of hard work. Obstacles do not frighten them. They forge ahead until they achieve what they set out for. The Scorpio man or woman has a strong will.

Although Scorpio may seem rather fixed and determined, inside he is often quite tender and loving. He can care very much for others. He believes in sincerity in all relationships. His feelings about someone tend to last; they are profound and not superficial.

The Scorpio person is someone who adheres to his principles no matter what happens. He will not be deterred from a path he believes to be right.

Because of his many positive strengths, the Scorpion can often achieve happiness for himself and for those that he loves.

He is a constructive person by nature. He often has a deep understanding of people and of life, in general. He is perceptive and unafraid. Obstacles often seem to spur him on. He is a positive person who enjoys winning. He has many strengths and resources; challenge of any sort often brings out the best in him.

The Negative Side of Scorpio

The Scorpio person is sometimes hypersensitive. Often he imagines injury when there is none. He feels that others do not bother to recognize him for his true worth. Sometimes he is given to excessive boasting in order to compensate for what he feels is neglect.

Scorpio can be proud, arrogant, and competitive. They can be sly when they put their minds to it and they enjoy outwitting persons or institutions noted for their cleverness.

Their tactics for getting what they want are sometimes devious and ruthless. They don't care too much about what others may think. If they feel others have done them an injustice, they will do their best to seek revenge. The Scorpion often has a sudden, violent temper; and this person's interest in sex is sometimes quite unbalanced or excessive.

Sagittarius: November 23–December 20

The Positive Side of Sagittarius

People born under this sign are honest and forthright. Their approach to life is earnest and open. Sagittarius is often quite adult in his way of seeing things. They are broad-minded and tolerant people. When dealing with others the person born under the sign of the Archer is almost always open and forthright. He doesn't believe in deceit or pretension. His standards are high. People who associate with Sagittarius generally admire and respect his tolerant viewpoint.

The Archer trusts others easily and expects them to trust him. He is never suspicious or envious and almost always thinks well of others. People always enjoy his company because he is so friendly and easygoing. The Sagittarius man or woman is often good-humored. He can always be depended upon by his friends, family, and co-workers.

The person born under this sign of the Zodiac likes a good joke every now and then. Sagittarius is eager for fun and laughs, which makes him very popular with others.

A lively person, he enjoys sports and outdoor life. The Archer is fond of animals. Intelligent and interesting, he can begin an

animated conversation with ease. He likes exchanging ideas and discussing various views.

He is not selfish or proud. If someone proposes an idea or plan that is better than his, he will immediately adopt it. Imaginative yet practical, he knows how to put ideas into practice.

The Archer enjoys sport and games, and it doesn't matter if he wins or loses. He is a forgiving person, and never sulks over something that has not worked out in his favor.

He is seldom critical, and is almost always generous.

The Negative Side of Sagittarius

Some Sagittarius are restless. They take foolish risks and seldom learn from the mistakes they make. They don't have heads for money and are often mismanaging their finances. Some of them devote much of their time to gambling.

Some are too outspoken and tactless, always putting their feet in their mouths. They hurt others carelessly by being honest at the wrong time. Sometimes they make promises which they don't keep. They don't stick close enough to their plans and go from one failure to another. They are undisciplined and waste a lot of energy.

Capricorn: December 21–January 19

The Positive Side of Capricorn

The person born under the sign of Capricorn, known variously as the Mountain Goat or Sea Goat, is usually very stable and patient. He sticks to whatever tasks he has and sees them through. He can always be relied upon and he is not averse to work.

An honest person, Capricorn is generally serious about whatever he does. He does not take his duties lightly. He is a practical person and believes in keeping his feet on the ground.

Quite often the person born under this sign is ambitious and knows how to get what he wants out of life. The Goat forges ahead and never gives up his goal. When he is determined about something, he almost always wins. He is a good worker—a hard worker. Although things may not come easy to him, he will not complain, but continue working until his chores are finished.

He is usually good at business matters and knows the value of money. He is not a spendthrift and knows how to put something away for a rainy day; he dislikes waste and unnecessary loss.

Capricorn knows how to make use of his self-control. He can apply himself to almost anything once he puts his mind to it. His ability to concentrate sometimes astounds others. He is diligent and does well when involved in detail work.

The Capricorn man or woman is charitable, generally speaking, and will do what is possible to help others less fortunate. As a friend, he is loyal and trustworthy. He never shirks his duties or responsibilities. He is self-reliant and never expects too much of the other fellow. He does what he can on his own. If someone does him a good turn, then he will do his best to return the favor.

The Negative Side of Capricorn

Like everyone, Capricorn, too, has faults. At times, the Goat can be overcritical of others. He expects others to live up to his own high standards. He thinks highly of himself and tends to look down on others.

His interest in material things may be exaggerated. The Capricorn man or woman thinks too much about getting on in the world and having something to show for it. He may even be a little greedy.

He sometimes thinks he knows what's best for everyone. He is too bossy. He is always trying to organize and correct others. He may be a little narrow in his thinking.

Aquarius: January 20–February 18

The Positive Side of Aquarius

The Aquarius man or woman is usually very honest and forthright. These are his two greatest qualities. His standards for himself are generally very high. He can always be relied upon by others. His word is his bond.

Aquarius is perhaps the most tolerant of all the Zodiac personalities. He respects other people's beliefs and feels that everyone is entitled to his own approach to life.

He would never do anything to injure another's feelings. He is never unkind or cruel. Always considerate of others, the Water

Bearer is always willing to help a person in need. He feels a very strong tie between himself and all the other members of mankind.

The person born under this sign, called the Water Bearer, is almost always an individualist. He does not believe in teaming up with the masses, but prefers going his own way. His ideas about life and mankind are often quite advanced. There is a saying to the effect that the average Aquarius is fifty years ahead of his time.

Aquarius is community-minded. The problems of the world concern him greatly. He is interested in helping others no matter what part of the globe they live in. He is truly a humanitarian sort. He likes to be of service to others.

Giving, considerate, and without prejudice, Aquarius have no trouble getting along with others.

The Negative Side of Aquarius

Aquarius may be too much of a dreamer. He makes plans but seldom carries them out. He is rather unrealistic. His imagination has a tendency to run away with him. Because many of his plans are impractical, he is always in some sort of a dither.

Others may not approve of him at all times because of his unconventional behavior. He may be a bit eccentric. Sometimes he is so busy with his own thoughts that he loses touch with the realities of existence.

Some Aquarius feel they are more clever and intelligent than others. They seldom admit to their own faults, even when they are quite apparent. Some become rather fanatic in their views. Their criticism of others is sometimes destructive and negative.

Pisces: February 19–March 20

The Positive Side of Pisces

Known as the sign of the Fishes, Pisces has a sympathetic nature. Kindly, he is often dedicated in the way he goes about helping others. The sick and the troubled often turn to him for advice and assistance. Possessing keen intuition, Pisces can easily understand people's deepest problems.

He is very broad-minded and does not criticize others for their faults. He knows how to accept people for what they are. On the whole, he is a trustworthy and earnest person. He is loyal to his friends and will do what he can to help them in time of need. Generous and good-natured, he is a lover of peace; he is often willing to help others solve their differences. People who have taken a wrong turn in life often interest him and he will do what he can to persuade them to rehabilitate themselves.

He has a strong intuitive sense and most of the time he knows how to make it work for him. Pisces is unusually perceptive and often knows what is bothering someone before that person, himself, is aware of it. The Pisces man or woman is an idealistic person, basically, and is interested in making the world a better place in which to live. Pisces believes that everyone should help each other. He is willing to do more than his share in order to achieve cooperation with others.

The person born under this sign often is talented in music or art. He is a receptive person; he is able to take the ups and downs of life with philosophic calm.

The Negative Side of Pisces

Some Pisces are often depressed; their outlook on life is rather glum. They may feel that they have been given a bad deal in life and that others are always taking unfair advantage of them. Pisces sometimes feel that the world is a cold and cruel place. The Fishes can be easily discouraged. The Pisces man or woman may even withdraw from the harshness of reality into a secret shell of his own where he dreams and idles away a good deal of his time.

Pisces can be lazy. He lets things happen without giving the least bit of resistance. He drifts along, whether on the high road or on the low. He can be lacking in willpower.

Some Pisces people seek escape through drugs or alcohol. When temptation comes along they find it hard to resist. In matters of sex, they can be rather permissive.

Sun Sign Personalities

ARIES: Hans Christian Andersen, Pearl Bailey, Marlon Brando, Wernher Von Braun, Charlie Chaplin, Joan Crawford, Da Vinci, Bette Davis, Doris Day, W. C. Fields, Alec Guinness, Adolf Hitler, William Holden, Thomas Jefferson, Nikita Khrushchev, Elton John, Arturo Toscanini, J. P. Morgan, Paul Robeson, Gloria Steinem, Sarah Vaughn, Vincent van Gogh, Tennessee Williams

TAURUS: Fred Astaire, Charlote Brontë, Carol Burnett, Irving Berlin, Bing Crosby, Salvador Dali, Tchaikovsky, Queen Elizabeth II, Duke Ellington, Ella Fitzgerald, Henry Fonda, Sigmund Freud, Orson Welles, Joe Louis, Lenin, Karl Marx, Golda Meir, Eva Peron, Bertrand Russell, Shakespeare, Kate Smith, Benjamin Spock, Barbra Streisand, Shirley Temple, Harry Truman

GEMINI: Mikhail Baryshnikov, Ruth Benedict, Josephine Baker, Carlos Chavez, Walt Whitman, Bob Dylan, Ralph Waldo Emerson, Judy Garland, Paul Gauguin, Allen Ginsberg, Benny Goodman, Bob Hope, Burl Ives, John F. Kennedy, Peggy Lee, Marilyn Monroe, Joe Namath, Cole Porter, Laurence Olivier, Harriet Beecher Stowe, Queen Victoria, John Wayne, Frank Lloyd Wright

CANCER: "Dear Abby," Lizzie Borden, David Brinkley, Yul Brynner, Pearl Buck, Marc Chagall, Jack Dempsey, Babe Didrikson, Mary Baker Eddy, Henry VIII, John Glenn, Ernest Hemingway, Lena Horne, Oscar Hammerstein, Helen Keller, Ann Landers, George Orwell, Nancy Reagan, Rembrandt, Richard Rodgers, Ginger Rogers, Rubens, Jean-Paul Sartre, O. J. Simpson

LEO: Neil Armstrong, James Baldwin, Lucille Ball, Emily Brontë, Wilt Chamberlain, Julia Child, William J. Clinton, Cecil B. De Mille, Ogden Nash, Amelia Earhart, Edna Ferber, Arthur Goldberg, Alfred Hitchcock, Mick Jagger, George Meany, Annie Oakley, George Bernard Shaw, Napoleon, Jacqueline Onassis, Henry Ford, Francis Scott Key, Andy Warhol, Mae West, Orville Wright

VIRGO: Ingrid Bergman, Warren Burger, Maurice Chevalier, Agatha Christie, Sean Connery, Lafayette, Peter Falk, Greta Garbo, Althea Gibson, Arthur Godfrey, Goethe, Buddy Hackett, Michael Jackson, Lyndon Johnson, D. H. Lawrence, Sophia Loren, Grandma Moses, Arnold Palmer, Queen Elizabeth I, Walter Reuther, Peter Sellers, Lily Tomlin, George Wallace

LIBRA: Brigitte Bardot, Art Buchwald, Truman Capote, Dwight D. Eisenhower, William Faulkner, F. Scott Fitzgerald, Gandhi, George Gershwin, Micky Mantle, Helen Hayes, Vladimir Horowitz, Doris Lessing, Martina Navratalova, Eugene O'Neill, Luciano Pavarotti, Emily Post, Eleanor Roosevelt, Bruce Springsteen, Margaret Thatcher, Gore Vidal, Barbara Walters, Oscar Wilde

SCORPIO: Vivien Leigh, Richard Burton, Art Carney, Johnny Carson, Billy Graham, Grace Kelly, Walter Cronkite, Marie Curie, Charles de Gaulle, Linda Evans, Indira Gandhi, Theodore Roosevelt, Rock Hudson, Katherine Hepburn, Robert F. Kennedy, Billie Jean King, Martin Luther, Georgia O'Keeffe, Pablo Picasso, Jonas Salk, Alan Shepard, Robert Louis Stevenson

SAGITTARIUS: Jane Austen, Louisa May Alcott, Woody Allen, Beethoven, Willy Brandt, Mary Martin, William F. Buckley, Maria Callas, Winston Churchill, Noel Coward, Emily Dickinson, Walt Disney, Benjamin Disraeli, James Doolittle, Kirk Douglas, Chet Huntley, Jane Fonda, Chris Evert Lloyd, Margaret Mead, Charles Schulz, John Milton, Frank Sinatra, Steven Spielberg

CAPRICORN: Muhammad Ali, Isaac Asimov, Pablo Casals, Dizzy Dean, Marlene Dietrich, James Farmer, Ava Gardner, Barry Goldwater, Cary Grant, J. Edgar Hoover, Howard Hughes, Joan of Arc, Gypsy Rose Lee, Martin Luther King, Jr., Rudyard Kipling, Mao Tse-tung, Richard Nixon, Gamal Nasser, Louis Pasteur, Albert Schweitzer, Stalin, Benjamin Franklin, Elvis Presley

AQUARIUS: Marian Anderson, Susan B. Anthony, Jack Benny, Charles Darwin, Charles Dickens, Thomas Edison, John Barrymore, Clark Gable, Jascha Heifetz, Abraham Lincoln, John McEnroe, Yehudi Menuhin, Mozart, Jack Nicklaus, Ronald Reagan, Jackie Robinson, Norman Rockwell, Franklin D. Roosevelt, Gertrude Stein, Charles Lindbergh, Margaret Truman

PISCES: Edward Albee, Harry Belafonte, Alexander Graham Bell, Chopin, Adelle Davis, Albert Einstein, Golda Meir, Jackie Gleason, Winslow Homer, Edward M. Kennedy, Victor Hugo, Mike Mansfield, Michelangelo, Edna St. Vincent Millay, Liza Minelli, John Steinbeck, Linus Pauling, Ravel, Renoir, Diana Ross, William Shirer, Elizabeth Taylor, George Washington

The Signs and Their Key Words

		POSITIVE	NEGATIVE
ARIES	self	courage, initiative, pioneer instinct	brash rudeness, selfish impetuosity
TAURUS	money	endurance, loyalty, wealth	obstinacy, gluttony
GEMINI	mind	versatility	capriciousness, unreliability
CANCER	family	sympathy, homing instinct	clannishness, childishness
LEO	children	love, authority, integrity	egotism, force
VIRGO	work	purity, industry, analysis	faultfinding, cynicism
LIBRA	marriage	harmony, justice	vacillation, superficiality
SCORPIO	sex	survival, regeneration	vengeance, discord
SAGITTARIUS	travel	optimism, higher learning	lawlessness
CAPRICORN	career	depth	narrowness, gloom
AQUARIUS	friends	human fellowship, genius	perverse unpredictability
PISCES	confine-ment	spiritual love, universality	diffusion, escapism

The Elements and Qualities of The Signs

Every sign has both an *element* and a *quality* associated with it. The element indicates the basic makeup of the sign, and the quality describes the kind of activity associated with each.

Element	Sign	Quality	Sign
FIRE	ARIES LEO SAGITTARIUS	CARDINAL	ARIES LIBRA CANCER CAPRICORN
EARTH	TAURUS VIRGO CAPRICORN	FIXED	TAURUS LEO SCORPIO AQUARIUS
AIR.........	GEMINI LIBRA AQUARIUS		
WATER....	CANCER SCORPIO PISCES	MUTABLE	GEMINI VIRGO SAGITTARIUS PISCES

Signs can be grouped together according to their element and quality. Signs of the same element share many basic traits in common. They tend to form stable configurations and ultimately harmonious relationships. Signs of the same quality are often less harmonious, but they share many dynamic potentials for growth as well as profound fulfillment.

Further discussion of each of these sign groupings is provided on the following pages.

The Fire Signs

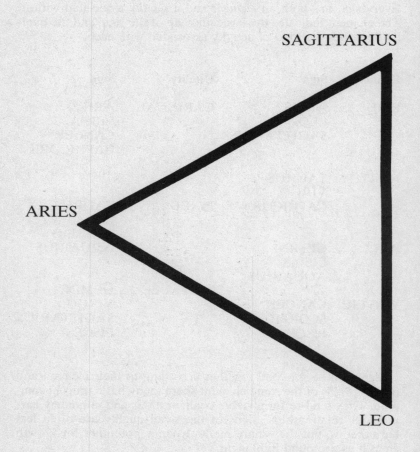

This is the fire group. On the whole these are emotional, volatile types, quick to anger, quick to forgive. They are adventurous, powerful people and act as a source of inspiration for everyone. They spark into action with immediate exuberant impulses. They are intelligent, self-involved, creative, and idealistic. They all share a certain vibrancy and glow that outwardly reflects an inner flame and passion for living.

The Earth Signs

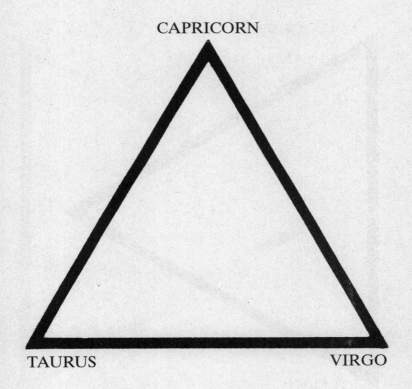

CAPRICORN

TAURUS   VIRGO

This is the earth group. They are in constant touch with the material world and tend to be conservative. Although they are all capable of spartan self-discipline, they are earthy, sensual people who are stimulated by the tangible, elegant, and luxurious. The thread of their lives is always practical, but they do fantasize and are often attracted to dark, mysterious, emotional people. They are like great cliffs overhanging the sea, forever married to the ocean but always resisting erosion from the dark, emotional forces that thunder at their feet.

The Air Signs

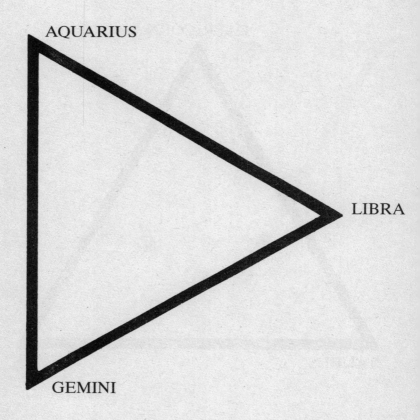

AQUARIUS

LIBRA

GEMINI

This is the air group. They are light, mental creatures desirous of contact, communication, and relationship. They are involved with people and the forming of ties on many levels. Original thinkers, they are the bearers of human news. Their language is their sense of word, color, style, and beauty. They provide an atmosphere suitable and pleasant for living. They add change and versatility to the scene, and it is through them that we can explore new territory of human intelligence and experience.

The Water Signs

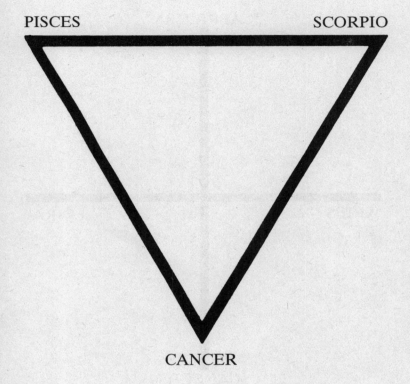

PISCES   SCORPIO

CANCER

This is the water group. Through the water people, we are all joined together on emotional, nonverbal levels. They are silent, mysterious types whose magic hypnotizes even the most determined realist. They have uncanny perceptions about people and are as rich as the oceans when it comes to feeling, emotion, or imagination. They are sensitive, mystical creatures with memories that go back beyond time. Through water, life is sustained. These people have the potential for the depths of darkness or the heights of mysticism and art.

The Cardinal Signs

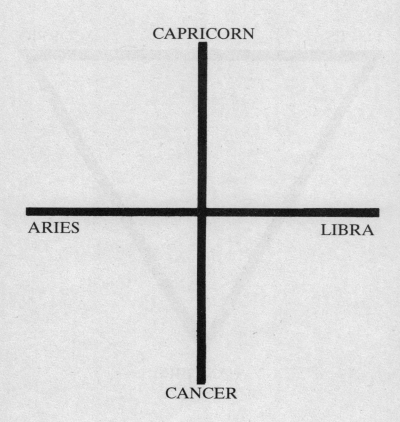

CAPRICORN

ARIES   LIBRA

CANCER

Put together, this is a clear-cut picture of dynamism, activity, tremendous stress, and remarkable achievement. These people know the meaning of great change since their lives are often characterized by significant crises and major successes. This combination is like a simultaneous storm of summer, fall, winter, and spring. The danger is chaotic diffusion of energy; the potential is irrepressible growth and victory.

The Fixed Signs

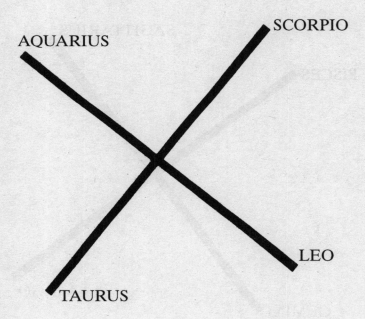

Fixed signs are always establishing themselves in a given place or area of experience. Like explorers who arrive and plant a flag, these people claim a position from which they do not enjoy being deposed. They are staunch, stalwart, upright, trusty, honorable people, although their obstinacy is well-known. Their contribution is fixity, and they are the angels who support our visible world.

The Mutable Signs

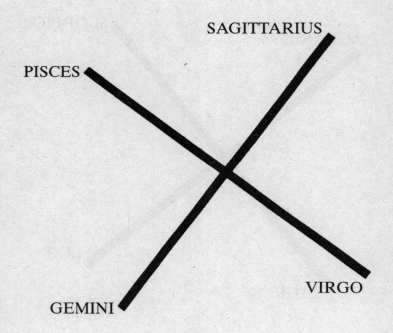

Mutable people are versatile, sensitive, intelligent, nervous, and deeply curious about life. They are the translators of all energy. They often carry out or complete tasks initiated by others. Combinations of these signs have highly developed minds; they are imaginative and jumpy and think and talk a lot. At worst their lives are a Tower of Babel. At best they are adaptable and ready creatures who can assimilate one kind of experience and enjoy it while anticipating coming changes.

THE PLANETS
OF THE SOLAR SYSTEM

This section describes the planets of the solar system. In astrology, both the Sun and the Moon are considered to be planets. Because of the Moon's influence in our day-to-day lives, the Moon is described in a separate section following this one.

The Planets and the Signs They Rule

The signs of the Zodiac are linked to the planets in the following way. Each sign is governed or ruled by one or more planets. No matter where the planets are located in the sky at any given moment, they still rule their respective signs, and when they travel through the signs they rule, they have special dignity and their effects are stronger.

Following is a list of the planets and the signs they rule. After looking at the list, read the definitions of the planets and see if you can determine how the planet ruling *your* Sun sign has affected your life.

SIGNS	RULING PLANETS
Aries	Mars, Pluto
Taurus	Venus
Gemini	Mercury
Cancer	Moon
Leo	Sun
Virgo	Mercury
Libra	Venus
Scorpio	Mars, Pluto
Sagittarius	Jupiter
Capricorn	Saturn
Aquarius	Saturn, Uranus
Pisces	Jupiter, Neptune

Characteristics of the Planets

The following pages give the meaning and characteristics of the planets of the solar system. They all travel around the Sun at different speeds and different distances. Taken with the Sun, they all distribute individual intelligence and ability throughout the entire chart.

The planets modify the influence of the Sun in a chart according to their own particular natures, strengths, and positions. Their positions must be calculated for each year and day, and their function and expression in a horoscope will change as they move from one area of the Zodiac to another.

We start with a description of the sun.

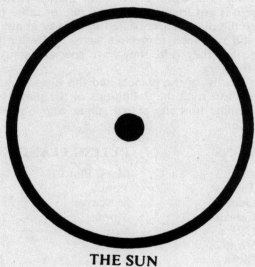

THE SUN

SUN

This is the center of existence. Around this flaming sphere all the planets revolve in endless orbits. Our star is constantly sending out its beams of light and energy without which no life on Earth would be possible. In astrology it symbolizes everything we are trying to become, the center around which all of our activity in life will always revolve. It is the symbol of our basic nature and describes the natural and constant thread that runs through everything that we do from birth to death on this planet.

To early astrologers, the Sun seemed to be another planet because it crossed the heavens every day, just like the rest of the bodies in the sky.

It is the only star near enough to be seen well—it is, in fact, a dwarf star. Approximately 860,000 miles in diameter, it is about ten times as wide as the giant planet Jupiter. The next nearest star is nearly 300,000 times as far away, and if the Sun were located as far away as most of the bright stars, it would be too faint to be seen without a telescope.

Everything in the horoscope ultimately revolves around this singular body. Although other forces may be prominent in the charts of some individuals, still the Sun is the total nucleus of being and symbolizes the complete potential of every human being alive. It is vitality and the life force. Your whole essence comes from the position of the Sun.

You are always trying to express the Sun according to its position by house and sign. Possibility for all development is found in the Sun, and it marks the fundamental character of your personal radiations all around you.

It is the symbol of strength, vigor, wisdom, dignity, ardor, and generosity, and the ability for a person to function as a mature individual. It is also a creative force in society. It is consciousness of the gift of life.

The underdeveloped solar nature is arrogant, pushy, undependable, and proud, and is constantly using force.

MERCURY

Mercury is the planet closest to the Sun. It races around our star, gathering information and translating it to the rest of the system. Mercury represents your capacity to understand the desires of your own will and to translate those desires into action.

In other words it is the planet of mind and the power of communication. Through Mercury we develop an ability to think, write, speak, and observe—to become aware of the world around us. It colors our attitudes and vision of the world, as well as our capacity to communicate our inner responses to the outside world. Some people who have serious disabilities in their power of verbal communication have often wrongly been described as people lacking intelligence.

Although this planet (and its position in the horoscope) indicates your power to communicate your thoughts and perceptions to the world, intelligence is something deeper. Intelligence is distributed throughout all the planets. It is the relationship of the planets to each other that truly describes what we call intelligence. Mercury rules speaking, language, mathematics, draft and design, students, messengers, young people, offices, teachers, and any pursuits where the mind of man has wings.

VENUS

Venus is beauty. It symbolizes the harmony and radiance of a rare and elusive quality: beauty itself. It is refinement and delicacy, softness and charm. In astrology it indicates grace, balance, and the aesthetic sense. Where Venus is we see beauty, a gentle drawing in of energy and the need for satisfaction and completion. It is a special touch that finishes off rough edges. It is sensitivity, and affection, and it is always the place for that other elusive phenomenon: love. Venus describes our sense of what is beautiful and loving. Poorly developed, it is vulgar, tasteless, and self-indulgent. But its ideal is the flame of spiritual love—Aphrodite, goddess of love, and the sweetness and power of personal beauty.

MARS

Mars is raw, crude energy. The planet next to Earth but outward from the Sun is a fiery red sphere that charges through the horoscope with force and fury. It represents the way you reach out for new adventure and new experience. It is energy and drive, initiative, courage, and daring. It is the power to start something and see it through. It can be thoughtless, cruel and wild, angry and hostile, causing cuts, burns, scalds, and wounds. It can stab its way through a chart, or it can be the symbol of healthy spirited adventure, well-channeled constructive power to begin and keep up the drive. If you have trouble starting things, if you lack the get-up-and-go to start the ball rolling, if you lack aggressiveness and self-confidence, chances are there's another planet influencing your Mars. Mars rules soldiers, butchers, surgeons, salesmen—any field that requires daring, bold skill, operational technique, or self-promotion.

JUPITER

This is the largest planet of the solar system. Scientists have recently learned that Jupiter reflects more light than it receives from the Sun. In a sense it is like a star itself. In astrology it rules good luck and good cheer, health, wealth, optimism, happiness, success, and joy. It is the symbol of opportunity and always opens the way for new possibilities in your life. It rules exuberance, enthusiasm, wisdom, knowledge, generosity, and all forms of expansion in general. It rules actors, statesmen, clerics, professional people, religion, publishing, and the distribution of many people over large areas.

Sometimes Jupiter makes you think you deserve everything, and you become sloppy, wasteful, careless and rude, prodigal and lawless, in the illusion that nothing can ever go wrong. Then there is the danger of overconfidence, exaggeration, undependability, and overindulgence.

Jupiter is the minimization of limitation and the emphasis on spirituality and potential. It is the thirst for knowledge and higher learning.

SATURN

Saturn circles our system in dark splendor with its mysterious rings, forcing us to be awakened to whatever we have neglected in the past. It will present real puzzles and problems to be solved, causing delays, obstacles, and hindrances. By doing so, Saturn stirs our own sensitivity to those areas where we are laziest.

Here we must patiently develop *method*, and only through painstaking effort can our ends be achieved. It brings order to a horoscope and imposes reason just where we are feeling least reasonable. By creating limitations and boundary, Saturn shows the consequences of being human and demands that we accept the changing cycles inevitable in human life. Saturn rules time, old age, and sobriety. It can bring depression, gloom, jealousy, and greed, or serious acceptance of responsibilities out of which success will develop. With Saturn there is nothing to do but face facts. It rules laborers, stones, granite, rocks, and crystals of all kinds.

THE OUTER PLANETS:
URANUS, NEPTUNE, PLUTO

Uranus, Neptune, Pluto are the outer planets. They liberate human beings from cultural conditioning, and in that sense are the lawbreakers. In early times it was thought that Saturn was the last planet of the system—the outer limit beyond which we could never go. The discovery of the next three planets ushered in new phases of human history, revolution, and technology.

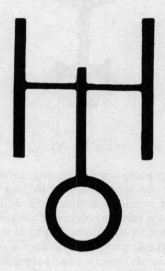

URANUS

Uranus rules unexpected change, upheaval, revolution. It is the symbol of total independence and asserts the freedom of an individual from all restriction and restraint. It is a breakthrough planet and indicates talent, originality, and genius in a horoscope. It usually causes last-minute reversals and changes of plan, unwanted separations, accidents, catastrophes, and eccentric behavior. It can add irrational rebelliousness and perverse bohemianism to a personality or a streak of unaffected brilliance in science and art. It rules technology, aviation, and all forms of electrical and electronic advancement. It governs great leaps forward and topsy-turvy situations, and *always* turns things around at the last minute. Its effects are difficult to predict, since it rules sudden last-minute decisions and events that come like lightning out of the blue.

NEPTUNE

Neptune dissolves existing reality the way the sea erodes the cliffs beside it. Its effects are subtle like the ringing of a buoy's bell in the fog. It suggests a reality higher than definition can usually describe. It awakens a sense of higher responsibility often causing guilt, worry, anxieties, or delusions. Neptune is associated with all forms of escape and can make things seem a certain way so convincingly that you are absolutely sure of something that eventually turns out to be quite different.

It is the planet of illusion and therefore governs the invisible realms that lie beyond our ordinary minds, beyond our simple factual ability to prove what is "real." Treachery, deceit, disillusionment, and disappointment are linked to Neptune. It describes a vague reality that promises eternity and the divine, yet in a manner so complex that we cannot really fathom it at all. At its worst Neptune is a cheap intoxicant; at its best it is the poetry, music, and inspiration of the higher planes of spiritual love. It has dominion over movies, photographs, and much of the arts.

PLUTO

Pluto lies at the outpost of our system and therefore rules finality in a horoscope—the final closing of chapters in your life, the passing of major milestones and points of development from which there is no return. It is a final wipeout, a closeout, an evacuation. It is a distant, subtle but powerful catalyst in all transformations that occur. It creates, destroys, then recreates. Sometimes Pluto starts its influence with a minor event or insignificant incident that might even go unnoticed. Slowly but surely, little by little, everything changes, until at last there has been a total transformation in the area of your life where Pluto has been operating. It rules mass thinking and the trends that society first rejects, then adopts, and finally outgrows.

Pluto rules the dead and the underworld—all the powerful forces of creation and destruction that go on all the time beneath, around, and above us. It can bring a lust for power with strong obsessions.

It is the planet that rules the metamorphosis of the caterpillar into a butterfly, for it symbolizes the capacity to change totally and forever a person's lifestyle, way of thought, and behavior.

THE MOON IN EACH SIGN

The Moon is the nearest planet to the Earth. It exerts more observable influence on us from day to day than any other planet. The effect is very personal, very intimate, and if we are not aware of how it works it can make us quite unstable in our ideas. And the annoying thing is that at these times we often see our own instability but can do nothing about it. A knowledge of what can be expected may help considerably. We can then be prepared to stand strong against the Moon's negative influences and use its positive ones to help us to get ahead. Who has not heard of going with the tide?

The Moon reflects, has no light of its own. It reflects the Sun—the life giver—in the form of vital movement. The Moon controls the tides, the blood rhythm, the movement of sap in trees and plants. Its nature is inconstancy and change so it signifies our moods, our superficial behavior—walking, talking, and especially thinking. Being a true reflector of other forces, the Moon is cold, watery like the surface of a still lake, brilliant and scintillating at times, but easily ruffled and disturbed by the winds of change.

The Moon takes about 27⅓ days to make a complete transit of the Zodiac. It spends just over 2¼ days in each sign. During that time it reflects the qualities, energies, and characteristics of the sign and, to a degree, the planet which rules the sign. When the Moon in its transit occupies a sign incompatible with our own birth sign, we can expect to feel a vague uneasiness, perhaps a touch of irritableness. We should not be discouraged nor let the feeling get us down, or, worse still, allow ourselves to take the discomfort out on others. Try to remember that the Moon has to change signs within 55 hours and, provided you are not physically ill, your mood will probably change with it. It is amazing how frequently depression lifts with the shift in the Moon's position. And, of course, when the Moon is transiting a sign compatible or sympathetic to yours, you will probably feel some sort of stimulation or just be plain happy to be alive.

In the horoscope, the Moon is such a powerful indicator that competent astrologers often use the sign it occupied at birth as the birth sign of the person. This is done particularly when the Sun is on the cusp, or edge, of two signs. Most experienced astrologers, however, coordinate both Sun and Moon signs by reading and confirming from one to the other and secure a far more accurate and personalized analysis.

For these reasons, the Moon tables which follow this section (see pages 86–92) are of great importance to the individual. They show the days and the exact times the Moon will enter each sign of the Zodiac for the year. Remember, you have to adjust the indicated times to local time. The corrections, already calculated for most of the main cities, are at the beginning of the tables. What follows now is a guide to the influences that will be reflected to the Earth by the Moon while it transits each of the twelve signs. The influence is at its peak about 26 hours after the Moon enters a sign. As you read the daily forecast, check the Moon sign for any given day and glance back at this guide.

MOON IN ARIES

This is a time for action, for reaching out beyond the usual self-imposed limitations and faint-hearted cautions. If you have plans in your head or on your desk, put them into practice. New ventures, applications, new jobs, new starts of any kind—all have a good chance of success. This is the period when original and dynamic impulses are being reflected onto Earth. Such energies are extremely vital and favor the pursuit of pleasure and adventure in practically every form. Sick people should feel an improvement. Those who are well will probably find themselves exuding confidence and optimism. People fond of physical exercise should find their bodies growing with tone and well-being. Boldness, strength, determination should characterize most of your activities with a readiness to face up to old challenges. Yesterday's problems may seem petty and exaggerated—so deal with them. Strike out alone. Self-reliance will attract others to you. This is a good time for making friends. Business and marriage partners are more likely to be impressed with the man and woman of action. Opposition will be overcome or thrown aside with much less effort than usual. CAUTION: Be dominant but not domineering.

MOON IN TAURUS

The spontaneous, action-packed person of yesterday gives way to the cautious, diligent, hardworking "thinker." In this period ideas will probably be concentrated on ways of improving finances. A great deal of time may be spent figuring out and going over schemes and plans. It is the right time to be careful with detail.

People will find themselves working longer than usual at their desks. Or devoting more time to serious thought about the future. A strong desire to put order into business and financial arrangements may cause extra work. Loved ones may complain of being neglected and may fail to appreciate that your efforts are for their ultimate benefit. Your desire for system may extend to criticism of arrangements in the home and lead to minor upsets. Health may be affected through overwork. Try to secure a reasonable amount of rest and relaxation, although the tendency will be to "keep going" despite good advice. Work done conscientiously in this period should result in a solid contribution to your future security. CAUTION: Try not to be as serious with people as the work you are engaged in.

MOON IN GEMINI
The humdrum of routine and too much work should suddenly end. You are likely to find yourself in an expansive, quicksilver world of change and self-expression. Urges to write, to paint, to experience the freedom of some sort of artistic outpouring, may be very strong. Take full advantage of them. You may find yourself finishing something you began and put aside long ago. Or embarking on something new which could easily be prompted by a chance meeting, a new acquaintance, or even an advertisement. There may be a yearning for a change of scenery, the feeling to visit another country (not too far away), or at least to get away for a few days. This may result in short, quick journeys. Or, if you are planning a single visit, there may be some unexpected changes or detours on the way. Familiar activities will seem to give little satisfaction unless they contain a fresh element of excitement or expectation. The inclination will be toward untried pursuits, particularly those that allow you to express your inner nature. The accent is on new faces, new places. CAUTION: Do not be too quick to commit yourself emotionally.

MOON IN CANCER
Feelings of uncertainty and vague insecurity are likely to cause problems while the Moon is in Cancer. Thoughts may turn frequently to the warmth of the home and the comfort of loved ones. Nostalgic impulses could cause you to bring out old photographs and letters and reflect on the days when your life seemed to be much more rewarding and less demanding. The love and understanding of parents and family may be important, and, if it is not forthcoming, you may have to fight against bouts of self-pity. The cordiality of friends and the thought of good times with them that are sure to be repeated will help to restore you to a happier frame

of mind. The desire to be alone may follow minor setbacks or rebuffs at this time, but solitude is unlikely to help. Better to get on the telephone or visit someone. This period often causes peculiar dreams and upsurges of imaginative thinking which can be helpful to authors of occult and mystical works. Preoccupation with the personal world of simple human needs can overshadow any material strivings. CAUTION: Do not spend too much time thinking—seek the company of loved ones or close friends.

MOON IN LEO

New horizons of exciting and rather extravagant activity open up. This is the time for exhilarating entertainment, glamorous and lavish parties, and expensive shopping sprees. Any merrymaking that relies upon your generosity as a host has every chance of being a spectacular success. You should find yourself right in the center of the fun, either as the life of the party or simply as a person whom happy people like to be with. Romance thrives in this heady atmosphere and friendships are likely to explode unexpectedly into serious attachments. Children and younger people should be attracted to you and you may find yourself organizing a picnic or a visit to a fun-fair, the movies, or the beach. The sunny company and vitality of youthful companions should help you to find some unsuspected energy. In career, you could find an opening for promotion or advancement. This should be the time to make a direct approach. The period favors those engaged in original research. CAUTION: Bask in popularity, not in flattery.

MOON IN VIRGO

Off comes the party cap and out steps the busy, practical worker. He wants to get his personal affairs straight, to rearrange them, if necessary, for more efficiency, so he will have more time for more work. He clears up his correspondence, pays outstanding bills, makes numerous phone calls. He is likely to make inquiries, or sign up for some new insurance and put money into gilt-edged investment. Thoughts probably revolve around the need for future security—to tie up loose ends and clear the decks. There may be a tendency to be "finicky," to interfere in the routine of others, particularly friends and family members. The motive may be a genuine desire to help with suggestions for updating or streamlining their affairs, but these will probably not be welcomed. Sympathy may be felt for less fortunate sections of the community and a flurry of some sort of voluntary service is likely. This may be accompanied by strong feelings of responsibility on several fronts and health may suffer from extra efforts made. CAUTION: Everyone may not want your help or advice.

MOON IN LIBRA

These are days of harmony and agreement and you should find yourself at peace with most others. Relationships tend to be smooth and sweet-flowing. Friends may become closer and bonds deepen in mutual understanding. Hopes will be shared. Progress by cooperation could be the secret of success in every sphere. In business, established partnerships may flourish and new ones get off to a good start. Acquaintances could discover similar interests that lead to congenial discussions and rewarding exchanges of some sort. Love, as a unifying force, reaches its optimum. Marriage partners should find accord. Those who wed at this time face the prospect of a happy union. Cooperation and tolerance are felt to be stronger than dissension and impatience. The argumentative are not quite so loud in their bellowings, nor as inflexible in their attitudes. In the home, there should be a greater recognition of the other point of view and a readiness to put the wishes of the group before selfish insistence. This is a favorable time to join an art group. CAUTION: Do not be too independent—let others help you if they want to.

MOON IN SCORPIO

Driving impulses to make money and to economize are likely to cause upsets all around. No area of expenditure is likely to be spared the ax, including the household budget. This is a time when the desire to cut down on extravagance can become near fanatical. Care must be exercised to try to keep the aim in reasonable perspective. Others may not feel the same urgent need to save and may retaliate. There is a danger that possessions of sentimental value will be sold to realize cash for investment. Buying and selling of stock for quick profit is also likely. The attention turns to organizing, reorganizing, tidying up at home and at work. Neglected jobs could suddenly be done with great bursts of energy. The desire for solitude may intervene. Self-searching thoughts could disturb. The sense of invisible and mysterious energies in play could cause some excitability. The reassurance of loves ones may help. CAUTION: Be kind to the people you love.

MOON IN SAGITTARIUS

These are days when you are likely to be stirred and elevated by discussions and reflections of a religious and philosophical nature. Ideas of faraway places may cause unusual response and excitement. A decision may be made to visit someone overseas, perhaps a person whose influence was important to your earlier character development. There could be a strong resolution to get away from present intellectual patterns, to learn new subjects, and to meet more interesting people. The superficial may be rejected in all its forms. An impatience with old ideas and unimaginative contacts could lead to a change of companions and interests. There may be an upsurge of religious feeling and metaphysical inquiry. Even a new insight into the significance of astrology and other occult studies is likely under the curious stimulus of the Moon in Sagittarius. Physically, you may express this need for fundamental change by spending more time outdoors: sports, gardening, long walks appeal. CAUTION: Try to channel any restlessness into worthwhile study.

MOON IN CAPRICORN

Life in these hours may seem to pivot around the importance of gaining prestige and honor in the career, as well as maintaining a spotless reputation. Ambitious urges may be excessive and could be accompanied by quite acquisitive drives for money. Effort should be directed along strictly ethical lines where there is no possibility of reproach or scandal. All endeavors are likely to be characterized by great earnestness, and an air of authority and purpose which should impress those who are looking for leadership or reliability. The desire to conform to accepted standards may extend to sharp criticism of family members. Frivolity and unconventional actions are unlikely to amuse while the Moon is in Capricorn. Moderation and seriousness are the orders of the day. Achievement and recognition in this period could come through community work or organizing for the benefit of some amateur group. CAUTION: Dignity and esteem are not always self-awarded.

MOON IN AQUARIUS

Moon in Aquarius is in the second last sign of the Zodiac where ideas can become disturbingly fine and subtle. The result is often a mental "no-man's land" where imagination cannot be trusted with the same certitude as other times. The dangers for the individual are the extremes of optimism and pessimism. Unless the imagination is held in check, situations are likely to be misread, and rosy conclusions drawn where they do not exist. Consequences for the unwary can be costly in career and business. Best to think twice and not speak or act until you think again. Pessimism can be a cruel self-inflicted penalty for delusion at this time. Between the two extremes are strange areas of self-deception which, for example, can make the selfish person think he is actually being generous. Eerie dreams which resemble the reality and even seem to continue into the waking state are also possible. CAUTION: Look for the fact and not just for the image in your mind.

MOON IN PISCES

Everything seems to come to the surface now. Memory may be crystal clear, throwing up long-forgotten information which could be valuable in the career or business. Flashes of clairvoyance and intuition are possible along with sudden realizations of one's own nature, which may be used for self-improvement. A talent, never before suspected, may be discovered. Qualities not evident before in friends and marriage partners are likely to be noticed. As this is a period in which the truth seems to emerge, the discovery of false characteristics is likely to lead to disenchantment or a shift in attachments. However, when qualities are accepted, it should lead to happiness and deeper feeling. Surprise solutions could bob up for old problems. There may be a public announcement of the solving of a crime or mystery. People with secrets may find someone has "guessed" correctly. The secrets of the soul or the inner self also tend to reveal themselves. Religious and philosophical groups may make some interesting discoveries. CAUTION: Not a time for activities that depend on secrecy.

NOTE: When you read your daily forecasts, use the Moon Sign Dates that are provided in the following section of Moon Tables. Then you may want to glance back here for the Moon's influence in a given sign.

MOON TABLES

CORRECTION FOR NEW YORK TIME, FIVE HOURS WEST OF GREENWICH

Atlanta, Boston, Detroit, Miami, Washington, Montreal, Ottawa, Quebec, Bogota, Havana, Lima, Santiago..Same time

Chicago, New Orleans, Houston, Winnipeg, Churchill, Mexico City .... Deduct 1 hour

Albuquerque, Denver, Phoenix, El Paso, Edmonton, Helena .... Deduct 2 hours

Los Angeles, San Francisco, Reno, Portland, Seattle, Vancouver .... Deduct 3 hours

Honolulu, Anchorage, Fairbanks, Kodiak .... Deduct 5 hours

Nome, Samoa, Tonga, Midway.................... Deduct 6 hours

Halifax, Bermuda, San Juan, Caracas, La Paz, Barbados ....Add 1 hour

St. John's, Brasilia, Rio de Janeiro, Sao Paulo, Buenos Aires, Montevideo..........................Add 2 hours

Azores, Cape Verde Islands...........................Add 3 hours

Canary Islands, Madeira, Reykjavik ....Add 4 hours

London, Paris, Amsterdam, Madrid, Lisbon, Gibraltar, Belfast, Rabat ....Add 5 hours

Frankfurt, Rome, Oslo, Stockholm, Prague, Belgrade...Add 6 hours

Bucharest, Beirut, Tel Aviv, Athens, Istanbul, Cairo, Alexandria, Cape Town, Johannesburg ....Add 7 hours

Moscow, Leningrad, Baghdad, Dhahran, Addis Ababa, Nairobi, Teheran, Zanzibar.........Add 8 hours

Bombay, Calcutta, Sri Lanka..................... Add 10 ½ hours

Hong Kong, Shanghai, Manila, Peking, Perth...... Add 13 hours

Tokyo, Okinawa, Darwin, Pusan.................... Add 14 hours

Sydney, Melbourne, Port Moresby, Guam.......... Add 15 hours

Auckland, Wellington, Suva, Wake................. Add 17 hours

1998 MOON SIGN DATES— NEW YORK TIME

JANUARY Day Moon Enters		FEBRUARY Day Moon Enters		MARCH Day Moon Enters	
1. Aquar.		1. Aries		1. Aries	
2. Pisces	4:57 am	2. Taurus	4:26 pm	2. Taurus	0:01 am
3. Pisces		3. Taurus		3. Taurus	
4. Aries	7:44 am	4. Gemini	8:10 pm	4. Gemini	2:16 am
5. Aries		5. Gemini		5. Gemini	
6. Taurus	10:53 am	6. Gemini		6. Cancer	7:28 am
7. Taurus		7. Cancer	1:58 am	7. Cancer	
8. Gemini	2:43 pm	8. Cancer		8. Leo	3:47 pm
9. Gemini		9. Leo	9:58 am	9. Leo	
10. Cancer	7:44 pm	10. Leo		10. Leo	
11. Cancer		11. Virgo	8:10 pm	11. Virgo	2:36 am
12. Cancer		12. Virgo		12. Virgo	
13. Leo	2:46 am	13. Virgo		13. Libra	2:59 pm
14. Leo		14. Libra	8:18 am	14. Libra	
15. Virgo	0:32 pm	15. Libra		15. Libra	
16. Virgo		16. Scorp.	9:14 pm	16. Scorp.	3:52 am
17. Virgo		17. Scorp.		17. Scorp.	
18. Libra	0:45 am	18. Scorp.		18. Sagitt.	3:57 pm
19. Libra		19. Sagitt.	8:57 am	19. Sagitt.	
20. Scorp.	1:35 pm	20. Sagitt.		20. Sagitt.	
21. Scorp.		21. Capric.	5:31 pm	21. Capric.	1:44 am
22. Scorp.		22. Capric.		22. Capric.	
23. Sagitt.	0:26 am	23. Aquar.	10:11 pm	23. Aquar.	8:02 am
24. Sagitt.		24. Aquar.		24. Aquar.	
25. Capric.	7:40 am	25. Pisces	11:43 pm	25. Pisces	10:44 am
26. Capric.		26. Pisces		26. Pisces	
27. Aquar.	11:28 am	27. Aries	11:43 pm	27. Aries	10:50 am
28. Aquar.		28. Aries		28. Aries	
29. Pisces	1:09 pm			29. Taurus	10:07 am
30. Pisces				30. Taurus	
31. Aries	2:22 pm			31. Gemini	10:39 am

Summer time to be considered where applicable.

1998 MOON SIGN DATES—
NEW YORK TIME

APRIL		MAY		JUNE	
Day Moon Enters		**Day Moon Enters**		**Day Moon Enters**	
1. Gemini		1. Cancer		1. Virgo	
2. Cancer	2:11 pm	2. Leo	4:50 am	2. Virgo	
3. Cancer		3. Leo		3. Libra	10:18 am
4. Leo	9:37 pm	4. Virgo	2:48 pm	4. Libra	
5. Leo		5. Virgo		5. Scorp.	11:07 pm
6. Leo		6. Virgo		6. Scorp.	
7. Virgo	8:26 am	7. Libra	3:20 am	7. Scorp.	
8. Virgo		8. Libra		8. Sagitt.	10:35 am
9. Libra	9:05 pm	9. Scorp.	4:11 pm	9. Sagitt.	
10. Libra		10. Scorp.		10. Capric.	7:51 pm
11. Libra		11. Scorp.		11. Capric.	
12. Scorp.	9:57 am	12. Sagitt.	3:49 am	12. Capric.	
13. Scorp.		13. Sagitt.		13. Aquar.	3:04 am
14. Sagitt.	9:53 pm	14. Capric.	1:40 pm	14. Aquar.	
15. Sagitt.		15. Capric.		15. Pisces	8:32 am
16. Sagitt.		16. Aquar.	9:31 pm	16. Pisces	
17. Capric.	8:06 am	17. Aquar.		17. Aries	0:24 pm
18. Capric.		18. Aquar.		18. Aries	
19. Aquar.	3:42 pm	19. Pisces	3:04 am	19. Taurus	2:48 pm
20. Aquar.		20. Pisces		20. Taurus	
21. Pisces	8:07 pm	21. Aries	6:07 am	21. Gemini	4:27 pm
22. Pisces		22. Aries		22. Gemini	
23. Aries	9:31 pm	23. Taurus	7:07 am	23. Cancer	6:40 pm
24. Aries		24. Taurus		24. Cancer	
25. Taurus	9:10 pm	25. Gemini	7:26 am	25. Leo	11:05 pm
26. Taurus		26. Gemini		26. Leo	
27. Gemini	8:56 pm	27. Cancer	8:59 am	27. Leo	
28. Gemini		28. Cancer		28. Virgo	6:55 am
29. Cancer	10:58 pm	29. Leo	1:39 pm	29. Virgo	
30. Cancer		30. Leo		30. Libra	6:06 pm
31. Virgo	10:22 pm				

Summer time to be considered where applicable.

1998 MOON SIGN DATES—
NEW YORK TIME

JULY Day Moon Enters		AUGUST Day Moon Enters		SEPTEMBER Day Moon Enters	
1. Libra		1. Scorp.		1. Capric.	
2. Libra		2. Sagitt.	2:49 am	2. Capric.	
3. Scorp.	6:46 am	3. Sagitt.		3. Aquar.	4:22 am
4. Scorp.		4. Capric.	0:19 pm	4. Aquar.	
5. Sagitt.	6:25 pm	5. Capric.		5. Pisces	7:49 am
6. Sagitt.		6. Aquar.	6:32 pm	6. Pisces	
7. Sagitt.		7. Aquar.		7. Aries	8:53 am
8. Capric.	3:28 am	8. Pisces	10:05 pm	8. Aries	
9. Capric.		9. Pisces		9. Taurus	9:17 am
10. Aquar.	9:53 am	10. Pisces		10. Taurus	
11. Aquar.		11. Aries	0:11 am	11. Gemini	10:41 am
12. Pisces	2:23 pm	12. Aries		12. Gemini	
13. Pisces		13. Taurus	2:05 am	13. Cancer	2:21 pm
14. Aries	5:46 pm	14. Taurus		14. Cancer	
15. Aries		15. Gemini	4:47 am	15. Leo	8:49 pm
16. Taurus	8:34 pm	16. Gemini		16. Leo	
17. Taurus		17. Cancer	1:56 am	17. Leo	
18. Gemini	11:19 pm	18. Cancer		18. Virgo	5:53 am
19. Gemini		19. Leo	3:02 pm	19. Virgo	
20. Gemini		20. Leo		20. Libra	4:58 pm
21. Cancer	2:44 am	21. Virgo	11:22 pm	21. Libra	
22. Cancer		22. Virgo		22. Libra	
23. Leo	7:50 am	23. Virgo		23. Scorp.	5:23 am
24. Leo		24. Libra	10:03 am	24. Scorp.	
25. Virgo	3:35 pm	25. Libra		25. Sagitt.	6:06 pm
26. Virgo		26. Scorp.	10:26 pm	26. Sagitt.	
27. Virgo		27. Scorp.		27. Sagitt.	
28. Libra	2:15 am	28. Scorp.		28. Capric.	5:31 am
29. Libra		29. Sagitt.	10:56 am	29. Capric.	
30. Scorp.	2:45 pm	30. Sagitt.		30. Aquar.	1:54 pm
31. Scorp.		31. Capric.	9:24 pm		

Summer time to be considered where applicable.

1998 MOON SIGN DATES— NEW YORK TIME

OCTOBER		NOVEMBER		DECEMBER	
Day Moon Enters		**Day Moon Enters**		**Day Moon Enters**	
1. Aquar.		1. Aries	6:28 am	1. Taurus	
2. Pisces	6:24 pm	2. Aries		2. Gemini	4:31 pm
3. Pisces		3. Taurus	6:13 am	3. Gemini	
4. Aries	7:33 pm	4. Taurus		4. Cancer	4:29 pm
5. Aries		5. Gemini	5:12 am	5. Cancer	
6. Taurus	6:58 pm	6. Gemini		6. Leo	6:56 pm
7. Taurus		7. Cancer	5:40 am	7. Leo	
8. Gemini	6:45 pm	8. Cancer		8. Leo	
9. Gemini		9. Leo	9:34 am	9. Virgo	1:22 am
10. Cancer	8:49 pm	10. Leo		10. Virgo	
11. Cancer		11. Virgo	5:38 pm	11. Libra	11:44 am
12. Cancer		12. Virgo		12. Libra	
13. Leo	2:26 am	13. Virgo		13. Libra	
14. Leo		14. Libra	4:59 am	14. Scorp.	0:17 am
15. Virgo	11:33 am	15. Libra		15. Scorp.	
16. Virgo		16. Scorp.	5:42 pm	16. Sagitt.	0:48 pm
17. Libra	11:03 pm	17. Scorp.		17. Sagitt.	
18. Libra		18. Scorp.		18. Capric.	11:56 pm
19. Libra		19. Sagitt.	6:14 am	19. Capric.	
20. Scorp.	11:37 am	20. Sagitt.		20. Capric.	
21. Scorp.		21. Capric.	5:46 am	21. Aquar.	9:18 am
22. Scorp.		22. Capric.		22. Aquar.	
23. Sagitt.	0:17 am	23. Capric.		23. Pisces	4:46 pm
24. Sagitt.		24. Aquar.	3:44 am	24. Pisces	
25. Capric.	0:06 pm	25. Aquar.		25. Aries	10:05 pm
26. Capric.		26. Pisces	11:15 am	26. Aries	
27. Aquar.	9:45 pm	27. Pisces		27. Aries	
28. Aquar.		28. Aries	3:35 pm	28. Taurus	1:06 am
29. Aquar.		29. Aries		29. Taurus	
30. Pisces	3:59 am	30. Taurus	4:54 pm	30. Gemini	2:23 am
31. Pisces				31. Gemini	

Summer time to be considered where applicable.

1998 PHASES OF THE MOON— NEW YORK TIME

New Moon	First Quarter	Full Moon	Last Quarter
Dec. 29 ('97)	Jan. 5	Jan. 12	Jan. 20
Jan. 28	Feb. 3	Feb. 11	Feb. 19
Feb. 26	Mar. 5	Mar. 12	Mar. 21
Mar. 27	Apr. 3	Apr. 11	Apr. 19
Apr. 26	May 3	May 11	May 18
May 25	June 1	June 9	June 17
June 23	July 1	July 9	July 16
July 23	July 31	Aug. 7	Aug. 14
Aug. 21	Aug. 30	Sept. 6	Sept. 12
Sept. 20	Sept. 28	Oct. 5	Oct. 12
Oct. 20	Oct. 28	Nov. 4	Nov. 10
Nov. 18	Nov. 26	Dec. 3	Dec. 10
Dec. 18	Dec. 26	Jan. 1 ('99)	Jan. 9 ('99)

Each phase of the Moon lasts approximately seven to eight days, during which the Moon's shape gradually changes as it comes out of one phase and goes into the next.

There will be a partial solar eclipse during the New Moon phase on February 26 and August 21.

1998 FISHING GUIDE

	Good	Best
January	5-9-10-13-14-15-28	11-12-20
February	9-10-11-12-13-14	3-8
March	5-10-11-12-13-28	14-15-16-21
April	8-9-19	3-10-11-12-13-14-26
May	3-12-13-14-25	8-9-10-11-19
June	2-8-9-10-13-17	7-11-12-24
July	6-7-10-11-12-16-23	1-8-9-31
August	7-8-11-22-30	5-6-9-10-14
September	3-4-5-7-8-9-13-20-28	6
October	2-5-6-28	3-4-7-8-12-20
November	1-2-3-5-6-7-11-19-30	4-27
December	2-3-4-10-18-26	1-5-6

1998 PLANTING GUIDE

	Aboveground Crops	Root Crops
January	2-3-7-11-30	18-19-20-21-22-26
February	3-4-7-8-27	15-16-17-18-22-23
March	2-3-7-11-12-30	14-15-16-17-21-22-26
April	3-4-10-11-27-30	12-13-14-18-22-23
May	1-7-8-9-10-28	15-16-19-20-24
June	4-5-6-7-24-25	11-12-16-20
July	1-2-3-4-5-8-28-29-30-31	13-17-18-21-22
August	1-5-6-25-26-27-28	9-10-13-14-18
September	1-2-21-22-23-24-25-29	10-14-15
October	3-4-21-22-26-27-30-31	7-8-11-12-18-19
November	22-23-27	4-8-14-15-16-17-18
December	1-19-20-24-25-28-29	5-6-12-13-14-15

	Pruning	Weeds and Pests
January	21-22	13-14-15-16-17-23-24
February	17-18	12-13-20-21-24-25
March	16-17-26	19-20-24
April	13-14-22-23	15-16-20-21-24-25
May	19-20	12-13-17-18-22
June	16	10-13-14-18-22-23
July	13-21-22	11-15-16-19-20
August	9-10-18	8-11-12-15-16-20-21
September	14-15	8-12-16-17-18-19
October	11-12	6-9-10-13-14-15-16-17
November	8-17-18	6-10-11-12-13
December	5-6-14-15	7-8-9-10-17-18

MOON'S INFLUENCE OVER PLANTS

Centuries ago it was established that seeds planted when the Moon is in signs and phases called Fruitful will produce more growth than seeds planted when the Moon is in a Barren sign.

Fruitful Signs: Taurus, Cancer, Libra, Scorpio, Capricorn, Pisces
Barren Signs: Aries, Gemini, Leo, Virgo, Sagittarius, Aquarius
Dry Signs: Aries, Gemini, Sagittarius, Aquarius

Activity	Moon In
Mow lawn, trim plants	**Fruitful sign:** 1st & 2nd quarter
Plant flowers	**Fruitful sign:** 2nd quarter; best in Cancer and Libra
Prune	**Fruitful sign:** 3rd & 4th quarter
Destroy pests; spray	**Barren sign:** 4th quarter
Harvest potatoes, root crops	**Dry sign:** 3rd & 4th quarter; Taurus, Leo, and Aquarius

MOON'S INFLUENCE OVER YOUR HEALTH

ARIES	Head, brain, face, upper jaw
TAURUS	Throat, neck, lower jaw
GEMINI	Hands, arms, lungs, shoulders, nervous system
CANCER	Esophagus, stomach, breasts, womb, liver
LEO	Heart, spine
VIRGO	Intestines, liver
LIBRA	Kidneys, lower back
SCORPIO	Sex and eliminative organs
SAGITTARIUS	Hips, thighs, liver
CAPRICORN	Skin, bones, teeth, knees
AQUARIUS	Circulatory system, lower legs
PISCES	Feet, tone of being

Try to avoid work being done on that part of the body when the Moon is in the sign governing that part.

MOON'S INFLUENCE OVER DAILY AFFAIRS

The Moon makes a complete transit of the Zodiac every 27 days 7 hours and 43 minutes. In making this transit the Moon forms different aspects with the planets and consequently has favorable or unfavorable bearings on affairs and events for persons according to the sign of the Zodiac under which they were born.

When the Moon is in conjunction with the Sun it is called a New Moon; when the Moon and Sun are in opposition it is called a Full Moon. From New Moon to Full Moon, first and second quarter—which takes about two weeks—the Moon is increasing or waxing. From Full Moon to New Moon, third and fourth quarter, the Moon is decreasing or waning.

Activity	Moon In
Business: buying and selling new, requiring public support	Sagittarius, Aries, Gemini, Virgo 1st and 2nd quarter
meant to be kept quiet	3rd and 4th quarter
Investigation	3rd and 4th quarter
Signing documents	1st & 2nd quarter, Cancer, Scorpio, Pisces
Advertising	2nd quarter, Sagittarius
Journeys and trips	1st & 2nd quarter, Gemini, Virgo
Renting offices, etc.	Taurus, Leo, Scorpio, Aquarius
Painting of house/apartment	3rd & 4th quarter, Taurus, Scorpio, Aquarius
Decorating	Gemini, Libra, Aquarius
Buying clothes and accessories	Taurus, Virgo
Beauty salon or barber shop visit	1st & 2nd quarter, Taurus, Leo, Libra, Scorpio, Aquarius
Weddings	1st & 2nd quarter

SCORPIO

SCORPIO

Character Analysis

The central thread of the Scorpio character is the struggle to release intense personal energy. Scorpios have the capacity to use personal energy either creatively or destructively, and sometimes self-destructively. No other sign of the Zodiac has the potential to change things for good or evil. Perhaps that is why Scorpio is denoted variously by three astrological symbols—the Scorpion, the Serpent, and the Eagle.

Like the stinging Scorpion, Scorpio individuals can be defensive in their reactions and devious in their motives. But the Scorpio man or woman can be as wise as the Serpent, and extremely successful in everyday life. And, like the Eagle, Scorpio can soar to exalted heights of service to humanity.

The Scorpion side of the mysterious and fascinating Scorpio individual naturally attracts the most attention, even notoriety. Such a reputation is certainly irritating to the very intelligent and reflective person born under the eighth sign of the Zodiac.

People born under the sign of Scorpio are usually gifted with a very strong personality. Of all the signs, they are perhaps the most goal-directed and relentless. Often they are quite dominating.

Some people find Scorpio hard to like or appreciate. But Scorpios are not afraid of being disliked. They just do not want to be ignored. They know what they want, generally speaking, and do not give up the struggle until they have it. They can be quite belligerent in stating their views. They aren't afraid of conflict or disapproval.

Scorpios have their own way of doing things—their own laws to follow. As long as they are true to themselves, they are happy. Scorpio seldom dances to someone else's tune. The Scorpio is a person who perseveres. It may take some time before they achieve their ends, but they'll wait. He or she pushes ahead, ignoring the setbacks, the disappointments.

Many people find it difficult to understand the personality of the person born under the sign of Scorpio. It is a subtle combination of intelligence and ruthlessness. Quite often people of this sign are seized by profound and revealing thoughts that are too complex to express. At such moments, the Scorpio is likely to draw within himself and remain silent.

Scorpios may spend such quiet moments within their own private world—a realm with its own rules and regulations. Scorpio is intrigued by the mysteries of life. He or she has an irrepressible desire to discover the truth. Some Scorpios have a deep almost intuitive understanding of life and death.

Scorpios tend to be consistent in all that they do. They never do things halfway. They are not afraid of conflict situations or emergencies. Under duress they can be relied upon to handle things in a calm manner. Scorpios are very constructive and positive in the way they channel their forces. They guard against waste and feel committed to make every gesture, every action, count.

In spite of a good sense of purpose and direction, Scorpio is sometimes the victim of conflicting moods. He may contradict himself several times a day without feeling that he is being untrue to himself and his beliefs. He or she believes that every moment has its own truth. They feel their moods strongly and believe that it is necessary to obey them in order to remain fixed. Scorpio is an organizer. He or she likes to have things their own way or not at all. On the whole, Scorpio is what you would call a principled person. They holds fast to their ideals.

The Scorpio understanding of life is sometimes remarkable. They are not short on insight and often can analyze a human situation accurately long before others. Their knowledge of things in general is often superior to that of others. In spite of their intelligence, they do not take the easy way toward a goal. They seem to have a penchant for argumentation. In some instances, Scorpio seems to bring about quarrels just for the enjoyment derived from crossing swords.

The Scorpio's ability to fly into a rage is considerable. People sometimes wind up disliking them intensely after having witnessed a fit of their temper. This does not bother Scorpio. If they lose a friend or two along the road of life, they are not apt to let it upset them. They keep moving on—the ultimate goal always in sight.

Scorpios do not believe in using fancy or complicated language. They go right to the point—not really caring how blunt they may sound to sensitive ears. Power—and how to get it—is what is most important to Scorpio. They do not try to hide this fact.

In spite of being being straight-off-the-shoulder in most of their dealings, the Scorpio man or woman is capable of holding back a fact or two—especially if it is to his or her advantage.

Health

On the whole, Scorpio men and women are quite healthy and have amazing recuperative powers. Their constitution is generally strong. They seldom have to worry about common ailments. They are capable of great spurts of energy. They can apply themselves to a strenuous task for a long period of time without tiring. The Scorpio man or woman enjoys stress and strain. It proves their mettle.

The Scorpio man or woman is seldom bothered by illnesses; their resistance is remarkably strong. When they do become ill—really ill—they have to give in in order to recuperate. Illness is a sort of weakness or frailty to Scorpio. They are ashamed when sick and do all they can to quickly recover. If they try to fight it—that is, act as though they aren't incapacitated—they often wind up worse off. It is difficult at times for Scorpio to realize that even he or she has limits.

In spite of the fact that he or she can take on a lot, it is also important that Scorpio learn how to relax. Often, Scorpio people push themselves to the limit—and sometimes there are serious consequences to pay. Overworked Scorpios are highly susceptible to breakdowns of various sorts. It is the cultivated Scorpio man or woman who knows when and how to relax. Because of their serious attitude toward most things, Scorpio when young often seems much older than he or she really is.

The Scorpio man or woman is sturdily built. There is usually something powerful about them. They are often large-boned and have deepset interesting eyes. In general, they could best be described as sensuous in their appearance and behavior. Scorpio women are often beautiful in a seductive way. Their voices are sometimes husky and rather sexy.

The weakest part of the Scorpio's anatomy is the digestive system. Whenever they become ill, this is the area usually affected. The sensible person born under this sign pays attention to minor warnings of an oncoming illness and does something about it while there is still time. Some Scorpio men and women pick up infections easily, but just as quickly throw them off.

Occupation

The Scorpio man or woman is a very industrious person. They enjoy keeping busy and always finish what they start. They do not believe in turning out slipshod work. Scorpio is a pro at whatever they do. They do not lack energy or push. They take their work seriously and want to be recognized for their deeds.

Quite often the person born under the sign of Scorpio dislikes heavy work. They would much rather leave that to someone else. They are goal-directed. It is important to achieve what they desire. In some instances, it does not matter how. When Scorpios set their minds to it—and they usually do—they can accomplish almost anything they wish.

Obstacles do not frighten Scorpio men and women. In fact, the threat of opposition seems to spur them on. Scorpio is no quitter. He or she will hang on until the bitter end. Their never-say-die attitude helps them scale heights that would frighten other people.

Scorpios are confident of themselves and of the moves they make.

The Scorpio person is ambitious. They can make work even when there isn't any—just to keep busy. Idleness tends to bore them and make them disagreeable. They are fascinated by difficult tasks. He or she enjoys figuring out ways of how to attack a project or a chore. Scorpio doesn't always choose the easiest route—but they choose the most challenging one.

Scorpio's intellectual ability is quite superior. There is almost no subject that would stump them. They are not afraid of learning something new and are quite capable of applying new or different trains of thought if they feel that will help them achieve their ends.

Generally speaking Scorpio people prefer to work for themselves. They don't like to share tasks, but will if it is absolutely necessary. People who work with them are not apt to find this relationship an enjoyable one, for the Scorpio is always ready to bring about a quarrel or argument if things are not going exactly the way they like.

Often people born under this sign do extremely well in the field of medicine or science. They have a deep interest in exploration of all sorts and are willing to devote their whole lives to something that is somewhat elusive and mysterious. Scorpio has an open mind, and this helps them to succeed in the things they do. They like to make tests, to prove things through experimentation. Scorpio isn't afraid of taking risks. He or she is always sure of himself—sure that they will come out a winner. Some people born under the sign of Scorpio make good detectives and lawyers.

The Scorpio person feels deeply whenever involved socially. They can either hate someone or love them; there is no middle of the road. They cannot afford to be indifferent. They will admire someone if that person deserves to be admired. Scorpio makes a strong leader. The people working under Scorpio may dislike him or her intensely, but they will not try to usurp authority. Scorpio won't put up with any nonsense from subordinates and lets them know that right from the start.

In whatever Scorpio undertakes, he or she forges ahead with no thought of quitting until the goal has been reached. Their powers of concentration are amazingly strong. They seldom allow themselves to be distracted from the path they have chosen. They expect the people working under them to have the same strength and devotion to purpose they have. They can be a hard driver at times. If others are not up to their standards, they won't waste time pampering and protecting. They will simply discard them and take on new people.

Some Scorpios have a bit of the genius in them. They are quite perceptive and often can accurately guess what someone else is thinking—particularly in a conflict situation.

People born under this sign are basically materialists. They are quite fond of money and what it can do and make no effort to disguise their interest. They are extremely power-oriented. Money seldom presents a problem to them. One way or another, they almost always come by the finances they feel they need or deserve. They are fond of luxuries as well, of course. They are sometimes deeply involved in such power games as keeping up with the Joneses. In most instances the Joneses wind up trying to keep up with them.

Scorpios are careful in the way they handle their finances. They do not believe in waste, although at times they are given to being extravagant. When they are wealthy, they can become a show-off about it. They can easily detect a false friend—someone who associates with them for the gain likely to be derived from the relationship.

Home and Family

In general, Scorpio men and women are not terribly interested in an intense domestic life. They do not like to feel tied down by home and family. However, they are adaptable and will be willing to sacrifice certain freedoms for the comforts and conveniences a home life can provide. Routine, though, bores them and can put them in a bad mood. They enjoy a home life that has a surprise in it now and again. Day-in day-out monotony is something Scorpio refuses to tolerate.

Scorpio individuals are as efficient and forceful in their homemaking as they are in other things. They see to it that everything runs well. The home may be glamorous in an ostentatious way. Scorpio is fond of a show of luxury. Their taste in furnishings is likely to be somewhat outspoken—at the very least, modern and daring. It may offend someone who has old-fashioned or traditional notions about decor.

Scorpio men and women are proud of their home, their possessions, and their loved ones. The family is geared to supporting the recreational and creative interests and studies of the Scorpio parent. Keeping the home attractive and luxurious is a full-time activity for many Scorpios. They are interested in having the latest appliances and the best trademark.

The Scorpio man likes to rule his own roost. His mate had better not try to take the head position. He wears the pants in the family and is apt to make that unmistakably clear before the marriage has taken place. All of the major decisions must be made by him. He'll listen to another's point of view, but will hardly take it into consideration when making up his mind.

Luxury helps the Scorpio man or woman to feel successful. It has definite psychological influence. The Scorpio in shabby surroundings is apt to be quite difficult to get along with. A show of affluence brightens their spirits and helps them to feel that they are on the right road.

The Scorpio person is often fond of large families. The Scorpio man may not be as responsible as he should be in caring for them. Quite often he is a strict parent and tolerates no misbehavior from his children. The children may resent his iron hand, especially when they are young. But as they reach adulthood they are likely to be thankful for his firmness. The Scorpio woman is concerned with instilling strong values in her children that will help them to go far in the battlefield of life. She can be quite a disciplinarian. Some Scorpio parents, both men and women, are quite possessive of their children.

Scorpios as children are often very affectionate. As a rule, they are sensitive children and should be handled in a considerate and loving way. Emotionally, they may not be as strong as children born under other signs. The observant and sensitive parent should have no trouble in bringing a youngster up in such a way that he or she is able to develop a personality along natural lines as they grow into the stage of independence.

At times the Scorpio child may be difficult to manage. They may be delinquent at times and cause some trouble at school. In spite of this, they are apt to show strong creative or artistic talent during the growing-up period. The wise parent or guardian will do everything to foster this interest in such a way that it develops along satisfactory lines.

Social Relationships

Scorpios often see life as one big fight. To them friends, casual acquaintances, and neighbors might become potential enemies. Often the Scorpio man or woman exhibits the iron control of a soldier. They are willing to undergo self-discipline in order to win out. They train themselves so that they are bound to be the victor if it comes to an all-out struggle, or even a minor skirmish.

Defeat is something the Scorpio man or woman cannot accept. They do their best to see to it that it never comes about. People born under this eighth sign of the Zodiac are skilled adversaries. Generally, they are gifted with brains and know how to put them to use. They can be clever and shrewd when the occasion calls for it.

Scorpios could hardly be called sensitive. Most of the time they are not terribly interested in how others might feel or react. Their nature is not a soft one. They can't be buttered up and sugared over. The Scorpio person generally says what he or she means. They can be quite cutting and when forced to can reduce an adversary to a pitiful state by just saying a few words. Scorpio is not the kind of person who encourages others with words of hope and best wishes. They're too concerned with their own aims for that.

Scorpio people are deeply interested in sex. They enjoy being physically involved with the people they feel themselves attracted to. They are often given to experimentation in sex. They are curious and want to know all there is to discover. They are, by and large, intensely passionate and intensely emotional.

Life without love is difficult for them to imagine. It is important to them that their sex life is well arranged and interesting. They may spend a great deal of time getting involved sexually with all kinds of people before they are satisfied and can concentrate their attention on just one person.

Love and Marriage

Scorpio can be quite a flirt. They may have quite a number of affairs before they think about settling down. In every romantic adventure they are quite sincere. They do not believe in being false or untrue when involved with someone. However, their interest may dissolve after they feel they have discovered everything there is to find out about a particular person. Scorpios are not interested in light romances. They mean business when it comes to love. They expect a lover to be honest and loyal.

Scorpio is in need of someone who is as passionate and understanding as they are. Their romances may be somewhat violent at times. An element of struggle and emotional drama may be quite definite. In fact, it is this quality that will perhaps keep Scorpio's interest alive in a love affair. They like to be admired and complimented by their partner. They hate criticism and may become difficult if a lover finds fault.

Scorpio does what he or she can to make a loved one comfortable and happy. They can be generous when in love and never without a gift or some token of their affection. They like to impress a loved one with a show of luxury. Often Scorpio's gifts are quite expensive.

It is important to Scorpios that the object of their affections be true during the relationship. They can be very jealous and possessive. If Scorpio suspects deceit, they can be violent.

The best partner for a Scorpio is one who can balance the Scorpio temperament—someone who does not mind being agreeable and supportive, someone who does not mind letting him or her make all of the decisions both large and small. A quiet, retiring sort of person sometimes makes the ideal mate for the man or woman born under Scorpio. Two Scorpios often clash. However, if they are cultivated and understand themselves well, they can go far together—helping each other out in various ways.

When the Scorpio man or woman sets their sights on someone, they generally succeed. They can be quite adversarial when dealing with someone who tries to stand between them and a loved one. Scorpios will do everything in their power to win the person who interests them. Some Scorpios will stop at nothing in order to eliminate competition and rivalry. Other Scorpios are jealous and suspicious when they really have no cause to be.

In married life, Scorpios seldom give themselves completely—even though they may expect this of a partner. There is always a corner, a secret side, that Scorpio protects. By nature, Scorpio men and women relish secrecy.

Scorpios are usually faithful, so a partner should not worry about the secrets or even absences from home and hearth. If home life is dull, Scorpio will not spend too much time there. There will be outside business or creative interests to keep them occupied.

Scorpio marries for keeps. They will not run to get a divorce or separation as soon as something goes wrong. Marriage is the most treasured bond in the world for a Scorpio. So they are willing to do whatever it takes to keep the relationship alive and fruitful.

Romance and the Scorpio Woman

The Scorpio woman is generally quite attractive and is often sought after by the opposite sex. Her attractiveness is sometimes more suggestive than real. Her voice is smooth, and mellow—her mannerisms dramatic.

She can be quite passionate when in love. She may be too much to handle for the man of moderate romantic interests. She does what she can to make a success of her love life. When in love, she does not hold back her affections. She expects the same honesty from her partner.

She is always serious when in love. She may have a great number of affairs before actually settling down. Romance is important to her. But more important is that she find a man who is compatible with her interests and needs. A man she desires, she usually wins. She is sure of herself in matters of the heart and can be very persuasive when necessary. Men find her difficult to ignore or resist. She may be jealous and possessive. If she suspects her lover of not being true, she can become quite angry and vindictive.

She is usually accurate when sizing up someone who interests her. She seldom chooses the wrong man. She is usually very faithful when married. She does all she can to help her man get ahead in his career. She supports him in all his interests and often is able to supply him with some very good advice. She will never let her husband down even in difficult times. She will fight for her husband and even take a job outside the home if it is necessary to make ends meet.

Scorpios have so much intense energy that they can handle the triple tasks of homemaker, mother, and career woman. But some Scorpio women have old-fashioned attitudes about marriage. She will be content with her role as wife and mother, and she will use her extraordinary creative talents in managing the household.

The Scorpio mother is an all-around homemaker, providing the children with all their material needs even if she has to go out and take a job to do so. If this is the case, the youngsters' emotional needs might suffer from lack of attention. Although the Scorpio mother idolizes her children, she can be quite strict, especially when they are young. As they grow older, they will understand and appreciate her better.

Romance and the Scorpio Man

The Scorpio man is often popular with women. There is something magnetic about his charm. He is protective and adventurous. His passionate way in love often sweeps women off their feet. Love— in each affair—is a matter of life and death. He does not believe in being lighthearted.

As a rule, he is warm and generous. He knows how to make a woman feel loved and wanted. He expects his loved one to be as demonstrative as he is in expressing her love. By nature, he is possessive and resents another's interest in his woman. He can easily become jealous. His anger can be quite frightening to a sensitive woman.

The Scorpio man makes a good husband and father. He is a good provider, most often, and sees to it that his family has everything it needs. His married life is apt to be full of ups and downs. He is affectionate, though, and true in his desire to be a good husband; this sometimes makes it easier for his wife to accept his changeable nature.

He is faithful. Once settled down he is apt to stay true to his wife. The cultivated Scorpio man is often successful in marriage. He knows how to withhold his negative traits so that they do not seriously affect the relationship.

He is fond of large families. Even though he may father one himself, he may not have enough interest in his children—especially when they are young—to make them feel secure and well loved. As the children grow older, however, and reach an adult stage, his interest is likely to increase considerably. At any rate, he will always see to it that they never want for anything.

Woman—Man

SCORPIO WOMAN
ARIES MAN

Scorpio and Aries are astrologically related through the planet Mars, so when you meet each other you recognize a kindred spirit. You both may believe you have found your true soul mate—for a while. Although it's possible you could find happiness with a man as rambunctious as his zodiacal symbol the Ram, it's uncertain how long that happiness would last.

An Aries who has made his mark in the world and is somewhat steadfast in his outlooks and attitudes could be quite a catch for you. On the other hand, men under this sign are often swift-footed and quick-minded. Their industrious mannerisms may fail to impress you, especially if you feel that much of their get-up-and-go often leads nowhere.

When it comes to a fine romance, you want someone with a nice, broad shoulder to lean on. You are likely to find a relationship with someone who doesn't like to stay put for too long somewhat upsetting.

The Aries man may have a little trouble in understanding you, too, at least in the beginning of the relationship. He may find you a bit too shy and moody. Aries men tend to speak their minds thoughtlessly. He might criticize you at the drop of a hat.

You may find a man born under this sign too demanding. He may give you the impression that he expects you to be at his beck and call. You have a lot of patience at your disposal and he may try every last bit of it. He is apt to be not as thorough as you in everything he does. In order to achieve success or a goal quickly, he will overlook small but important details—and regret it when it is too late.

Being married to an Aries does not mean that you'll have a secure and safe life as far as finances are concerned. Not all Aries are rash with cash, but they lack the sound head you perhaps have for putting away something for that inevitable rainy day. He'll do his best, however, to see that you're adequately provided for—even though his efforts may leave something to be desired as far as you're concerned.

With an Aries man for a mate, you'll find yourself constantly among people. Aries people generally have many friends, and you may not heartily approve of them all. Rams are often more interested in interesting people than they are in influential ones. Although there may be a family squabble from time to time, you are stable enough to be able to take it in your stride.

Kids take to Aries like ducks to water. His quick mind and

energetic behavior appeal to the young. His ability to jump from one thing to another will delight the kids and keep them active. The Aries father is young at heart and will spoil children every chance he gets. You must see to it that the youngsters stick to something until it is finished instead of abandoning one project after another with little to show for it.

SCORPIO WOMAN
TAURUS MAN

Taurus is your zodiacal mate in the astrological scheme of things, but also your zodiacal opposite. If you've got your heart set on a man born under the sign of Taurus, you'll have to learn the art of being patient. Taurus take their time about everything—even love.

The steady and deliberate Taurus man is a little slow on the draw. It may take him quite a while before he gets around to popping that question. For the woman who doesn't mind twiddling her thumbs, the waiting and anticipating almost always pays off. Taurus men want to make sure that every step they take is a good one, particularly if they feel that the path they're on leads to the altar.

If you are in the mood for a whirlwind romance, you had better cast your net in shallower waters. Moreover, most Taurus prefer to do the angling themselves. They are not keen on women taking the lead. Once she does, he may drop her like a dead fish. If you let yourself get caught on his terms, you'll find that he's fallen for you—hook, line, and sinker.

The Taurus man is fond of a comfortable home life. It is very important to him. If you keep those home fires burning, you will have no trouble keeping that flame in your Taurus mate's heart aglow. You have a talent for homemaking; use it. Your taste in furnishings is excellent. You know how to make a house come to life with colors and decorations.

Taurus, the strong, steady, and protective Bull, may not be your idea of a man on the move. Still he's reliable. Perhaps he could be the anchor for your dreams and plans. He could help you to acquire a more balanced outlook and approach to your life. If you're given to impulsiveness, he could help you to curb it. He's the man who is always there when you need him.

When you tie the knot with a man born under Taurus, you can put away fears about creditors pounding on the door. Taurus are practical about everything including bill paying. When he carries you over that threshold, you can be certain that the entire house is paid for, not only the doorsill.

As a wife, you won't have to worry about putting aside your many interests for the sake of back-breaking house chores. Your

Taurus hubby will see to it that you have all the latest time-saving appliances and comforts.

Astrologically linked together, the Scorpio-Taurus couple will make wonderful parents together. Taurus has much affection for the children, and has no trouble demonstrating his love and warmth. Yet the Taurus father does not believe in spoiling the kids. He thinks that children have a place, which is mainly to behave properly at all times. He is an excellent disciplinarian. Your Taurus husband will share with you the responsibility for bringing up obedient and polite youngsters.

SCORPIO WOMAN
GEMINI MAN

Gemini men, in spite of their charm and dashing manner, may leave you puzzled and unsatisfied. They may seem to lack the sort of common sense you set so much store in. Their tendency to start something out of boredom but never finish it may do nothing more than exasperate you.

You may be inclined to interpret a Gemini's jumping around from here to there as childish if not downright neurotic. A man born under the sign of the Twins will seldom stay put. If you should take it upon yourself to try and make him sit still, he will resent it and say so.

On the other hand, the Gemini man may think you're an opportunist—someone far too interested in security and material things. He's attracted to airy pleasures and doesn't want to get too deep about anything. You, with your intense way of looking at things most of the time, are likely to seem too serious for this gadabout. If you're looking for a life of security and permanence, you'd better look elsewhere for your Mr. Right.

Chances are you'll be taken by his charming ways and facile wit. Few women can resist Gemini magic. But after you've seen through his live-for-today, gossamer facade, you'll most likely be very happy to turn your attention to someone more stable, even if he is not as interesting. You want a man who is there when you need him. You need someone on whom you can fully rely. Keeping track of a Gemini's movements will make you dizzy. Still, if you are a patient woman, you should be able to put up with someone contrary—especially if you feel the experience may be well worth the effort.

A successful and serious Gemini could make you a very happy woman, perhaps if you gave him half a chance. Although you may think he's got bats in his belfry, the Gemini man generally has a good brain and can make good use of it when he wants. Some Geminis who have learned the importance of being diligent have risen to great heights, professionally. President Kennedy was a

Gemini as was Thomas Mann and William Butler Yeats. Once you can convince yourself that not all people born under the sign of the Twins are witless grasshoppers, you'll find that you've come a long way in trying to understand them.

Life with a Gemini man can be more fun than a barrel of clowns. You'll never experience a dull moment. He's always the life of the party. He's a little scatterbrained when it comes to handling money most of the time. You'd better handle the budgeting and bookkeeping.

The Gemini father is a pushover for the kids. He loves them so much, he generally lets them do what they want. His sense of humor is infectious, so the youngsters will naturally come to see the fun and funny sides of life. He will help to develop the children's mental and verbal skills at an early age. You will have to focus on the full emotional development of your young, which your Gemini mate might ignore.

SCORPIO WOMAN
CANCER MAN

The man born under the sign of Cancer may very well be the man after your own heart. Generally, Cancer people are steady. They are interested in security and practicality. Despite their seemingly grouchy exterior, men born under the sign of the Crab are sensitive and kind individuals. They are amost always hard workers and are very interested in becoming successful in business as well as in society.

You'll find that his conservative outlook on many things often agrees with yours. He'll be a man on whom you can depend come rain or shine. He'll never shirk his responsibilities as a provider and he'll always see to it that his wife and family never want.

Your patience will come in handy if you decide it's a Cancer man you want for a mate. He isn't the type that rushes headlong into romance. He wants to be sure about love as you do. If after the first couple of months of dating, he suggests that you take a walk with him down lovers' lane, don't jump to the conclusion that he's about to make his great play. Chances are he'll only hold your hand and seriously observe the stars.

Don't let his coolness fool you, though. Beneath his starched reserve lies a very warm heart. He's just not interested in showing off as far as affection is concerned. Don't think his interest is wandering if he doesn't kiss you goodnight at the front door; that just isn't his style. For him, affection should only be displayed for two sets of eyes—yours and his. He's passionate only in private.

He will never step out of line. He's too much of a gentleman for that. When you're alone with him and there's no chance of you being disturbed or spied upon, he'll pull out an engagement ring (the one that belonged to his grandmother) and slip it on your trembling finger.

Speaking of relatives, you'll have to get pretty much used to the fact that Cancer men are overly fond of their mothers. When he says his mother is the most wonderful woman in the world, you'd better agree with him—that is, if you want to become his wife.

He'll always be a faithful husband. Cancer men never play around after they've taken that marriage vow. They don't take marriage responsibilities lightly. He'll see to it that everything in the house runs smoothly and that bills are paid promptly—never put aside. He may take all kinds of insurance policies out on his family and property. He'll arrange it so that when retirement time rolls around, you'll both be very well off.

Cancers make proud, patient, and protective fathers. But they can be a little too protective. Their sheltering instincts can interfere with a youngster's natural inclination to test the waters outside the home. Still, the Cancer father doesn't want to see his kids learning about life the hard way from the streets. Scorpio courage, steadfastness, and knowledge of right and wrong will help the youngsters cope with a variety of life situations.

SCORPIO WOMAN
LEO MAN

To know a man born under the sign of the Lion is not necessarily to love him, even though the temptation may be great. When he fixes most girls with his leonine double-whammy, it causes their hearts to pitter-pat and their minds to cloud over.

You are a little too sensible to allow yourself to be bowled over by a regal strut and a roar. Still, there's no denying that Leo has a way with women—even sensible women like yourself. Once he's swept a girl off her feet, it may be hard for her to scramble upright again. However, you are no pushover for romantic charm—especially if you feel it's all show.

He'll wine you and dine you in the fanciest places. He'll croon to you under the moon and shower you with diamonds if he can get a hold of them. But it would be wise to find out just how long that shower is going to last before consenting to be his wife.

Lions in love are hard to ignore, let alone brush off. Your resistance will have a way of nudging him on until he feels he has you completely under his spell. Once mesmerized by this romantic powerhouse, you will most likely find yourself doing things you never dreamed of. Leos can be like vain pussycats when involved romantically. They like to be cuddled and adored. This may not be your cup of tea romantically.

Although he may be big and magnanimous while trying to win you, he'll whine if he thinks he's not getting the tender love and care he feels is his due. If you keep him well supplied with affection, you can be sure his eyes will never look for someone else and his heart will never wander.

Leo men often tend to be authoritarian. They are born to lord it over others in one way or another, it seems. If he is the top banana at his firm, he'll most likely do everything he can to stay on top. If he's not number one, he's most likely working on it and will be sitting on the throne before long.

You'll have more security than you can use if he is in a position to support you in the manner to which he feels you should be accustomed. He is apt to be too lavish, at least by your standards.

You'll always have plenty of friends when you have a Leo for a mate. He's a natural-born wheeler-dealer and entertainer. He loves to kick up his heels at a party.

Leo fathers have a tendency to spoil the children—up to a point. That point is reached when the children become the center of attention, and Leo feels neglected. Then the Leo father becomes strict and insists that his rules be followed. You will have your hands full pampering both your Leo mate and the children. As long as he comes first in your affections, the family will be happy and loving.

SCORPIO WOMAN
VIRGO MAN

Although the Virgo man may be a bit of a fussbudget at times, his seriousness and dedication to common sense may help you to overlook his tendency to sometimes be overcritical about minor things.

Virgo men are often quiet, respectable types who set great store in conservative behavior and levelheadedness. He'll admire you for your practicality and tenacity—perhaps even more than for your good looks. He's seldom bowled over by a glamour-puss. When he gets his courage up, he turns to a serious and reliable woman for romance. He'll be far from a Valentino while dating. In fact, you may wind up making all the passes. Once he does get his motor running, however, he can be a warm and wonderful fellow—to the right lover.

He's gradual about love. Chances are your romance with him will most likely start out looking like an ordinary friendship. Once he's sure you're no fly-by-night flirt and have no plans of taking him for a ride, he'll open up and rain sunshine all over your heart.

Virgo men tend to marry late in life. He believes in holding out until he's met the right mate. He may not have many names in his little black book. In fact, he may not even have a black book. He's not interested in playing the field; leave that to men of the more flamboyant signs.

The Virgo man is so particular that he may remain romantically inactive for a long period. His mate has to be perfect or it's no go. If you find yourself feeling weak-kneed for a Virgo man, do your best to convince him that perfect is not so important when it comes to love. Help him to realize that he's missing out on a great deal by not considering the near-perfect or whatever it is you consider yourself to be. With your surefire perseverance, you will most likely make him listen to reason and he'll wind up reciprocating your romantic interests.

The Virgo man is no block of ice. He'll respond to what he feels to be the right feminine flame. Once your love life with a Virgo man starts to bubble, don't give it a chance to fall flat. You may never have a second chance at winning his heart.

If you should ever have a separation from him, forget about patching up. He'd prefer to let the pieces lie scattered. Once married, though, he'll stay that way—even if it hurts. He's too conscientious to try to back out of a legal deal of any sort.

The Virgo father appreciates good manners and courtesy. He will instill a sense of order in the household, and he expects the children to respect his wishes. He is very concerned about the kids' health and hygiene, so he may try to restrict their freedom. You have a magic touch in matters of health, so you can reassure your Virgo mate and allow the children some leeway.

SCORPIO WOMAN
LIBRA MAN

You are apt to find men born under the sign of Libra too wrapped up in their own private dreams to be really interesting as far as love and romance are concerned. Quite often, he is a difficult person to bring back down to earth. It is hard for him to face reality at times. Although he may be very cautious about weighing both sides of an argument, he may never really come to a reasonable decision about anything.

Decision making is something that often makes the Libra man uncomfortable. He would rather leave that job to someone else. Don't ask him why for he probably doesn't know himself.

Qualities such as permanance and constancy are important to you in a love relationship. The Libra man may be quite a puzzle for you. One moment he comes on hard and strong with declarations of his love; the next moment you find he's left you like yesterday's mashed potatoes. It does no good to wonder what went wrong. Chances are nothing, really. It's just one of Libra's strange ways.

He is not exactly what you would call an ambitious person. You are perhaps looking for a mate or friend with more drive and fidelity. You are the sort of person who is interested in getting ahead—in making some headway in the areas that interest you.

Libra is often contented just to drift along. He does have drive, however, but it's not the long-range kind.

He's interested in material things. He appreciates luxuries and the like, but he may not be willing to work hard enough to obtain them. Beauty and harmony interest him. He'll dedicate a lot of time arranging things so that they are aesthetically pleasing. It would be difficult to accuse the Libra man of being practical; nine times out of ten, he isn't.

If you do begin a relationship with a man born under this sign, you will have to coax him now and again to face various situations in a realistic manner. You'll have your hands full, that's for sure. But if you love him, you'll undoubtedly do your best to understand him—no matter how difficult this may be.

If you take up with a Libra man, either temporarily or permanently, you'd better take over the task of managing his money. Often he has little understanding of financial matters. He tends to spend without thinking, following his whims.

The Libra father is patient and fair. He can be firm without exercising undue strictness or discipline. Although he can be a harsh judge at times, with the kids he will radiate sweetness and light in the hope that they will grow up imitating his gentle manner. In the interest of harmony, the Libra father may hide a few unpleasant facts of life from the youngsters. You will have to intervene and teach the kids about the birds and the bees, as well as the education needed to prepare them for real life.

SCORPIO WOMAN
SCORPIO MAN

When two Scorpios get together, it's either too much of a good thing or it's nothing at all. Can you put up with someone who is as explosive, as powerful, as possessive as you are? Perhaps you understand yourself better than you understand a Scorpio man. He's a lot like you in many ways, but there are lots of little ways he has that can irritate and madden you.

The Scorpio man hates being tied down to home life—he would rather be out on the battlefield of life, belting away at whatever he feels is a just and worthy cause, instead of staying home nestled in a comfortable armchair with the evening paper. As passionate as he is in business affairs and politics, the Scorpio man still has plenty of pep and ginger stored away for lovemaking.

Most women are easily attracted to him—perhaps you are no exception. Those who allow a man born under this sign to sweep them off their feet soon find that they're dealing with a pepper pot of seething excitement.

The Scorpio man is passionate with a capital P, but your passion is a match for his. Both of you are capable of dishing out emotional pain while you enjoy the sensual pleasure you have come to expect from this steamy combination of two water signs.

You both can complement each other's strengths, or prey on each other's weaknesses. You both are blunt, angry individuals. The Scorpion sting can insult each other, wound each other—yet remarkably it can heal each other. One of you will have to keep a stiff upper lip, take it on the chin, turn a deaf ear at times. You both are under each other's love spell in spite of everything.

If you have decided to take the bitter with the sweet, prepare yourself for a lot of ups and downs. Chances are you won't have as much time for your own affairs and interests as you'd like. The Scorpio man's love of power may cause you to be at his constant beck and call.

Scorpios like fathering large families. He is proud of his children, but often he fails to live up to his responsibilities as a parent. In spite of the extremes in his personality, the Scorpio man is able to transform the conflicting characteristics within himself when he becomes a father. When he takes his fatherly duties seriously, he is a powerful teacher. He believes in preparing his children for the hard knocks life sometimes delivers. He is adept with difficult youngsters because he knows how to tap the best in each child.

SCORPIO WOMAN
SAGITTARIUS MAN

Sagittarius men are not easy to catch. They get cold feet whenever visions of the altar enter the romance. You'll most likely be attracted to the Sagittarius because of his sunny nature. He's lots of laughs and easy to get along with. But as soon as the relationship begins to take on a serious hue, you may feel disappointed a little when Sagittarius starts to back away.

Sagittarius are full of bounce, perhaps too much bounce to suit you. They are often hard to pin down; they dislike staying put. If he ever has a chance to be on the move, he'll latch onto it without so much as a how-do-you-do. Sagittarius are quick people, both in mind and spirit. If ever they do make mistakes, it's because of their zip. They leap before they look.

If you offer him good advice, he most likely won't follow it. Saigittarius men like to rely on their own wits and ways.

His up-and-at-'em manner about most things is likely to drive you up the wall. He's likely to find you a little too intense and deliberate. Your competitive streak and compulsion to win will ruin the joy of the game for him. He can't abide an equally matched rival, especially one like you who against any odds may beat him.

At times you'll find him too much like a kid—too breezy. Don't mistake his youthful zest for premature senility. Sagittarius is equipped with first-class brainpower and knows how to use it.

They are often full of good ideas and drive. Generally, they are very broad-minded people and very much concerned with fair play and equality.

In the romance department, he's quite capable of loving you wholeheartedly while treating you like a good pal. His hail-fellow-well-met manner in the arena of love is likely to insult the deeply sexual Scorpio woman. However, a woman who knows that his heart is in the right place won't mind it too much if he behaves like a schoolboy once in a while.

He's not so much of a homebody. He's got ants in his pants and enjoys being on the move. Humdrum routine—especially at home—bores him silly. At the drop of a hat, he may ask you to dine out for a change. He's a past master in the instant surprise department. He'll love to keep you guessing. His friendly, candid nature will win him many friends. He'll expect his friends to be yours, and vice versa.

The Sagittarius father can be all thumbs when it comes to tiny tots. He will dote on any son or daughter dutifully, but he may be bewildered by the newborn. The Archer usually becomes comfortable with youngsters once they have passed through the baby stage. As soon as the children are old enough to walk and talk, the Sagittarius dad encourages each and every visible sign of talent and skill in his kids.

SCORPIO WOMAN
CAPRICORN MAN

The Capricorn man is quite often not the romantic kind of lover that attracts most women. Still, with his reserve and calm, he is capable of giving his heart completely once he has found the right woman. The Capricorn man is thorough and deliberate in all that he does; he is slow and sure.

He doesn't believe in flirting and would never lead a heart on a merry chase just for the game of it. If you win his trust, he'll give you his heart on a platter. Quite often, it is the woman who has to take the lead when romance is in the air. As long as he knows you're making the advances in earnest, he won't mind. In fact, he'll probably be grateful.

Don't get to thinking he's all reserve and reason. He's just inhibited. While some Capricorns are indeed quite capable of expressing passion, others often have difficulty in trying to display affection. He should have no trouble in this area, however, once he has found a patient and understanding lover.

The Capricorn man is very interested in getting ahead. He's quite ambitious and usually knows how to apply himself well to whatever task he undertakes. He's far from being a spendthrift. Like you, he knows how to handle money with extreme care. You, with your knack for putting away pennies for that rainy day, should have no difficulty understanding his way with money.

The Capricorn man thinks in terms of future security. He wants to make sure that he and his wife have something to fall back on when they reach retirement. There's nothing wrong with that. In fact, it's a plus quality.

The Capricorn man will want you to handle household matters efficiently. The dynamic and creative Scorpio woman will have no trouble in doing this. If he should check up on you from time to time, don't let it irritate you. Once you assure him that you can handle it all to his liking, he'll leave you alone.

The Capricorn man likes to be liked. He may seem dull to some, but underneath his reserve there is sometimes an adventurous streak that has never had a chance to express itself. He may be a real dare-devil in his heart of hearts. The right woman—the affectionate, adoring woman—can bring out that hidden zest in his nature.

The Capricorn father is a dutiful parent and takes a lifelong interest in seeing that his children make something of themselves. He may not understand their hopes and dreams because he often tries to put his head on their shoulders. The Capricorn father believes that there are certain goals to be achieved, and there is a traditional path to achieving them. He can be quite a scold if the youngsters break the rules. You will have to soften his sometimes rigid approach and smooth things over for the kids.

SCORPIO WOMAN
AQUARIUS MAN

You may find the Aquarius man the most broad-minded man you have ever met. On the other hand, you may also find him the most impractical. Oftentimes, he's more of a dreamer than a doer. If you don't mind putting up with a man whose heart and mind are as wide as the universe but whose head is usually only in the clouds, then start dating that Aquarius who has somehow captured your fancy.

He's no dumbbell, make no mistake about that. He can be busy making some very complicated and idealistic plans when he's got that out-to-lunch look in his eyes. But more than likely, he'll never execute them. After he's shared one or two of his progressive ideas with you, you may think he's crazy. But don't go jumping to conclusions. There's a saying that Aquarius are a half-century ahead of everybody else in the thinking department.

If you decide to marry him you'll find out how right his zany whims are on or about your 50th anniversary. Maybe the waiting will be worth it. Could be that you have an Einstein on your hands—and heart.

Life with an Aquarius won't be one of total despair if you can learn to temper his airiness. Aquarius always maintains an open mind. He'll entertain the ideas and opinions of everybody although he may not agree with all of them.

His broad-mindedness doesn't stop when it comes to you and your personal freedom. You won't have to give up any of your hobbies or projects after you're married. He'll encourage you to continue in your interests.

He'll be a kind and generous husband. He'll never quibble over petty things. Keep track of the money you both spend. He can't. Money burns a hole in his pockets.

At times, you may feel like calling it quits because he fails to satisfy your intense feelings. Chances are, though, that you'll always give him another chance.

The Aquarius father has an almost intuitive understanding of children. He sees them as individuals in their own right, not as extensions of himself or as beings who are supposed to take a certain place in the world. He can talk to the kids on a variety of subjects, and his knowledge can be awe-inspiring. You will sometimes have to bring the youngsters back down to earth, but you will appreciate the lessons of justice and tolerance your Aquarius mate has transmitted to the children.

SCORPIO WOMAN
PISCES MAN

The Pisces man could be the man you've looked for high and low and thought never existed. He's terribly sensitive and terribly romantic. Still, he has a very strong individual character and is well aware that the moon is not made of green cheese. He'll be very considerate of your every wish and will do his best to see to it that your relationship is a happy one.

The Pisces man is great for showering the object of his affection with all kinds of little gifts and tokens of his love.

He's just the right mixture of dreamer and realist. He's capable of pleasing most women's hearts. When it comes to earning bread and butter, the strong Pisces will do all right in the world. Quite often they are capable of rising to the very top. Some do extremely well as writers or psychiatrists.

He'll be as patient and understanding with you as you will undoubtedly be with him. One thing a Pisces man dislikes is pettiness. Anyone who delights in running another into the ground is almost immediately crossed off his list of possible mates. If you have any grievances with anyone, don't tell him. He couldn't care less and will think less of you if you do.

If you fall in love with a weak kind of Pisces, don't give up your job at the office before you get married. Better hang onto it until a good time after the honeymoon; you may still need it.

A funny thing about the man born under the sign of the Fishes is that he can be content almost anywhere. This is perhaps because he is quite inner-directed and places little value on material things. In a shack or a palace, the Pisces man is capable of making the best of all possible adjustments. He won't kick up a fuss if the roof leaks or if the fence is in sad need of repair. He's got more important things on his mind. At this point, you'll most likely feel like giving him a piece of your mind. Still and all, the Pisces man is not shiftless or aimless; it is important to understand that material gain is never a direct goal for him.

Pisces men have a way with the sick and troubled. He can listen to one hard-luck story after another without seeming to tire. He often knows what's bothering someone before that someone knows it himself.

As a lover, he'll be quite attentive. You'll never have cause to doubt his intentions or sincerity. Everything will be aboveboard in his romantic dealings with you.

Children are delighted with the Pisces father because of his permissiveness. Because of his live-and-let-live attitude, Pisces men are immensely popular with the young. For tots, the Pisces dad plays the double role of confidant and playmate. It will never enter his mind to discipline a child, no matter how spoiled or incorrigible the youngster becomes.

Man—Woman

SCORPIO MAN
ARIES WOMAN

Although Scorpio and Aries are kin, you both come from different sides of the family ruled by planet Mars. Both of you are ambitious and bossy. But the Aries way lacks foresight and calculation, so important to the steel-willed Scorpio.

Aries can become a little impatient with people who are more thorough and deliberate than they are—especially if they feel they're taking too much time. The Aries woman is a fast worker. Sometimes she's so fast she forgets to look where she's going. When she stumbles or falls, it would be nice if you were there to catch her.

Aries are proud women. They don't like to be criticized when they err. Tongue lashings can turn them into blocks of ice. Don't begin to think that the Aries woman frequently gets tripped up in her plans. Quite often they are capable of taking aim and hitting the bull's-eye. You'll be flabbergasted at times by their accuracy. On the other hand, you're apt to spot a flaw in the Aries woman's plans before she does.

You are more thoughtful and deliberate than the Aries in attaining your goals. You do not want to make mistakes along the way. You're almost always well prepared.

The Aries woman is sensitive. She likes to be handled with gentleness and respect. Let her know that you love her for her brains as well as for her good looks. Never give her cause to become jealous. Handle her with tender love and care, and she's yours.

The Aries woman can be giving if she feels her partner is deserving. She is no iceberg; she responds to the proper masculine flame. She needs a man she can look up to and feel proud of. If the shoe fits, put it on. If not, quietly tiptoe out of her sight. She can cause you plenty of heartache if you've made up your mind about her but she hasn't made up hers about you. Aries women are at times very demanding. Some of them tend to be highstrung. They can be difficult if they feel their independence is being hampered.

The cultivated Aries woman makes a wonderful homemaker and hostess. You'll find she's very clever in decorating and using color. Your house will be tastefully furnished; she'll see to it that it radiates harmony. The Aries wife knows how to make guests feel at home.

Although the Aries woman may not be keen on burdensome responsibilities, she is fond of children and the joy they bring. She is skilled at juggling both career and motherhood, so her kids will never feel that she is an absentee parent. In fact, as the youngsters grow older, they might want a little more of the liberation that is so important to her.

SCORPIO MAN
TAURUS WOMAN

The astrological link between Scorpio and Taurus draws you both together in the hopes of an ideal partnership, blessed by the stars. But the woman born under the sign of Taurus may lack a little of the sparkle and bubble you need for the challenge of love and romance.

The Taurus woman is generally down to earth and never flighty. It's important to her that she keep both feet flat on the ground. She is not fond of bounding all over the place, especially if she's under the impression that there's no profit in it.

On the other hand, if you hit it off with a Taurus woman, you won't be disappointed in romance. The Taurus woman is all woman and proud of it too. She can be very devoted and loving once she decides that her relationship with you is no fly-by-night romance. Basically, she's a passionate person.

In sex, she's direct and to the point. If she really loves you, she'll let you know she's yours—and without reservations. Better not flirt with other women once you've committed yourself to her. She is capable of being jealous and possessive, like you.

She'll stick by you through thick and thin. It's almost certain that if the going ever gets rough, she'll not go running home to her mother. She can adjust to hard times just as graciously as she can to the good times.

Taurus women are, on the whole, even-tempered and calm. They like to be treated with kindness and generosity. Luxurious things, soft and feminine, will please your Taurus mate.

You may find her too cautious and deliberate. She likes to be safe and sure about everything. Let her plod along if she likes. Don't coax her but just let her take her own sweet time. Everything she does is done thoroughly and, generally, without mistakes. Don't ride her for being habit-bound and a traditionalist by nature.

The Taurus woman doesn't anger readily but when prodded enough, she's capable of letting loose with a cyclone of anger. If you treat her with kindness and consideration, you'll have no cause for complaint.

The Taurus woman loves doing things for her man. She's a whiz in the kitchen and can whip up feasts fit for a king if she thinks they'll be royally appreciated. She may not fully understand you, but she'll adore you and be faithful to you if she feels you're worthy of it.

The woman born under Taurus will make a wonderful mother. She knows how to keep her children loved, cuddled, and warm. She may find them difficult to manage, however, when they are teenagers. The Taurus woman is your true zodiacal mate, so as parents you both will be dividing the responsibilities for the children. Whenever she has trouble understanding the kids, your ability to see beneath the surface of things will be invaluable.

SCORPIO MAN
GEMINI WOMAN

The Gemini woman may be too much of a flirt to ever strike your heart seriously. Then again, it depends on what kind of mood she's in. Gemini women can change from hot to cold quicker than a cat can wink its eye.

Chances are her fluctuations will tire you, and you'll pick up your heart—if it's not already broken into small pieces—and go elsewhere. Women born under the sign of the Twins have the talent of being able to change their moods and attitudes as frequently as they change their party dresses.

Sometimes, Gemini woman like to whoop it up. Some of them are good-time gals who love burning the candle at both ends. You'll see them at parties and gatherings, surrounded by men of all types, laughing gaily and kicking up their heels. Wallflowers, they're not. The next day you may bump into her at the neighborhood library and you'll hardly recognize her for her sensible attire. She'll probably have five or six books under her arm—on five or six different subjects. In fact, she may even work there.

You'll probably find her a dazzling and fascinating creature—for a time, at any rate. Most men do. But when it comes to being serious about love you may find that this sparkling Eve leaves quite a bit to be desired. It's not that she has anything against being serious, it's just that she might find it difficult trying to be serious with someone as intense as you.

At one moment, she'll be capable of praising you for your dynamic, inventive lovemaking. The next moment she'll tell you in a cutting way that you're too strange and devious.

Don't even begin to fathom the depths of her mercurial soul—it's full of false bottoms. She'll resent close investigation, anyway, and will make you rue the day you ever took it into your head to try to learn more about her than she feels is necessary.

Better keep the relationship fancy-free and full of fun until she gives you the go-ahead. Take as much of her as she is willing to give; don't ask for more. If she does take a serious interest in you, then she'll declare herself yours.

There will come a time when the Gemini woman will realize that she can't spend her entire life at the ball. The security and warmth you have to offer are just what she needs to be a happy, complete woman.

A Gemini mother is easygoing and enjoys her children, which can be the truest form of love. Like them, she's often restless, adventurous, and easily bored. She will never complain about their fleeting interests because she understands the changes they will go through as they mature.

SCORPIO MAN
CANCER WOMAN

The woman born under Cancer needs to be protected from the cold, cruel world. She'll love you for your masculine yet gentle manner; you make her feel safe and secure.

You don't have to pull any he-man or heroic stunts to win her heart; that's not what interests her. She's more likely to be impressed by your sure, steady ways—that way you have of putting your arm around her and making her feel that she's the only one in the world. When she's feeling glum and tears begin to well up in her eyes, you have that knack of saying just the right thing—you know how to calm her fears, no matter how silly some of them may seem.

The Cancer female is inclined to have her ups and downs. You have that talent for smoothing out the ruffles in her sea of life. She'll most likely worship the ground you walk on or put you on a terribly high pedestal. Don't disappoint her if you can help it. She'll never disappoint you.

Your Cancer mate will take great pleasure in devoting the rest of her natural life to you. She'll darn your socks, mend your overalls, scrub floors, wash windows, shop, cook, and do just about anything short of murder in order to please you and to let you know that she loves you. Sounds like that legendary good old-fashioned girl, doesn't it? Contrary to popular belief, there are still a good number of them around—and many of them are Cancer people.

There's one thing you should be warned about: never be unkind to your mother-in-law. It will be the only golden rule your Cancer wife will probably expect you to live up to. No mother-in-law jokes in the presence of your wife, please. With her, they'll go over like a lead balloon. Mother is something special for her. She may be the crankiest and nosiest relative in the whole clan. Still, she's your wife's mother, so you'd better treat her like she's one of the landed gentry. Sometimes this may be difficult to swallow, but if you want to keep your home together and your wife happy, you'd better learn to grin and bear it.

Treat your Cancer wife like a queen and she'll treat you royally.

Of all the signs of the Zodiac, the women under the Cancer sign are the most maternal. In caring for and bringing up children, they know just how to combine the right amount of tenderness with the proper dash of discipline. A child couldn't ask for a better mother. Cancer women are sympathetic, affectionate, and patient with their children.

SCORPIO MAN
LEO WOMAN

If you can manage a dame who likes to kick up her heels every now and again, then the Leo woman was made for you. You'll have to learn to put away jealous fears—or at least forget about them—when you take up with a woman born under this sign. The Lioness makes heads turn and tongues wag. You don't necessarily have to believe any of what you hear—it's most likely just jealous gossip or wishful thinking.

Take up with a Leo woman and you'll be taking off on a romance full of fire and ice. Be prepared to take the good things with the bad—the bitter with the sweet.

Lady Leo has more than a fair share of grace and glamour. She is aware of her charms and knows how to put them to good use. Needless to say, other women in her vicinity turn green with envy and will try anything to put her out of commission.

If she's captured your heart and fancy, woo her intensely if your intention is to eventually win her. Shower her with expensive gifts and promise her the moon—if you're in a position to go that far. Then you'll find her resistance beginning to weaken. She will probably make a fuss over you once she's decided you're the man for her. But she does enjoy a lot of attention. What's more, she feels she's entitled to it. Her mild arrogance, though, is becoming. The Leo woman knows how to transform the crime of excessive pride into a very charming misdemeanor. It sweeps most men right off their feet. Those who do not succumb to her leonine charm are few and far between.

If you've got an important business deal to clinch and you have doubts as to whether or not it will go over well, bring your Leo lover along to that business luncheon and it's a cinch that the contract will be yours. She won't have to do or say anything—just be there, at your side. The grouchiest oil magnate can be transformed into a gushing, obedient schoolboy if there's a Leo woman in the room.

If you're rich and want to stay that way, don't give your Leo mate a free hand with the charge accounts and credit cards. If you're poor, the luxury-loving Leo will most likely never enter your life.

A Leo mother can be so proud of her children that she is sometimes blind to their faults. Yet when she wants them to learn and take their rightful place in the social scheme of things, the Leo mother can be strict. She is a patient teacher, lovingly explaining the rules the youngsters are expected to follow. Easygoing and friendly, she loves to pal around with the kids and show them off on every occasion.

SCORPIO MAN
VIRGO WOMAN

The Virgo woman may be a little too difficult for you to understand at first. Her waters run deep. Even when you think you know her, don't take any bets on it. She's capable of keeping things hidden in the deep recesses of her womanly soul—things she'll only release when she's sure that you're the man she's been looking for.

It may take her some time to come around to this decision. Virgo women are finicky about almost everything. Everything has to be letter-perfect before they're satisfied. Many of them have the idea that the only people who can do things right are Virgos.

Nothing offends a Virgo woman more than slovenly dress, sloppy character, or a careless display of affection. Make sure your tie is not crooked and your shoes sport a bright shine before you go calling on this lady. Keep your off-color jokes for the locker room, she'll have none of that.

Don't rush the romance. Trying to corner her in the back of a cab may be one way of striking out. Never criticize the way she looks. In fact, the best policy would be to agree with her as much as possible. Still, there's just so much a man can take. All those dos and don'ts you'll have to follow if you want to get to first base can turn off the passionate Scorpio man.

After a few dates, you may come to the conclusion that she just isn't worth all that trouble. However, the Virgo woman is mysterious enough, generally speaking, to keep her men running back for more. Chances are you'll be intrigued by her airs and graces.

If lovemaking means a lot to you, you'll be disappointed at first in the cool ways of your Virgo woman. However, under her glacial facade there lies a cauldron of seething excitement. If you're patient and artful in your romantic approach, you'll find that all that caution was well worth the trouble. When Virgos love, they don't stint. It's all or nothing as far as they're concerned. Once they're convinced that they love you, they go all the way, tossing caution to the wind.

One thing a Virgo woman can't stand in love is hypocrisy. They don't give a hoot about what the neighbors say when their hearts tell them to go ahead. They're very concerned with human truths, just as you are. So if their hearts stumble upon another fancy, they will be true to that new heartthrob and leave you standing in the rain. She's honest to her heart and will be as true to you as you are with her, generally. Do her wrong once, however, and it's farewell.

The Virgo mother has high expectations for her children, and she will strive to bring out the very best in them. She is more tender than strict, though, and will nag rather than discipline. But youngsters sense her unconditional love for them, and usually turn out just as she hoped they would.

SCORPIO MAN
LIBRA WOMAN

As the saying goes, it's a woman's prerogative to change her mind. Whoever said it must have had the Libra woman in mind. Her changeability, in spite of its undeniable charm, could actually drive even a man of your patience up the wall. She's capable of smothering you with love and kisses one day, and on the next avoid you like the plague.

Scorpio is a man of steel nerves, so you probably can tolerate her sometime-ness without suffering too much. However, if you own up to the fact that you're only a mere mortal who can only take so much, then you'd better fasten your attention on a woman who's somewhat more constant.

But don't get the wrong idea. A love affair with a Libra is not bad at all. In fact, it can have an awful lot of pluses to it. Libra women are soft, very feminine, and warm. She doesn't have to vamp all over the place in order to gain a man's attention. Her delicate presence is enough to warm the cockles of any man's heart. One smile, and you're putty in the palm of her hand.

She can be fluffy and affectionate—things you like in a woman. On the other hand, her indecision about which dress to wear, what to cook for dinner, or whether to redo the rumpus room could make you tear your hair out. What will perhaps be more exasperating is her flat denial of the accusation that she cannot make even the simplest decision. The trouble is that she wants to be fair or just in all matters. She'll spend hours weighing pros and cons. Don't make her rush into a decision; that will only irritate her.

The Libra woman likes to be surrounded by beautiful things. Money is no object where beauty is concerned. There will always be plenty of flowers in the house. She'll know how to arrange them tastefully, too. Women born under this graceful sign are fond of beautiful clothes and furnishings. They will run up bills without batting an eye—if given the chance.

Once she's cottoned to you, the Libra woman will do everything in her power to make you happy. She'll wait on you hand and foot when you're sick and bring you breakfast in bed. She'll be very thoughtful and devoted. If anyone dares suggest you're not the grandest man in the world, your Libra wife will give that person a piece of her mind.

The Libra mother is well-balanced and moderate, and will overcome any extremes or disharmony in the family household. She will create an environment sensitive to the needs of every child. The Libra mother understands that young ones need both guidance and encouragement as they grow and change. Her youngsters will never lack for anything that would make their lives easier and richer.

SCORPIO MAN
SCORPIO WOMAN

The Scorpio woman can be a whirlwind of passion, but never too much passion to suit the Scorpio man. As long as your timing together is right, you won't have to worry about satisfying each other. It is when a love affair between you gets out of the bedroom and into the boardroom that the trouble can start.

She may not see eye-to-eye with you on a multitude of matters, ranging from the most monumental issue to the most minor one. But try never to cross her on even the most trivial thing. When it comes to revenge, she's an eye-for-an-eye woman—as you well know.

The Scorpio woman may have less control over her temper than you do. And her moods will baffle even you, with your own tendency to go to extremes. She can be as hot as a tamale one minute, then cool as a cucumber the next. And you know her moods are for real, so you better cater to them if you want the affair to last.

Life with the Scorpio woman will be a challenge. When prompted, she can unleash a gale of venom. Generally, she'll have the good grace to keep family battles within the walls of your home. When company visits, she's apt to give the impression that married life with you is one great big joyride. It's just one of her ways of expressing her loyalty to you—at least in front of others. She may fight you tooth and nail in the confines of home, but during an evening out, she'll hang onto your arm and have stars in her eyes.

The Scorpio woman is sultry and seductive. Her femme fatale charm can pierce the hardest of hearts like a laser beam. She may not look like Mata Hari, but she possesses all the allure and tradecraft of the perfect secret agent—the successful spy who will uncover all your private desires while never revealing any of her own.

Scorpio women are adept at keeping secrets. She may even keep a few buried from you while she is cleverly unearthing facts of your life that you thought were carefully hidden.

You are well advised not to give your Scorpio mate any cause to be jealous. When she sees green, your life will be made far from rosy. She's not keen on forgiving and forgetting—especially if she feels she's been wronged unfairly.

You may find life with a Scorpio woman one explosive scene after another. On the other hand, once the two of you understand and respect each other's deep swirling undercurrents, you can get along very nicely and lovingly.

When you both decide to spend the rest of your natural days with each other, you can be flexible and mutually helpful. You can take the highs with the lows, the rough with the smooth, the calm with the storm. Your Scorpio woman can be a demon, but she also can be a heavenly angel when she ministers to your care.

Although the Scorpio mother loves her children, she will not put them on a pedestal. She is devoted to developing her youngsters' talents. The Scorpio mother is protective yet encouraging. The opposites within her nature mirror the contradictions within life itself. Under her skillful guidance, the children will learn how to cope with extremes and will grow up to become well-rounded individuals. She will teach her young ones to be courageous and steadfast.

SCORPIO MAN
SAGITTARIUS WOMAN

The Sagittarius woman is hard to keep track of. First she's here, then she's there. She's a woman with a severe case of itchy feet. She's got to keep on the move.

People generally like her because of her hail-fellow-well-met manner and breezy charm. She is constantly good-natured and almost never cross. She is the kind of gal with whom you can be palsy-walsy. You might not be interested in letting the relationship go any farther. She probably won't sulk if you leave it on a friendly basis, either. Treat her like a kid sister and she'll eat it up like candy.

She'll probably be attracted to you because of your restful, self-assured manner. She'll need a friend like you to help her over the rough spots in her life. She'll most likely turn to you for advice.

There is nothing malicious about a Sagittarius woman. She is full of bounce and good cheer. Her sunshiny disposition can be relied upon on even the rainiest of days. No matter what she says or does, you'll always know that she means well.

Sagittarius is sometimes short on tact. Some of them will say anything that comes into their heads, no matter what the occasion. Sometimes the words that tumble out of their mouths seem downright cutting and cruel. They mean well, but often everything they say comes out wrong. She's quite capable of losing her friends—and perhaps even yours—through a careless slip of the lip. Always remember that she is full of good intentions. Stick with her if you like her and try to help her mend her ways.

She's not a woman you'd most likely be interested in marrying, but she'll certainly be lots of fun to pal around with. Quite often, Sagittarius women are outdoor types. They're crazy about sports, especially wilderness activities such as fishing, camping, and mountain climbing. They love the wide open spaces. They are fond of all kinds of animals. Make no mistake about it, this busy little lady is no slouch. She's full of fire and fun.

She's great company most of the time. She's more fun than a three-ring circus when she's in the right company. You'll like her for her candid and direct manner. On the whole, Sagittarius are very kind and sympathetic women.

If you do wind up marrying this girl-next-door type, you'd better see to it that you handle all of the financial matters. Sagittarius often let money run through their fingers like sand.

The Sagittarius mother is a wonderful and loving friend to her children. She'll smother them with love and give them all of the freedom they think they need. She is not afraid if a youngster learns some street smarts along the way. She will broaden her children's knowledge and see that they get a well-rounded education.

SCORPIO MAN
CAPRICORN WOMAN

The Capricorn may not be the most romantic woman of the Zodiac, but she's far from frigid when she meets the right man. She believes in true love. She doesn't appreciate getting involved in flings. To her, they're just a waste of time. She's looking for a man who means business—in life as well as in love.

Although she can be very affectionate with her boyfriend or mate, she tends to let her head govern her heart. That is not to say she is a cool, calculating cucumber. On the contrary, she just feels she can be more honest about love if she consults her brains first. She wants to size up the situation before throwing her heart in the ring. She wants to make sure it won't get stepped on.

The Capricorn woman is faithful, dependable, and systematic in just about everything she undertakes. She is quite concerned with security and sees to it that every penny she spends is spent wisely. She is very economical about using her time, too. She does not believe in whittling away her energy on a scheme that is not going to pay off.

Ambitious themselves, they are quite often attracted to ambitious men—men who are interested in getting somewhere in life. If a man of this sort wins her heart, she'll stick by him and do all she can to help him get to the top.

The Capricorn woman is almost always diplomatic. She makes an excellent hostess. She can be very influential when your business acquaintances come to dinner.

The Capricorn woman is likely to be very concerned, if not downright proud, about her family tree. Relatives are important to her, particularly if they're socially prominent. Never say a cross word about one of her family. That can really go against her grain, and she'll punish you by not talking to you for days.

She's generally thorough in whatever she does. Capricorn women are well-mannered and gracious, no matter what their backgrounds. They seem to have it in their natures always to behave properly.

If you should marry a Capricorn woman, you need never worry about her going on a wild shopping spree. She understands the value of money better than most women. If you turn over your paycheck to her at the end of the week, you can be sure that a good hunk of it will wind up in the bank.

The Capricorn mother is very ambitious for her children. She wants them to have every advantage and to benefit from things she perhaps lacked as a child. She will train her youngsters to be polite and kind and to honor traditional codes of conduct.

SCORPIO MAN
AQUARIUS WOMAN

If you find that you've fallen head over heels for a woman born under the sign of the Water Bearer, you'd better fasten your safety belt. It may take you quite a while to actually discover what this creature is like. Even then, you may have nothing to go on but a string of vague hunches.

The Aquarius woman is like a rainbow, full of bright and shining hues. She's like no one you've ever known. There is something elusive about her—something delightfully mysterious. You'll most likely never be able to put your finger on it. It's nothing calculated, either. Aquarius doesn't believe in phony charm.

There will never be a dull moment in your life with this Water Bearer woman. She seems to radiate adventure and magic. She'll most likely be the most open-minded and tolerant woman you've ever met. She has a strong dislike for injustice and prejudice. Narrow-mindedness runs against her grain.

She is very independent by nature and quite capable of shifting for herself if necessary. She may receive many proposals for marriage from all sorts of people without ever really taking them seriously. Marriage is a very big step for her. She wants to be sure she knows what she's getting into. If she thinks that it will seriously curb her independence and love of freedom, she will return the engagement ring—if indeed she's let the romance get that far.

The line between friendship and romance is a pretty fuzzy one for an Aquarius. It's not difficult for her to remain buddy-buddy with an ex-lover. She's tolerant, remember? So, if you should see her on the arm of an old love, don't jump to any hasty conclusions.

She's not a jealous person herself and doesn't expect you to be, either. You'll find her pretty much of a free spirit most of the time. Just when you think you know her inside out, you'll discover that you don't really know her at all.

She's a very sympathetic and warm person. She can be helpful to people in need of assistance and advice.

She'll seldom be suspicious even if she has every right to be. If the man she loves slips and allows himself a little fling, chances are she'll just turn her head the other way. Her tolerance does have its limits, however, and her man should never press his luck at hanky-panky.

The Aquarius mother is bighearted and seldom refuses her children anything. Her open-minded attitude is easily transmitted to her youngsters. They have every chance of growing up as respectful and tolerant individuals who feel at ease anywhere.

SCORPIO MAN
PISCES WOMAN

The Pisces woman places great value on love and romance. She's gentle, kind, and romantic. Perhaps she's the ideal mate you've been dreaming about all these years. Like you, she has very high ideals. She will only give her heart to a man who she feels can live up to her expectations.

Your Pisces mate will let you be the brains of the family; she's contented to play a behind-the-scenes role in order to help you achieve your goals. The illusion that you are the master of the household is the kind of magic that the Pisces woman is adept at creating.

She can be very ladylike and proper. Your business associates and friends will be dazzled by her warmth and femininity. Although she's a charmer, there is a lot more to her than just a pretty exterior. There is a brain ticking away behind that soft, womanly facade. You may never become aware of it—that is, until you're married to her. It's no cause for alarm, however; she'll most likely never use it against you, only to help you and possibly set you on a more successful path.

If she feels you're botching up your married life through careless behavior or if she feels you could be earning more money than you do, she'll tell you about it. But any wife would, really. She will never try to usurp your position as head and breadwinner of the family.

No one had better dare say one uncomplimentary word about you in her presence. It's likely to cause her to break into tears. Pisces women are usually very sensitive beings. Their reaction to adversity, frustration, or anger is just a plain, good, old-fashioned cry. They can weep buckets when inclined.

She can do wonders with a house. She is very fond of dramatic and beautiful things. There will always be plenty of fresh-cut flowers around the house. She will choose charming artwork and antiques, if they are affordable. She'll see to it that the house is decorated in a dazzling yet welcoming style.

She'll have an extra special dinner prepared for you when you come home from an important business meeting. Don't dwell on the boring details of the meeting, though. But if you need that grand vision, the big idea, to seal a contract or make a conquest, your Pisces woman is sure to confide a secret that will guarantee your success. She is canny and shrewd with money, and once you are on her wavelength you can manage the intricacies on your own.

Treat her with tenderness and generosity and your relationship will be an enjoyable one. She's most likely fond of chocolates. A bunch of beautiful flowers will never fail to make her eyes light up. See to it that you never forget her birthday or your anniversary. These things are very important to her. If you let them slip your mind, you'll send her into a crying fit that could last a considerable length of time.

If you are patient and kind, you can keep a Pisces woman happy for a lifetime. She, however, is not without her faults. Her sensitivity may get on your nerves after a while. You may find her lacking in practicality and good old-fashioned stoicism. You may even feel that she uses her tears as a method of getting her own way.

The Pisces mother has total faith in her children. She makes a strong, self-sacrificing mother. She will teach her children the value of service to the community while not letting them lose their individuality.

SCORPIO
LUCKY NUMBERS 1998

Lucky numbers and astrology can be linked through the movements of the Moon. Each phase of the thirteen Moon cycles vibrates with a sequence of numbers for your Sign of the Zodiac over the course of the year. Using your lucky numbers is a fun system that connects you with tradition.

New Moon	First Quarter	Full Moon	Last Quarter
Dec. 29 ('97)	Jan. 5	Jan. 12	Jan. 20
9 6 1 4	4 5 8 7	7 7 2 9	4 0 8 5
Jan. 28	Feb. 3	Feb. 11	Feb. 19
2 6 9 1	1 4 3 3	8 7 9 0	9 2 8 5
Feb. 26	March 5	March 12	March 21
9 3 4 7	7 6 1 0	3 7 3 4	1 0 7 2
March 27	April 3	April 11	April 19
5 0 6 9	8 8 3 5	5 0 9 4	7 4 8 2
April 26	May 3	May 11	May 18
3 6 5 5	5 9 2 0	0 1 7 4	8 2 1 2
May 25	June 1	June 9	June 17
5 4 4 8	8 1 0 9	4 6 3 1	7 2 5 1
June 23	July 1	July 9	July 16
1 1 0 5	7 0 6 3	1 9 4 7	8 2 1 9
July 23	July 31	August 7	August 14
4 6 1 0	0 1 5 2	7 3 6 7	7 1 0 9
August 21	August 30	Sept. 6	Sept. 12
4 8 0 5	9 6 3 7	2 1 2 5	4 4 8 9
Sept. 20	Sept. 28	Oct. 5	Oct. 12
1 2 6 0	1 4 8 2	5 3 6 5	5 5 9 2
Oct. 20	Oct. 28	Nov. 4	Nov. 10
9 1 4 5	7 2 5 6	6 0 9 8	8 3 5 0
Nov. 18	Nov. 26	Dec. 3	Dec. 10
0 4 4 1	5 8 9 0	9 0 2 6	6 8 3 7
Dec. 18	Dec. 26	Jan. 1 ('99)	Jan. 9 ('99)
7 4 6 1	0 4 5 8	8 7 2 4	4 8 3 9

SCORPIO
YEARLY FORECAST 1998

*Forecast for 1998 Concerning Business
and Financial Affairs, Job Prospects,
Travel, Health, Romance and Marriage
for Those Born with the Sun
in the Zodiacal Sign of Scorpio.
October 23–November 22*

For those born under the influence of the Sun in the zodiacal sign
of Scorpio, ruled by both Mars, the planet of action, drive, and
initiative, and by Pluto, the planet of hidden depths, this promises
to be a busy and pleasurable year. There should be more opportunities overall to develop new hobbies and other creative pursuits
which interest you. Being able to manage your time more effectively is part of your key to success. The other vital factor is noticing golden opportunities when they arise. It is a good idea to
become more social, offering and accepting invitations from a
wide range of people. Work must be given priority in your daily
life so that you maintain maximum efficiency. Your spare time,
however, should be devoted to enjoying yourself more. For Scorpio business people, this is the year to grasp unusual opportunities
and develop diverse interests. Innovative ideas can bring excellent
long-term results if sufficiently developed. Avoid spreading yourself too thin, however, or you will probably not get down to anything solid and lasting. In relation to finances, this is a year to
build up a nest egg. You may have cause to fall back on savings
occasionally, but make a point of budgeting carefully on a regular
basis. It is unwise to put all your eggs in one basket where both
income and investments are concerned. You will feel more secure
if you have a number of options. Where routine occupational affairs are concerned, you get the best results when you put in sustained effort. Changing routines on a frequent basis is not a
particularly good idea. The support of work colleagues is vital if
you are to keep on the ball with major projects. Travel opportu-

nities abound during 1998, although some of your plans may get no further than the dream stage. This does not necessarily matter, since you can develop them further into the future. However, ensure that you have at least a few breaks from everyday surroundings during the year, even if only on occasional weekends. Your health is likely to benefit if you stick to proper eating and maintain a regular exercise regime. Snacks and too much time in front of the television can make you listless and lacking in energy. In love and romance, this is the year when Scorpio people who have not committed to a relationship could decide to take the plunge and tie the knot. There is a greater chance of finding a partner with whom you want to' settle down.

For professional Scorpio men and women, this year provides the opportunity to be innovative and move into new areas. Be open to unique opportunities which come your way. The more varied your interests from those you have already explored, the more likely you are to be successful. If you want to ensure good long-term returns, it is important to work hard at creating a stable foundation. New projects need a firm structure within which to be successfully developed. While it is a good idea to move into new areas, it is also important not to take on more than you can comfortably handle. The tendency this year is to say yes to everything and wind up overextending yourself. If you spread yourself too thin it may be impossible to develop new projects in sufficient depth. When dealing with others in the business world, it is more important than usual to pin them down to specific commitments. Try to get agreements in writing rather than relying solely on verbal promises. Long-distance work-related travel, especially to foreign countries, can lead to discovering new interests which are potentially lucrative for the future. Make the most of existing foreign contacts who can help point you in the right direction. If you become involved in any type of legal dispute or proceedings this year, you are apt to come out better than you expect. Luck tends to be on your side more than usual in this respect. An unexpected turnaround in a tricky situation can work out to your advantage. Nevertheless, this is not a year when you should take a lot for granted. Lucky as your breaks may be, the risks you take are likely to be open-ended. Not being sufficiently well organized could be a serious drawback. However, it is surprising how well you can pick up the pieces when you have no other choice. The period between January 26 and February 4 is a key time for pooling resources successfully with other people, especially in order to develop a new business venture.

Where your personal finances are concerned, watch spending carefully. Heavy demands on your resources, particularly toward the end of the year, can lead you to consider dipping into savings designated for a special purpose. If you can budget carefully on a regular basis, this can be avoided. Your security will be greater this year if you have a number of options open to you where both earnings and investments are concerned. If you have money to invest, spread it around rather than plowing it all into one option. This can help to guarantee the return you are looking for. Likewise, if you have more than one source of income, even if the secondary source is minor, you can cope with periods of heavy expenditure more easily. Should you lose income in relation to one area of work or investment, at least you will have the opportunity to try to develop another without so much panic or time delay. Be most careful about spending between November 23 and December 22, when the Christmas spirit can destroy the best budget.

In routine occupational affairs, this is a year of hard work for little initial return. At times you may doubt the usefulness of what you are doing. However, the long-term rewards are something to look forward to with confidence. It is important to fix your mind firmly on an overall goal and stick to this course. Sustained effort ought to bring excellent results in the long run. Out of boredom or frustration, you may be tempted to change your mind on the spur of the moment and vary where you invest your energies. However, this is not a good idea. The more single-minded you can be about achieving one particular goal, no matter how tedious the route, the better chance you have of succeeding. Much new responsibility is likely to fall on you this year. Be thoughtful in organizing your schedule. If you can gain greater support from colleagues, particularly for the most difficult tasks and projects, you should find the overall responsibility a lot easier to handle. Scorpio people often choose to go it alone in order to maintain a greater degree of control over any given situation. This year, however, it is important to create a sound base of support so that you are not continually pushing yourself too hard or too far.

There is likely to be more than the usual number of opportunities to travel this year, particularly abroad. Nevertheless, some of the plans you have to travel overseas may not develop fully this year. You may not have the time or money to fulfill all of your desires in this respect. Combining business with pleasure is a valuable a way of getting the best of both worlds when it comes to foreign travel. Be sure, however, that you have some control over the planning. A major vacation planned for early in the year, between January 26 and February 4, is likely to be very pleasurable. Your busiest period of travel is between July 7 and August 20. Since business and work commitments are quite heavy this year, it is a good idea to take weekend breaks fairly frequently during the year if you can. In this way you give yourself a chance to break away from routine work and stressful tasks. Peace and quiet are vital when it comes to being able to switch off and relax.

To safeguard your health this year, maintain strict regimes. Regular nutritious eating should help keep your energy high. Try to avoid junk food eaten on the run between appointments. A planned exercise routine would keep you strong overall. Keeping fit is important this year because you have more demands on your time than usual. If you allow yourself to remain sedentary for much of the time, you could end up feeling sluggish all too often. Walking rather than driving is likely to be more stimulating but less stressful.

Where love and romance are concerned, this year should be very rewarding for both married and unattached Scorpios. Giving greater commitment to a relationship that has been rather casual is a sign that you feel certain that you are with the right person. You could even go so far as to get married because the time is right. For single Scorpio men and women, this year offers a good chance of finding someone you want to be with for a lifetime. For married Scorpios, life at home is likely to be more demanding than usual, probably because your partner needs you more. Your commitment to make the relationship work is bound to be rewarding.

SCORPIO
DAILY FORECAST

January–December 1998

JANUARY

1. THURSDAY. Good. A discussion with the folks at home can potentially help you solve a financial dilemma or a property-related problem. This is a particularly fortunate time if you are thinking of making a major move of any kind. As you enter the new year you are more mentally free from old problems and able to recognize and seize new opportunities. Some gifts are still likely to come your way, even though the Christmas celebration is over. Take the time to do a favor for someone you love; you are likely to be repaid in several ways in the coming months.

2. FRIDAY. Disquieting. Keep away from new year sales if you can resist them. You are apt to come away broke and without a great deal of true value to show for having spent so much. If you are harboring second thoughts about a romantic involvement, there is probably a very good reason. However, do not be in a hurry to call it quits before you have thought the situation through carefully. A thorough cleaning around the home is a good idea, and may alert you to a problem that needs to be handled by a professional. Since replacing worn furniture or appliances could prove costly if purchased all at once, put together a long-term budget so that you can buy them over time and with cash.

3. SATURDAY. Confusing. A mix-up in arrangements could leave you financially out of pocket. To help avoid this, it is a good idea to double-check meeting times and places before buying tickets for yourself and other people or making reservations for a group. A child who is misbehaving could be upset because you have not kept your word about something important. Rather than try to figure out what the problem might be, talk about it openly; you will probably be able to sort it out. Single Scorpio people need to guard against a fast-talking would-be suitor who is not crystal clear about future intentions. It is all too easy to believe what you hope is true.

4. SUNDAY. Fair. This is a great day for entertainment and leisure activities. A neighbor or relative's gathering is well worth attending. If you are restless, do something fun with family members or friends, such as ice skating or sledding. Getting some outdoor exercise can lift your spirits as well as being good for you physically. If you are stuck at home, make an effort to get your place shipshape. You may find something valuable which you thought you had lost while you are cleaning closets and drawers. Do not let words take the place of action when it comes to evening romance.

5. MONDAY. Variable. You may have an urge to throw away papers and other accumulation, but be careful not to be overly thorough. You can be ruthless at the best of times. An extra strong tendency toward this trait at the moment means you could discard items you later wish you still had. If a neighbor or relative wants to chat or sends an invitation your way, make an effort to be accommodating even if you are short of time. If you end up missing out on a chance to help or on a social event you could have regrets later on. Only give advice if specifically asked for it. Being a willing listener is often more important.

6. TUESDAY. Deceptive. Crossed wires in the workplace can cause you problems. If the boss or a colleague has left you a message but is not around when you need to check details, be careful how you proceed. Delay might be your best tactic until you can be sure of what you are to do. Your mate or partner may be in a strange mood, possibly because of a struggle to understand something quite deep. Scorpio people are gifted at drawing out people and then helping them sort out problems. Do your best to be supportive. Although another person's lack of confidence can sometimes irritate you, keep in mind that you, too, at times feel uncertain. Try not to expect more from someone than they can possibly give.

7. WEDNESDAY. Changeable. Avoid discussing important matters regarding your home or work situation. It is unlikely that you will be able to reach an agreement on anything at the moment. A friend or relative is a good adviser when it comes to arbitrating a dispute. This is a favorable day for making travel plans for the not too distant future, particularly if they involve loved ones. A heart-to-heart talk with your mate, in which you discuss very personal feelings, is likely to bring you closer together. An accountant, lawyer, or other professional who has not been cooperative lately is now ready to take your side.

8. THURSDAY. Easygoing. This promises to be a smoother day than yesterday where partnership matters are concerned. Although you experienced some stressful moments yesterday, some friction on the domestic scene should be out of the way now. This is an excellent time for increasing your involvement in a joint financial or business venture. Your receptive Scorpio nature should be well received, helping to open the door for more intense negotiations. If you are trying to win over a client at work, use some of your entertainment budget to create the right atmosphere for important discussions. Your keen sense of humor can overcome stumbling blocks in record time.

9. FRIDAY. Productive. This is another highly favorable day for business matters. Important developments are likely if you make a greater effort to set the right kind of scene. If you are signing a contract, be sure to read through the small print, tiring as it may seem. This can help avoid misunderstandings in the future. If you are thinking of buying a costly item for your home, shop around for the best deal rather than make the decision based on a salesperson. If the item is likely to benefit both you and other family members, such as a larger car or a backyard swimming pool, consider sharing the expense.

10. SATURDAY. Misleading. This is a day of ups and downs where money matters are concerned. What you gain through shopping for one item or deal, you may lose through someone else's neglect at not doing the same thing. As a Scorpio you find it hard to trust others at the best of times, and it is doubly difficult when someone in whom you placed your trust does not make the best decision. Try to chalk it off to experience. Family members are there to comfort you when it comes to needing someone to take your side in a dispute. To avoid a mix-up where a social meeting is concerned, leave nothing to chance; one phone call just before an event can ward off disappointment.

11. SUNDAY. Disconcerting. A trip which you had hoped would be exciting could turn out to be rather boring. If things are not going well, a last-minute change of plan might save the day. If you are planning to spend the day at home, do not schedule too many tasks. It is better to stick to handling one or two problems rather than create a huge amount of work for yourself. Besides, you are apt to run out of time with a major job half-done. If you are setting out on a long distance journey, make allowances for possible traffic delays. Even if you are using public transport, consider that there may be holdups to contend with.

12. MONDAY. Frustrating. Scorpios are likely to feel very restless. If you are scheduled to leave on a trip, the change of scene is bound to do you a lot of good. However, there are a number of routine matters to tie up before you can even consider leaving town. Good communications are a key to success in the business world. If you are passing on information or instructions to another person, be sure to make the details crystal clear. Hearing from an old flame or a former employer could cause you to reconsider a current major plan. It is vital at the moment to keep your options wide open and avoid making any spontaneous commitments.

13. TUESDAY. Variable. This is a much simpler day than yesterday when it comes to business matters. A meeting with a key authority figure is likely to prove fruitful. However, do not expect to be able to finalize a business or financial deal immediately. It is likely that a snag will develop; you may even have to draw up an entirely new contract. These new developments are likely to turn out to be positive in the long run. Your home life may seem more unsettled than usual, probably due to a family member's moodiness or worry about money and future security. It should help to talk things over this evening in a calm, relaxed manner.

14. WEDNESDAY. Mixed. Today is excellent for getting down to some solid work. You should make good progress, especially when handling detailed and intricate matters. If you have neglected filing away important papers, do so now. Excellent headway can be made with tasks of a technical or practical nature. Domestic matters may again trouble you more than usual. Worrying about home concerns can negatively affect your professional life if you are not careful. The less you allow fleeting thoughts to bother you, the better. Similarly, it is a mistake to take your business attitude home. Be compassionate and extra understanding with loved ones. Give them the benefit of all doubts.

15. THURSDAY. Good. Friends and acquaintances are likely to be a source of inspiration to you. This is a starred time for making new contacts as well. Some of the people you are introduced to now are likely to become key players in your future plans and schemes. Make an extra effort to cultivate relationships which you sense could be highly useful in the months ahead. Something important to you, which you have so far only been dreaming about, can be at least started today. Help from friends and relatives can be the push you need. A local social event is likely to turn out to be not only interesting but important to your ongoing advancement in the political community.

16. FRIDAY. Pleasant. Relationships with colleagues and friends should be especially cordial. This is an excellent time for teamwork. Through joint effort you are likely to make more progress than if you work alone. This is another favorable day for attending a social gathering organized by people you know well. Taking part more fully in local community affairs is likely to enhance your feeling of security. It could also put you in touch with someone who could become a close friend or partner. Take advantage of the opportunity to meet new people and expand your horizons.

17. SATURDAY. Enjoyable. This is a great day for doing something just a little bit out of the ordinary. Work on fulfilling a special plan or scheme. If you are not feeling physically active, spend more time relaxing and dreaming. It is a good idea to give your mind a rest from time to time. Traveling to a peaceful destination can be enjoyable; so can simply lounging around at home, doing nothing. Socializing arranged for this weekend ought to go with a swing. Where a birthday party is concerned, there is a magical air to the day that affects adults and children alike. Go out of your way to make a newcomer feel welcome.

18. SUNDAY. Fair. It is necessary to keep a number of matters to yourself. Discretion is your ally and best source of protection. Nevertheless, it is all too easy to let a secret slip out without noticing while chatting with a neighbor or friend. The key is to be on guard. Other people can pry when they do not really mean to do so. Indiscretions can also occur if a person who is a friend of yours unwittingly lets slip another person's secret, assuming that you have already been told. It is best to try to forget what was said; when you meet up with the person whose secret you learned, act as though you know nothing. Refuse to take sides in a family dispute that does not involve you directly.

19. MONDAY. Suspenseful. Rumors floating around at work or in your neighborhood can be unsettling. Try your best to ignore them. It is possible that one particularly meddlesome person is spreading incorrect information. A colleague pointing an accusing finger at you for something they believe you did or did not do is clearly in the wrong. Nevertheless, it is discomforting to have the finger pointed. Take the person aside and make it clear that you do not appreciate their accusation. Also explain how embarrassed you feel. It is likely that you will end up receiving an apology and having your name fully cleared. If you are currently out of work, take a rest from job interviewing for a day, but send out some resumes.

20. TUESDAY. Mixed. A private discussion with a family member should help clear up a problem. If you are at home you are apt to feel quite restless. It is a good time to get some physical exercise by cleaning the house or washing the car. You have to work hard to achieve your goals at the moment. After much effort to finalize plans, you may feel that you are getting nowhere. Unless you are in the right frame of mind to really push things, try to take life at a slower pace both at home and at work. Avoid excessive spending; steer clear of tempting sales where you might not be able to resist impulse buys.

21. WEDNESDAY. Variable. You should be able to make some significant progress moving ahead with personal projects. However, your schedule could be a little disrupted due to too much noise from those around you. A visit to or from a neighbor or relative is likely to bring some light relief. This person may also be able to offer useful equipment or ideas for you to utilize. You can make the most headway, both in and out of the workplace, if you do not plan too tight a schedule. A trip can be surprisingly fruitful. Ongoing negotiations should help you advance toward a central goal. Give a little and you will get a lot in return.

22. THURSDAY. Uncertain. Trust your own good judgment; it is the best measure you have at the moment, especially in the business world. By being alert you can make an important contact or consolidate plans with existing contacts. Much is still hanging in the air both in your personal and professional life; do not expect any kind of finalization just now. Instead, focus on advancing plans step by step. Life at home may still be disruptive. A disagreement is likely with a loved one over your personal plans. Try to keep a cool head and discuss rather than argue.

23. FRIDAY. Slow. Money matters need careful handling. You are in a stronger position than you believe, largely due to having done some thorough background research. A contract or agreement which you have been trying to finalize could at last be signed today. You can trust a business associate with innovative ideas. It is important to establish mutually agreeable methods early in the stages of a new partnership in order to save a lot of grief and controversy later on. Concentrate on the ground rules. Home life should be much more harmonious. Surprise that special person in your life with the gift of your time and full attention.

24. SATURDAY. Quiet. Life should be relatively peaceful and trouble-free. This is a fine time to attend to money matters which have been neglected. If you are behind with personal or business accounting, make an effort to catch up while you have the time and energy to do so. Tranquil surroundings at home make it easier to handle intricate mental tasks and sort through paperwork. Do not hurry to make a decision about a financial investment you are considering. Think the matter through in greater depth, carefully comparing one option with another. Avoid any money decision that involves an element of gambling or pure guesswork.

25. SUNDAY. Good. This is a particularly favorable day for Scorpios to get out to visit people, especially close relatives. An invitation from a friend is well worth accepting. If you are new in the neighborhood, a local celebration could be your chance to get to know your neighbors a little better. For single Scorpio men and women, a gathering could lead to meeting a new partner or finding friends for socializing. This is generally a favorable day for traveling; a change of scene will do you a lot of good. A trip to a resort area ought to be refreshing and pleasant, especially if you are in congenial company.

26. MONDAY. Challenging. This is one of those days when you are likely to spend a lot of time on the telephone. Touch base with friends and associates, and get arrangements settled. It is also a favorable time for attending to correspondence which was put aside earlier in the month. Mental endeavors tend to produce better results at the moment than physical exertion. It may be difficult to push ahead with practical tasks, simply because you do not have all the equipment you require. It is also likely that your concentration will come in fits and starts because the telephone rings incessantly. It is best not to expect too much of yourself or of anyone else.

27. TUESDAY. Cautious. Although there is a magical quality in both your business and social worlds, be wary of getting overly enthusiastic about a new project or opportunity. All is not quite as it at first seems. It is vital not to rush into a long-term commitment or make up your mind about major decisions just yet. Wait until you understand more clearly what is really being offered and what will be expected of you. If you are out in a public place today, guard your wallet; there is a chance of losing it or of being pickpocketed; obviously the likelihood increases if you are careless. It is a better day for buying than for selling, but you need to shop around and compare prices.

28. WEDNESDAY. Productive. This is a favorable day for getting a number of projects finished. A pile of work that has seemed never ending should now be slimming down nicely. Business deals can be made; documents can be signed, sealed, and delivered. It is also a key time for completing tasks around the home. If you recently began a decorating project, make an effort to complete all the detailed work. You should make especially good progress with work which need careful attention and a steady hand. If you are concerned about an electrical problem, call a professional rather than try to solve it yourself. Get to bed earlier than usual tonight.

29. THURSDAY. Satisfactory. All the good work you put in yesterday, whether at home or in your professional life, may begin to pay off. Now, however, it would be all too easy to overdo and end up pulling a muscle or giving yourself a colossal headache. Move on to less strenuous and less intense projects and interests. Socially, the atmosphere is likely to be highly charged among a group of friends. Romantic sparks are in the air. For single Scorpios, some of those sparks could ignite a new passion. A newcomer that you meet will either be an inspiration or too hot to handle. Get to know one another as friends before becoming romantically involved.

30. FRIDAY. Calm. The children in your life are likely to be a source of great pleasure for you. Talk to them about their current schoolwork, their friends, and their hopes for the future. If you are thinking of turning a hobby into a business venture, selling advice and personal services could be the ideal outlet for your talents. Get out and mingle socially this evening, even if you have to attend a function without a companion. Quality conversation with people whose company you enjoy is likely to make the evening a real pleasure. Arrange a future luncheon date with someone you meet for the first time.

31. SATURDAY. Manageable. This is another excellent day for turning pleasure interests into a money-making business. Concentrate in particular on advertising and public relations. Promote yourself and your abilities. If you are already involved in a specific area of work from home, this promises to be a lucrative day. Scorpios with children at home may want to plan a day trip with educational overtones, perhaps to a museum or movie. If there has been tension around the household, getting out into a different environment should help ease the atmosphere at home. Where romance is concerned, this is a key time for getting closer to your loved one through considerate gestures.

FEBRUARY

1. SUNDAY. Stressful. This is one of those days when you can get so engrossed in what you are doing that you virtually end up working your fingers to the bone. The good progress that you make should be enough reward for your effort. However, do not miss out on a pleasurable social function with the excuse that you are too busy. You will benefit from a break, and could also meet someone who has been out of your life a while. Home-based tasks will be harder to tear yourself away from; in fact, you may not want to do so. This is a starred day for making headway with do-it-yourself projects, especially painting or wallpapering or rearranging furniture.

2. MONDAY. Confusing. Friends and associates are likely to be vague about their wishes and plans. It is pointless trying to pin them down to specific arrangements at the moment since no one is ready to make a firm commitment. Be satisfied with possible arrangements for the time being and get on with your own schedule. You should be able to make good progress with work projects since colleagues are more cooperative than usual. For Scorpios who are currently out of work, putting in new applications and following up old ones can lead to a good offer. A fresh opportunity is not to be missed, so keep your eyes and ears open.

3. TUESDAY. Unsettling. Home life is apt to be rather unsettled because your partner or another close family member is not seeing eye-to-eye with you. It is not worthwhile trying to change people's mind; they will most probably do just as they please. Lack of support or even being given the cold shoulder may upset you and make you feel alienated. Keep in mind that other people are just unavailable or too wrapped up in their own world at the moment. Pamper yourself as an antidote to feeling left out. It is possible that the mixed messages you are receiving reflect your own conflicting feelings. You cannot get what you want unless you know what you want.

4. WEDNESDAY. Variable. This is another day when your home life is unlikely to be as comfortable as you would like. People you are usually close to are lacking in generosity at the moment, possibly even being quite insensitive toward you. The good news is that a neighbor or relative is apt to help lift your spirits and give you a keener understanding of the situation. Forging stronger links in casual relationships that have not been so close or important to you in the past is likely to take the pressure off an intimate relationship that is not going well at the moment. The key to happiness just now is to look on the bright side and maintain a sense of optimism.

5. THURSDAY. Changeable. Think twice before making a major commitment, particularly one of a financial nature. You have more to lose by getting involved in a business venture than is obvious right now. An individual who is making light of a situation you see as quite serious is probably not viewing it in its true perspective. Trust yourself and your good Scorpio instincts. If you have to be forceful in order to get another person to act on your behalf, do so. Be careful if you are buying a gift for a child. You can easily get carried away, giving in to their whims for the latest trend and winding up spending too much. Be conservative in all financial matters, including spending on yourself.

6. FRIDAY. Quiet. Today promises to be a great relief after the mixed messages of the past few days. It is a time for reaching an understanding of one kind or another. Think about where your greatest support is coming from. Those people who are not really there for you and never really have been cannot be considered good friends. It is not worth investing much more of your energy in those relationships. Where work matters are concerned, clear off your desk and your work space. Do the same at home, getting rid of outdated paperwork. The more you clear out physically and materially, the calmer and more in control you will feel. If you go out tonight, opt for a quiet rendezvous rather than a raucous gathering or crowded bar.

7. SATURDAY. Enjoyable. This is an excellent day for taking a break from your usual routine and getting away to a different environment. A day spent with friends should be particularly invigorating. If peace and quiet appeals to you more, take off for some time alone. Being close to nature is likely to help clear your mind and put life back into perspective. News from a friend living far away ought to be pleasing and may be cause for celebration. If you have not heard from someone you miss, drop them a line or call them. Sometimes people are quietest when they have problems to handle. Reassurance that you are still there for them could be helpful.

8. SUNDAY. Disconcerting. Although being away from home may be stimulating at times, as the weekend goes on it is likely to be harder to ignore routine matters and work problems. Try not to allow your pleasure to be marred by worries you are going to have to face during the week ahead. If important responsibilities force you to stay at home, try to make the environment in which you have to handle them as pleasant as possible. The more comfortable your surroundings, the less disagreeable those difficult tasks and issues are likely to seem. A surprise visit or telephone call can give you a lift this evening.

9. MONDAY. Deceptive. It may be difficult to trust your own judgment and decision. Think twice before making any major move. What appears to be a good offer or an appealing course of action could turn out to be quite different in retrospect. If you are dieting at the moment, it is not necessary to avoid accepting a social invitation. Just let the hostess know what food you can and cannot eat. If you go out to a restaurant for lunch or dinner, a salad can be your best menu choice. You have less willpower now than usual, so resist being around temptation in any form.

10. TUESDAY. Mixed. An authority figure, most probably the boss at work, is likely to be argumentative. You may think this is going to mean more work for you, but it is likely that you can be paid for putting in overtime or will get help from someone else on the staff. If you are currently looking for work, this is a tricky day for interviews. Nervousness may keep you from making the best possible impression. As a Scorpio you are good at hiding your feelings, but when you are very stressed it generally shows. If you can turn the interview to talking about what you are good at, your true character should become apparent and your chances will improve measurably.

11. WEDNESDAY. Disquieting. You have to juggle your occupational commitments and private interests today. Try your best to fit everything in. It is important to maintain a totally professional image at work. The boss could criticize you for attending to private matters on work time. If you need to use the telephone to make a personal call, or if you receive a personal call, try to be inconspicuous about it. Keep it short and to the point. If a decision needs to be made regarding where you live or who you live with, base it largely on your instincts. In romance, too, go with what seems right to you.

12. THURSDAY. Rewarding. Neither borrow nor lend anything of value. In particular, it is unwise to get involved in complicated financial arrangements with friends. Although you may have the best of intentions in lending to someone in need, a strain could eventually develop in your relationship if the person has a problem paying you back. If you must borrow, set up a definite date for repayment and put this in writing. Doing so is likely to save a lot of grief in the long run. Efforts made to clinch a business deal should be rewarding, and efforts to complete a task at home are also positive. You can make as much progress as your patience permits.

13. FRIDAY. Pleasant. Today should be much easier than yesterday where your friendships and social life are concerned. Ongoing relationships should be especially congenial if you go out in a group this evening. This is also a propitious time for meeting new people and beginning new friendships. For single Scorpios opportunity is present to link up with someone new on the scene, provided that you get out and mingle. Do not turn down any invitation, even if it does not seem to be very appealing. It is surprising how an evening you expect to be routine can turn out to be stimulating when there are new people to meet. A blind date could lead to a memorable evening.

14. SATURDAY. Easygoing. This weekend is especially good for spending time alone. You need time to sort out minor tasks that have been neglected. Allow plenty of time for planning. If you are not in the mood to receive telephone calls, switch on the answer machine and monitor the calls. Sometimes you need to cut yourself off from the outside world in order to rest up and think.

The solution to a problem may suddenly become obvious when you consider new possibilities. A money situation which has been worrying you could be resolved quite easily. It is just a matter of looking in another place for an alternative source of funding.

15. SUNDAY. Frustrating. It is less easy today to get the time and space to yourself that you desire. The main problem is that work or another obligation is starting to press in on you at a time when you do not feel up to handling it. If you are emotionally upset about a situation at the moment, the last thing you want is to get down to mental tasks at home such as paying bills or balancing your checkbook. Nevertheless, try to keep an open mind. It is likely that once you focus on something other than what is distressing you, the problem will seem much less severe. A friend's refusal to see things your way may add to your frustration.

16. MONDAY. Misleading. Get an earlier start than usual so that you can begin to work on important matters. This is a favorable day for tackling tasks that you have shelved or avoided for one reason or another. If you are self-employed, a seemingly tedious task like figuring out your profit and expenses can turn out to be quite satisfying once you get into it. You can work most effectively when you are left alone to get on with the job in peaceful surroundings. Fortunately, you should not have to put up with too many interruptions from telephone callers or drop-in visitors.

17. TUESDAY. Unsettling. The right way for you to proceed is not easy to figure out just now. Much of your indecision may stem from a general sense of upset with your life. For example, if you are not happy with your home life at the moment, it is difficult to make social plans which are not primarily an excuse to get out of the house. Be open to change, particularly in allowing old friends back into your life. Someone you parted from months or years ago could reappear on the scene. You are likely to find that you have much in common now. The past can be forgotten and your relationship renewed with confidence. If you owe someone an apology, now is the time to make it.

18. WEDNESDAY. Good. The struggle you went through with personal direction yesterday is likely to be much less of a problem today. This is a particularly good time for advancing your personal goals. If you want to try to improve your image and appearance by losing weight, sports activities are likely to be the best method. Whatever sport you get involved in, you are bound to enjoy. Creative urges should be expressed in whatever way appeals to you.

If you work in a creative field, this promises to be an inspired time for you. Good communications with various contacts are vital to your success. Do not be shy about promoting yourself.

19. THURSDAY. Difficult. Arguments relating to money matters can make a new relationship seem more of a trial than a pleasure. However, friends or lovers sometimes come at a cost. It is a good idea to have a lighthearted, calm discussion about the problem, rather than get too businesslike or serious. Costs occurring in relation to the needs and desires of a family member may be more than you can afford. Put your foot down and agree only to what is necessary and within your budget. Family life is likely to be a lot easier than you expect due to the strong support of older loved ones. You can rely on their advice.

20. FRIDAY. Successful. The key to success is to keep your mind firmly fixed on your goals. Only make a financial investment if you feel sure about the scheme and about the company involved. You may need to look further into operating methods and procedures before you feel secure about investing a large sum of money. Issues with regard to family members and money which affected you yesterday may not yet be entirely resolved. Do not give in to pressure simply because you hope to avoid the hassle of thinking things through carefully. Long-term budgeting is vital to your overall financial well-being.

21. SATURDAY. Productive. You are likely to get a surprising amount done if you start the day with a definite strategy. Recent struggles which have been upsetting you are now dwindling, particularly where money matters are concerned. Socially, this is an excellent time for mixing. Accept any appealing invitation that comes your way, even if it is the last-minute variety. Spontaneous events are apt to be especially pleasurable. It is likely that you will meet interesting new people and even strike up a new friendship. This is also a great day for going somewhere special with one or more family members, including a child or pet.

22. SUNDAY. Fair. Today is likely to be somewhat tricky as people impinge on your plans. An unexpected visit from relatives or neighbors may throw your schedule out of kilter. Even if the visits are planned, you could find yourself running out of time while trying to get a lot of preliminaries out of the way. The key to a successful day is to avoid cramming in too many activities. Even if there is a great deal you would like to achieve, concentrate first and foremost on your top priorities. Less urgent matters can wait until a more convenient time. Enjoy some quiet reminiscing this evening about the good old days.

23. MONDAY. Lucky. Increased socializing can lead to making some useful links. Whether you are hoping for a business or romantic contact, you should be successful so long as you make the effort to get out and about. This is not a time to be turning down any invitation. It pays to be organized when it comes to social events. If you are going to an important meeting, allow enough time to relax beforehand. Too much rushing around is likely to leave you feeling flustered and not in top form. Single Scorpios who have been thinking about contacting an old flame should not hesitate to do so. Your call or letter is sure to be welcome.

24. TUESDAY. Demanding. A problem in relation to your finances can be resolved if you make the move you have been considering. All in all, this is a favorable time for tying up loose ends. A business deal can be completed with minimal effort. In fact, you are likely to be surprised at how simple it is to conclude matters that have dragged on for some time. One matter of importance at the moment is your financial situation. Be careful not to overspend when socializing. It can be tempting to do so in good company, but try to be restrained about paying for anyone's way except your own.

25. WEDNESDAY. Rewarding. This is another favorable day for completing tasks both at home and at work. You should find it easy to bring negotiations to a close. The more effort you put in, the more you are apt to enjoy any task you undertake. Past efforts should start paying off handsomely. Seeds you have planted where your social relationships are concerned should start to flourish. Follow up leads and contacts, particularly in order to reinforce or confirm information passed on to you by someone not directly involved. Who you know is as important now as what you know.

26. THURSDAY. Buoyant. Today is likely to be a lot of fun. Even the most basic, everyday things should bring you joy at the moment. It may be that you are seeing life in a different light. Make the most of your current optimistic mood. Plan for the future, particularly the long-term future. Dreams and schemes can be outlined and personal aims pinpointed. The more solidly your plans take shape now in mental or written fashion, the more likely you are to fulfill them in the not too distant future. Write down major intentions that you wish to follow through on during the remainder of the year.

27. FRIDAY. Exciting. If you receive an invitation to socialize this evening, accept it. This is a key time for making the most of social opportunities, particularly in getting to meet new people or reinforcing links with people you already know. You should find that business mixes well with pleasure at the moment. In fact, the best deals are likely to be worked out when there is plenty of good food and drink in a relaxed setting. Little touches mean a lot both in your social and professional life. Send out notes of thanks and general correspondence. Someone at a distance has important information to share with you.

28. SATURDAY. Fortunate. What you have been hoping for in your private or professional life is likely to start materializing now. Rumors that have been going on in the background are likely to turn out to be true, much to your pleasure. A project which you began not long ago can be picked up again now and much good progress made. Work is likely to be highly profitable. Extra money can come your way as the result of taking a well-calculated gamble. Regarding home-based efforts, you are likely to feel very satisfied with what you achieve, particularly if you are hosting a party or celebration of any kind. Go out of your way to make a newcomer feel welcome.

MARCH

1. SUNDAY. Sensitive. Do not expect to be able to focus on any difficult, complicated, or detailed task. It is one of those times when your mind is likely to flit from one matter to another; it will be hard to concentrate on any one thing for very long. Besides, the day is apt to be full of interruptions, with the telephone ringing incessantly and people dropping by to visit you. It may be very pleasant receiving guests and hearing from those with whom you like to chat, but nevertheless distracting. Be flexible and do not expect too much of yourself. Try breaking your day down into small, manageable parts so that you have some measure of success.

2. MONDAY. Fair. Family relationships may not be easygoing at the moment, but a romantic liaison or other close alliance is likely to be smooth. The home scene may be disruptive due to a household or family member's restlessness and general lack of cooperation. If you are trying to finalize a deal, such as buying property or a new car, expect the unexpected. Changes to your plans are almost inevitable; it pays to be fairly adaptable. Where social relationships are concerned, look forward to a satisfying time. Romance is likely to bring a great deal of pleasure, even if you are only involved as a go-between.

3. TUESDAY. Good. It is another harmonious and enjoyable day for all of your relationships, with the added bonus that unwanted disruptions should disappear. If you are planning a romantic rendezvous, take time to make special arrangements. Your choice of a meeting place, what you wear, and what you talk about are especially important on a first or second date. Scorpio men and women already in a long-term relationship or marriage have the opportunity to bridge a gap that has widened between you and your partner. Reach out even if you think you have nothing to apologize for; you should receive a warm response.

4. WEDNESDAY. Variable. Concentrate on advancing important personal goals and you are likely to make good progress. This is an especially helpful day for finishing off old jobs and starting out on new, more creative ventures. If you need financial backing, however, you may have to wait awhile to put your plans into operation. Try several different sources rather than just giving up often step one if you do not get the result you want. Traditional banking institutions could be more helpful than you think, particularly if you are seeking business funding. For more personal projects, parents and family members may offer to help you out with a loan. Social events of any kind should be enjoyable this evening, but do not stay out too late.

5. THURSDAY. Mixed. This is an excellent day for settling old scores in the nicest possible way. Efforts you have been making at work, whether to further your position or simply complete a project, should start to pay off. A project you have been worrying about may be a lot more straightforward than you expect. Likewise, a key meeting that you have been dreading is likely to turn out well. Much is in your favor at the moment. Be careful, however, if dealing with tricky financial matters. Lighthearted commitments or assurances may not be enough for one particular individual. Be honest about your situation and willing to put a promise in writing.

6. FRIDAY. Deceptive. The need to handle a lot of routine work and also go on a long-distance journey means that your day is likely to be rushed. If you can manage to reorganize matters so that one appointment is postponed, without doing too much damage, so much the better. If you are traveling by public transportation or using roads which you do not usually drive on, find out as much information as you can before you begin your journey. A timetable may be out of date or a plane canceled. Listen on the radio for road delays and suggested detours. It is also worthwhile making routine checks on your vehicle before driving any distance.

7. SATURDAY. Uncertain. A day out with family members, especially children, is likely to be highly enjoyable for all concerned. If you are carefree and unattached, this is an ideal day for getting away to a new environment with new people. You may meet someone you instantly like while on your travels. It is best to avoid irksome tasks if you can. If you get bogged down with paperwork or household chores, the day could go by in a flash and you may not feel as though you had any rest and relaxation at all. If you have to work during the day, make sure that you have something to look forward to in the evening. Do not wait for someone to call you with an invitation; get on the phone to them.

8. SUNDAY. Productive. Although traditionally this is a day of rest, you may need to handle a few business matters. You should be able to make some headway, but do not expect to finish any major task or undertaking that you begin today. Deals which are in the pipeline probably cannot be concluded just now. Nevertheless, discussions which take place at this stage are crucial and should contribute to a positive final result when the time comes. You should be able to make good progress with tasks around the home so long as they are small ones. Time spent with your family promises to be helpful as well as enjoyable.

9. MONDAY. Frustrating. Although a promotion you have been hoping for may not be forthcoming, do not give up entirely. It is likely that a higher-up is keeping a close watch on you and will put in a good word on your behalf later in the year. A tricky situation may take some time to negotiate thoroughly. People can be won over through the force of your persuasion, but you need to be patient. Where property matters are concerned, an unexpected development may force you to change your plans. Although this may seem to be a setback and make you feel negative, it is likely to be for the best in the long run.

10. TUESDAY. Calm. This is an excellent day for getting back on top of things both in and out of work. You should have a greater degree of success than yesterday in gaining the required approval of the boss or a governmental agency for plans you want to develop. Fewer disruptions mean that you have more time to spend planning and generally getting your house in order. Good organization is your key to success. The groundwork you put in now is likely to pay off handsomely at a later time. Going out of your way to help others should make you feel good about yourself.

11. WEDNESDAY. Disquieting. Do not get involved in complicated financial arrangements with friends or acquaintances. Neither loan money to them nor ask for investment advice. It is likely that you will later regret such action because somebody is likely to end up demanding a financial accounting. In the long term, this could strain your relationship. Keep all money matter open and aboveboard. Avoid any type of gambling. An associate making generous gestures may not have absolutely clear motives. If this is someone of the opposite sex, keep in mind that romantic interest could be one of the motivating factors, although not obvious or welcome.

12. THURSDAY. Unsettling. Today is like yesterday in that you sense some strain in a friendship, particularly with someone of the opposite sex. While their attention may be flattering in some ways, you may not particularly like or want to get to know the person in question. Although little is being said out loud, it is best to bring the matter out into the open as soon as possible. A decision needs to be made soon regarding a relationship that has been wavering between friendship and romance. Talk it over with a good friend who has your best interests at heart.

13. FRIDAY. Fortunate. A matter which has been troubling you for some time can be brought to a happy conclusion. Your recent efforts to smooth over the situation are at last producing positive results. Quiet time spent alone at home or elsewhere is also likely to yield productive results, particularly if you are hoping to get a pile of paperwork out of the way. Attending to neglected matters of various kinds without further delay is sure to lift a weight from your shoulders. The more you focus on tying up loose ends, the happier you are likely to feel. It is important to wipe the slate clean before beginning any new projects.

14. SATURDAY. Excellent. As was true yesterday, you can make good progress today bringing outstanding issues, problems, and even projects to a satisfying conclusion. A property deal which has looked shaky stands more of a chance of going through as hoped, with a contract drawn up for your signature. Money owed to you could be repaid in full, perhaps even earlier than you thought. It is worth chasing down outstanding debts and getting back items you loaned out. Watch that you do not spoil a situation that is going well by saying too much or asking too many questions. Leave details for another time.

15. SUNDAY. Slow. Yesterday it was useful to refrain from focusing on the details of a situation or opportunity, since this could have influenced other people in a negative way. This advice also holds true today. While you may imagine that you would feel more secure about a particular personal or business situation if you knew more, delving too deeply is likely to be a mistake. Similarly, resist attempting to organize other people in the way that you think is best. In any situation where a group of people is involved, a democratic approach is most likely to work out in the long run. Go along with the will of the majority.

16. MONDAY. Optimistic. You may start the day feeling a little uncertain about the right course of action for you and the motives and reactions of other people. Do not trouble yourself too much, however. In short order you should start to feel assured about all of these matters. A wonderful opportunity to express your creative Scorpio talents is likely to crop up; go after it wholeheartedly. For single Scorpio men and women, romance is in the air. Accept an invitation to a social event being held out of town. A newcomer is your best bet for finding happiness in love.

17. TUESDAY. Unsettling. The optimism of yesterday may not stay with you today. You are apt to revert back to feeling uncertain about the right moves to make. This is quite likely due to unexpected developments where other people are concerned. If a deal falls through, it is probably for very valid reasons. It is better to know about problems early on and have a chance to back out rather than go ahead blindly. Your self-esteem can easily be knocked off course, especially if your partner or a family member makes negative comments directed at you. Try to ignore them.

Once you have settled on a particular course of action, do not be swayed from it.

18. WEDNESDAY. Stimulating. You are likely to feel much more confident and on top of things today than you did yesterday. This is the perfect time for making new starts with projects, personal interests, work, and hobbies. Your creativity is your strong point at the moment. Someone in a position of influence, who could help you in the future, is likely to be impressed by your efforts. Scorpios interested in making a key financial or property investment are likely to have the opportunity to do just that. Where romance is concerned, positive sparks are flying between you and someone who is coming back into your life or has never really gone away.

19. THURSDAY. Fair. Be careful with your money; it can tend to run through your fingers all too fast when you are out socializing. Carry the amount that you intend to spend, and stick to that sum. If you are invited to a restaurant, find out the general price range so that you can decide whether it is within your budget. If not, do not hesitate to suggest an alternative. If you find yourself financially embarrassed in a situation where it is too late to do much about it, an old friend is likely to help out. Your progress with a work matter should be excellent, with the finish line well in sight ahead of the deadline date.

20. FRIDAY. Good. Your concentrated work efforts are sure to produce very good results. The opportunity to work at your own pace is just what you need in order to boost your finances. This is an excellent day for Scorpio people who have been temporarily out of work. Make a renewed effort to get the ball rolling with your job search. Get organized in terms of filling out applications, and consider redrafting your resume in a different format. It is worth paying more attention to both style and content if you are applying for various jobs which emphasize different skills. Persistence pays off in trying to get a break.

21. SATURDAY. Enjoyable. Social events planned for today as well as impromptu arrangements are likely to be enjoyable. This is the ideal time for a change of scene. You are likely to enjoy a trip to the movies or to a museum. Driving for pleasure should be relaxing. Running routine errands could bring you in contact with people you have not seen in a while; catch up on the latest news and gossip. If you have to buy a birthday or anniversary gift, this is one of the best days to shop for it. You are likely to find something that is just right for the occasion and within your price range at a craft store or show.

22. SUNDAY. Confusing. The smallest details need to be thought about carefully as you are making travel and social plans. This is one of those days when omitting to mention something which seems trivial can lead to missed connections or being stood up. Call and confirm arrangements if necessary, even if you feel slightly foolish about doing so. Communications generally can be off the mark, especially when it comes to family and household relationships and plans. Do not pay too much attention to the mixed messages you are receiving; before too long, all should become clear. However, it is a good idea to try to pin others down to a definite time and place.

23. MONDAY. Productive. Conditions are particularly good for finishing up outstanding work. If you are looking for a new job, this is a key day for sending out applications and going on an interview. Also finish writing letters which you previously drafted. Overdue money owed to you should turn up soon. It is also quite likely that you can get a debt cleared up, and it is especially important to pay it off if it is worrying you. Take advantage of the opportunity to settle down to solid work, especially solitary efforts. Teamwork may not be as productive. You are likely to feel a lot calmer than you have lately and can therefore plan more carefully and get more accomplished.

24. TUESDAY. Demanding. Property negotiations should go without a hitch. You can bring a deal to a final, amicable conclusion. Business matters are under similar influences. One particular agreement is likely to be brought to a close sooner than you expect. This is a helpful omen for the continuing, rapid progress of the venture as a whole. If you are beginning a new business enterprise, it stands every chance of continuing success in the future. Conversations with older colleagues can help you solve a work problem, but do not expect anything other than advice from them.

25. WEDNESDAY. Unsettling. Any difficulty you are encountering in making progress with creative endeavors is likely to be money based. If you work in an industry where deals have a way of falling through, such as in the media, film, or music industry, do not be surprised if yet another great deal bites the dust. Just because this one does not get off the ground does not mean that others will not work out. Pick yourself up, dust yourself off, and move on. A romantic relationship under some stress at the moment is likely to be easier going if each of you can reduce expectations and be more accepting.

26. THURSDAY. Successful. Combining business with pleasure could lead to special success. This is one of those days when you can enjoy yourself no matter what you are doing. If you are sports minded, this is an excellent time for participating actively rather than as a spectator. Scorpios are on a lucky streak at the moment. This, combined with your skill and talent, is bound to make you a winner. It is seldom wise to take unnecessary risks, but today you are less likely than usual to make a bad move. A new romantic involvement can be deepened by sharing more time together. Look for ways to create greater closeness without clinging.

27. FRIDAY. Rewarding. Today marks the beginning of a new cycle where business and professional matters are concerned. You have the opportunity now to make considerable progress in your work. Self-discipline is the key to success in this respect. Greater rewards are coming your way due to the extra efforts you are extending at the moment. An authority figure who has been keeping tabs on your performance is likely to act positively in your favor. Settling into a new routine should help you feel more organized. Do some long-term planning so that you can make the most of your available time. Having a variety of projects in the pipeline should stave off boredom.

28. SATURDAY. Profitable. This is another excellent day where work and routine matters are concerned. If you have tasks to attend to around the house, do so without delay. You can get plenty done if you put your mind to it. If you are at work, make an effort to get through a pile of tasks which seem irksome. The sooner you complete them, the sooner you can move on to something more interesting. Preparations for a party are likely to keep you very busy. The gathering should be a real success and worth all your effort. It is a good idea to involve family members or friends in the preparations in order to ease your burden and to make the whole experience more fun.

29. SUNDAY. Useful. Although this is a day of rest, a work offer that comes your way may be too good to refuse. Financial incentives are strong at the moment. If taking on a few extra tasks or putting in a few extra hours will help your cash flow, it is worth exerting yourself. Your relationship with a loved one may not be as settled as you would like. It does not take much for Scorpio people to become suspicious. However, before you jump to any conclusions, consider that your partner may not be feeling very strong physically or mentally. Their unusual behavior could simply be due to tiredness.

30. MONDAY. Mixed. This is a much better day than yesterday where close relationships are concerned. A loved one may make the most sincere romantic gestures. This could be to compensate for neglecting you lately. It is also a good time for you to be making thoughtful romantic overtures. Any demonstration of affection on your part is likely to be well received. It can be worthwhile to step back from the relationship and to try to understand the other person's situation or motivation. If your loved one is feeling insecure about the future, offer some reassurance without making any promises you may not be able to keep.

31. TUESDAY. Favorable. Today favors making decisions in relation to financial and property investments. It is not, however, a favorable day for actually moving money around. Only make verbal commitments; follow up with deposits or a down payment at a later time, once you feel absolutely certain you have made the right decision. Tax demands could worry you, or needed repairs on your home, particularly if paying them would leave you short of cash. Nevertheless, this may be an incentive to look for extra work to bring in the additional money that you require.

APRIL

1. WEDNESDAY. Exciting. Mixing business with pleasure is not an especially good idea. If you can manage to keep the two separate, business negotiations are likely to work more in your favor. On the other hand, forming a business partnership with a friend or acquaintance could be quite fortunate providing you segregate business from personal interests right from the start. If you are looking for work at the moment, a promising opportunity or phone call is likely. This could be a surprise development stemming from recent efforts you have made. Networking with others in your line of work can be very useful.

2. THURSDAY. Demanding. You are bound to be kept busy and on the go. You may need to travel a long distance in relation to work or your social life, and this is likely to be quite time consuming. Nevertheless, unlike yesterday, it is a favorable day for mixing business with pleasure. If you are traveling for any reason, the change of scene should do you a world of good. Your work and professional life is apt to be taxing. You may have to produce figures or a report by a deadline. In all matters there are time constraints being put on you, indicating that you have to work at top speed to get everything done. Be careful to be thorough as well as speedy.

3. FRIDAY. Challenging. There is opportunity to expand your social life. Accept an invitation to a party or other social gathering. It is also a fine time to pursue your cultural interests and personal hobbies. Your current creative streak allows you to enjoy artistic and craft hobbies which you might normally not have the patience to attempt. The only problem you are likely to encounter is not being able to be in two places at the same time. Being out of touch is not ideal when people are trying to get you to discuss a problem or make an instant decision. Leave a phone number for them to use in an emergency.

4. SATURDAY. Cautious. The problems that plagued you yesterday because you could not be in two places at the same time are still with you today. It is important that you prioritize and make sure that you attend to the most vital tasks. If you are driving a long distance, make basic checks on your vehicle before starting out. Delays due to traffic can be irritating, but if they are cause by something simple going wrong with your vehicle they could be infuriating. If you are involved in any type of self-improvement effort, such as dieting or weightlifting, take your time rather than overdoing it. Keep in mind how long it took you to get out of shape in the first place.

5. SUNDAY. Variable. Scorpio people are forever plotting and planning, coming up with ideas. However, avoid get-rich-quick schemes even if they seem quite sound when you first hear about them. As you probably suspect with your naturally detective-like mind, there is bound to be a catch. There is a career move to be made now which will enhance your status and income in the long term. It is all a matter of figuring out the right direction in which to proceed. A discussion with an older person, someone with an enterprising attitude coupled with plenty of past experience, is likely to be helpful. Keep in mind that you only have to consider advice, not take it.

6. MONDAY. Lucky. Nothing should go wrong or be unexpected. This is one of those trouble-free days when it is easy to achieve the goals you set for yourself. Influential people are the key to your career success. Opportunities for discussions with them should be used to your full advantage. If a boss wants to discuss budgetary matters and future staff planning, this would be a favorable time to ask about a pay increase or promotion. A colleague has some useful information to share with you. Work cooperatively with others as much as possible. With your Scorpio creativity and know-how and their connections you make an unbeatable team.

7. TUESDAY. Disquieting. If you suspect that there is an underlying problem in one of your friendships, you are probably right. An offbeat comment or even lack of contact from this person is the signal that something is wrong. It may be that one of your friends or acquaintances has romantic inclinations toward you. This could be someone you have known for a long time, but it is more likely to be a recent acquaintance. If this person's attentions are unwelcome, do not hesitate to say so, but be diplomatic about it. One possible way to begin such a discussion is to mention how much you value the relationship as it is but do not want to become more involved.

8. WEDNESDAY. Frustrating. Your hopes that a newfound acquaintance may soon become a close friend are not likely to be fulfilled. The same issues that were relevant yesterday still exist today. If the matter has not been discussed openly, the person in question may make an obvious move which brings the issue to a head. Friendship which turns into romance work for some people, but you must decide what you really want before changing the relationship to another level. In gaining a lover, you could lose a friend. This is not a favorable day for playing Cupid.

9. THURSDAY. Quiet. The worries troubling you over the past few days should vanish today. Any difficulties in your friendships are likely to fizzle away if they have not been consciously resolved. This is a starred time to focus on your own personal secret hopes and wishes. Make plans for the future, aiming to bring at least one important goal to fruition before summertime. Associating with friends this evening should be especially congenial. Being involved in a club activity should also be enjoyable. If you think of a way to make the world a better place, act on it rather than wishing someone else would do so.

10. FRIDAY. Fair. Your most profitable time today is likely to be spent alone. If you can tuck yourself away in a quiet corner you are bound to get a lot done. If you have recently been out of work, behind-the-scenes developments are likely to work in your favor. If you recently went on an interview, discussions about you are likely to be positive. It is not a good idea to try to follow up the situation too soon or pester the interviewer for a response right now. Allow others some thinking time, and let things develop at their own pace. You are right to treat no news as good news at the moment. Relax with friends this evening.

11. SATURDAY. Stressful. You are likely to struggle between a need to work and a desire to rest and relax. On the one hand you may want to get a lot done, while on the other your mind needs to unwind. You may feel lethargic even though you know that there is a lot you could and should be doing. If this reflects a longer term trend, start trying to rebalance the situation. If you neglect work and tasks that need attention for too long, you are apt to end up with a really big problem on your hands. Similarly, if you need rest and do not get it, you can exhaust yourself and lower your resistance. Aim at regaining some equilibrium.

12. SUNDAY. Mixed. Like yesterday, there is plenty to do, but you may not have the energy for tackling any of it. It is better to get some extra rest and not worry rather than exhaust yourself mentally through anxiety. As a Scorpio you are prone to extremes of behavior at times, and you sometimes push yourself too far. Recognize when you reach your breaking point, and take a rest at that point. If you relax and take things easy, you may be surprised at the way some problems start to disappear on their own. Any mental or practical tasks are best done in a slow, casual manner. Do not set a time limit on any activity.

13. MONDAY. Sensitive. Your self-esteem is lower than usual, making it difficult to move ahead with confidence in work or in your personal life. However, you have a profound creative streak at the moment that can be applied with success in all areas of your life. Try to make light of problems; sooner or later they are unlikely to seem as troubling as they do now. Time spent alone gives you the opportunity to get a lot done, but guard against becoming too insular and inward looking. If you do not achieve all that you set out to do, there is little point in berating yourself. Tomorrow is another day.

14. TUESDAY. Calm. The troubles and worries that have been troubling you lately should virtually disappear today. This is a time for stepping back from other people's concerns and concentrating more on your own interests. Do some planning for the future in relation to your personal life. Be prepared to say no to people who make demands on you which do not really appeal. You are doing nobody a favor if you take on commitments and burdens which seem irksome and uninteresting. You always have the choice of refusing. People tend to leave you alone when you are self-absorbed, so make the most of the opportunity to concentrate on yourself.

15. WEDNESDAY. Deceptive. You can get carried away with spending, particularly in relation to your social life. A good time is foreseen if you go out in a group this evening, but keep an eye on your expenditures. Otherwise you may regret the cost later. The main problem is that so much is tempting, and you are more easily swayed than usual. Draw on your strong natural Scorpio determination to prevent going too far. The same applies to your love life. If you are seeing someone new, you may be tempted to get deeply involved very quickly, but this is not a good idea. Take your time and allow all new relationships to develop naturally.

16. THURSDAY. Variable. Set spending limits for yourself, and stick to them. As with yesterday, this is a day to guard against spending foolishly. It can be tempting to splurge on lavish gifts for that special person in your life. However, first consider if you can really afford to do this. There are other ways of showing your affection. Your partner may be much more impressed by a sincere and emotional display of your feelings. If you have been looking for new work, a sound opportunity is likely to come your way through a friend, neighbor, or former colleague.

17. FRIDAY. Good. This is an excellent day for writing letters and for getting in touch with people by telephone. If you hope to extend your business interests, discuss your plans in general with recent contacts. You also have the opportunity to make potentially profitable new contacts through friends of friends. Where your social life is concerned, a group gathering as well as a one-to-one meeting should be enjoyable. For single Scorpios, this is a key time for getting out in order to meet new people. Accept an invitation to a casual get-together; you may be introduced to someone you would like to get to know better.

18. SATURDAY. Starred. This is another favorable day for contacting people both in your personal and professional life. Mail delivered to you is likely to contain either good news or perhaps a gift. If a reply or a thank you is needed, respond promptly. For single Scorpios there are good opportunities once again to link up with someone new. A person who attracts you can be pursued; it is worth making the effort to try to get to know this person better. A romantic invitation could come your way from someone you have already met. For married Scorpio people, this is an evening for intimate conversation and romance.

19. SUNDAY. Confusing. This is a day of mixed messages, particularly where travel plans and social arrangements are concerned. Double-check arrangements before you set out anywhere. Something could be bothering a family or household member. It may be difficult to bring up the matter directly with this person. To be supportive, it can help to offer a listening ear rather than specific advice for their problems. If you are buying anything for the home, check out information about guarantees and after-sales service. Buy only from a reputable dealer; you get what you pay for.

20. MONDAY. Fair. This is another day when home and family life may be up and down. Loved ones do not necessarily do what you expect. Avoid presuming too much, especially if you are relying on someone to do something specific for you or to be in a particular place at a particular time. If you are considering moving or buying property, this is a favorable day to look around. It is in your best interests, however, not to make an offer until you look into any prospective place in some depth. A cursory glance around is unlikely to give you sufficient information. It could be a mistake to be overly influenced by a superficial first impression or the glowing words of a selling agent.

21. TUESDAY. Useful. This is a good day for cleaning up and throwing out both around the home and at work. If you have a stack of papers to file, get to it now. Straighten out drawers and closets. Cleaning up can be carried out on a personal level, too. A dispute with a colleague can be resolved and put behind you. You should feel stronger about tackling tasks and subjects that you have previously avoided. A business agreement can be brought to a satisfactory conclusion. The last pieces of a project should fall into place with little effort on your part. All in all, this is a day of consolidation and finalization as you prepare for new starts.

22. WEDNESDAY. Happy. This promises to be a romantic day for both attached and unattached Scorpios. Your love partner is apt to spring a pleasant surprise on you. If you are single, accept a social invitation; it may lead to linking up with a new partner. Money could be a bit of a problem. This is one of those times when affording everything that you want to do may not be possible. Opt for the most important or most enjoyable. Where creative endeavors are concerned, you should feel unusually inspired, leading to exceptional end results. If you have to turn down a request, be gentle.

23. THURSDAY. Rewarding. Make an extra effort to finish a project or a report. You are likely to receive a special reward or recognition as a result. Routine tasks are likely to be easier to accomplish and complete if you have the help of someone else. If you are watching your weight, consider switching to a diet that provides a lifelong eating plan rather than a restricted choice. If you are entertaining at home, extra touches can make the evening special. If it is just you and your loved one, there is all the more reason to make it a romantic evening.

24. FRIDAY. Buoyant. You should be in top form where work matters are concerned. If you have been looking for new work, this is the perfect time to get back in touch with companies you interviewed with earlier in the month. If you have no clear idea of what you want to do, consider discussing the matter with a career counselor. Scorpio people intending to move from self-employment back to employee status should first seek advice from friends and also from experts such as a financial planner or tax accountant. Weigh the pros and cons carefully before making a final decision. In either case you have much to offer and much to gain.

25. SATURDAY. Unsettling. You are likely to be worrying more than usual about just about everything because you are taking a more serious attitude toward life. While it is good to take a responsible approach to crucial matters and decisions, try to refrain from becoming overly anxious. One key characteristic of Scorpio people is a tendency toward obsession. This can aid you in getting difficult tasks completed at times, but it is not always the best approach in other areas of your life. Relax and allow things to happen naturally rather than trying to manipulate them to your own agenda.

26. SUNDAY. Stressful. Relationships with other people may not be easygoing at the moment. In order to get along with people, you need to compromise more than usual. It is important to avoid a natural inclination to rebel. Part of the Scorpio nature is to be willful at times, often just to prove who is boss. However, in close partnerships, whether personal or professional, what is of mutual concern and interest must be taken into consideration. Your key to success lies in giving as well as taking, in making requests rather than demands, and in doing more than your fair share in any partnership arrangement.

27. MONDAY. Good. The results you get from your relationships may reflect the change of attitude you adopted yesterday. This is a very productive time when it comes to working hand in hand with others as part of a team. Your combined talents and creativity should bring unexpected and surprising results. For single Scorpio people, this is another key time for new contacts and attachments. Both business and social invitations could lead to romance. Scorpios involved in a long-term, committed relationship are likely to have cause for celebration.

28. TUESDAY. Changeable. Be extra careful where investments and expenditure are concerned. It is likely that you will not be able to go ahead with one particular financial plan due to people not coming up with money owed to you or with the backing that you need. This is likely to be temporary, however. It is simply a matter of waiting until you are on more solid ground, which may actually occur quicker than you expect. On this day of change, difficulties can turn into advantages in the blink of an eye. Be prepared to change direction an short notice.

29. WEDNESDAY. Sensitive. Extra work taken on now can do much to ensure your future economic security, especially if you concentrate on saving rather than spending. You are at risk of being encouraged to part with money you do not really want to spend. You could find yourself in a business or social situation where it might seem rude to opt out, even though you cannot really afford to be a part of what is going on. To save embarrassment and awkwardness, come up with a reasonable excuse or create a clever diversion. An argument can quickly escalate. Avoid making any type of threat; your credibility and good reputation are at stake.

30. THURSDAY. Fair. After the stresses and strains that have been part of your life lately at work and in your personal life, it is a good idea now to take a break from it all. If you have the opportunity to go away somewhere completely different, jump at the chance. Your partner could come up with some good ideas in this respect. Traveling a long distance with your partner or a good friend is ideal. Although you want to get away from it all, you do not want to be lonely. Ideally, choose a destination where you cannot be contacted regarding work problems or for other unwelcome reasons. Otherwise you are likely to find yourself pulled back into what you have tried to escape from temporarily. Hiding will not resolve the problem but can put it in perspective.

MAY

1. FRIDAY. Rewarding. This is a day for getting away from it all if you possibly can. A pleasure trip of any kind is likely to do you a world of good. if you have children, they are an ideal excuse to go somewhere special that you will all enjoy. For single Scorpios, opportunities to link up with a potential new romantic partner exist in places you have not been to before. Try to avoid doing the same old thing in the same old place with the same old crowd. Where work matters are concerned, focus on broadening your horizons. Going out of your way to visit an agent or adviser in order to discuss future possibilities is sure to be worthwhile.

2. SATURDAY. Satisfactory. Being misunderstood by a friend or relative can be annoying at a time when you could do with some support. Strive to make your plans and intentions clearer so that they see what you hope to accomplish. The more effort you put into explaining your situation and your ideas, the more others are likely to jump on the bandwagon and offer to help you. This is a positive day where money matters of all kinds are concerned. Rewards for your recent efforts are likely, whether you expected them or not. Taking on more responsibility than has been specifically assigned to you is likely to lead to more pay or a bonus.

3. SUNDAY. Unsettling. Loved ones may seem distant and preoccupied. Initially it is unlikely that you will receive the love and support that you want and need. Your partner may even take a rather patronizing or sarcastic stance. This stems more from their own frame of mind and worries than a direct reflection on you. Discussing mutual concerns and problems can help clear the air and alter the situation for the better. Any bad feelings could be about simple, routine tasks which need to be shared more equally so that you are both happy with the situation. Get to bed early tonight; the coming workweek is a busy one.

4. MONDAY. Manageable. Various tasks and responsibilities, both at work and at home, are sure to keep you busy. If you need the backing of your boss or colleagues, you can count on them being there for you. It is worthwhile to cultivate relations with people in high places who can help you achieve what you want in the long term. If you have been out of work, this is an excellent time to renew efforts to find a new job. Careers advisers can be helpful if you are unsure of what you are best suited to do. In all work matters a professional approach tends to pay dividends. Look your best from head to toe.

5. TUESDAY. Enjoyable. Friends are great company today. Through your partner's contacts you could be introduced to important new people. Do not be too quick to make judgments at the moment. You are likely to make a good impression and be immediately accepted into a new crowd. Because these people are apt to be quite different from those you normally associate with, you have the opportunity to branch out in an exciting new direction. Take the attitude that if others treat you well, it is worth making the effort to treat them the same way. For single Scorpios, friends are the key to meeting a new romantic partner, probably through a blind date that you initially resist.

6. WEDNESDAY. Changeable. New interests and involvement with people you recently met in your social life may begin to blossom. Being drawn into the crowd more, you are likely to be talked into things you would not normally consider doing. Be careful, however, that you do not end up spending too much on activities which, given the choice, you would usually avoid. A practical joker in your midst may try to encourage you to take part in a prank which you do not really approve of. Your strength of character gives you the option to duck out of this without losing face or seeming to be a poor sport.

7. THURSDAY. Fair. After this recent period of frequent socializing, you need to rest and catch up on your sleep. Indulgences are likely to be putting a strain on your entire body. Adhere to a light diet with foods that contain a lot of water, to help cleanse your system. Fruit and vegetables should not upset your digestion. Work tasks are demanding, and it is unlikely that you can shirk certain responsibilities. Plan a quiet evening at home so that you can rest, recuperate, and recharge your batteries. A good book is your best companion tonight.

8. FRIDAY. Variable. This promises to be a productive day, particularly at work. You should be left to your own devices more than usual. With certain individuals out of the workplace at the moment, you have the time and peaceful atmosphere to get on with tasks that require intense concentration. This is an excellent day for tying up loose ends and attending to various tasks which have been neglected. It is not such a favorable time, however, for matters which require constant back-and-forth communication with other people. If you telephone contacts to obtain specific information, you could have problems tying them down. Focus on more solitary duties where you only have to rely on yourself.

9. SATURDAY. Mixed. Yesterday you probably had too much to do and too little time, or did not feel up to handling a lot of responsibilities. Whether you are at work or home today, you have the energy to tackle jobs which need your undivided attention and cannot easily be avoided. It is important, however, that you also make some time for yourself to relax and wind down. Too much rushing around, trying to do everything in one day, can take a toll on your nerves and normally good judgment. Try to pin family members and friends down to exact arrangements, rather than waiting around for them to decide what they want to do and where they would like to go this evening.

10. SUNDAY. Disconcerting. Family members are likely to spring surprises on you. If you were hoping for some quiet time alone to pursue your own plans, you could be in for a shock. It is likely that you have been included in other people's plans, whether you like it or not. If you really do not want to take part, say so bluntly. However, you may decide that it is easier to put aside your own plans and go along for the sake of maintaining peace and harmony. If you want to try out a new image by changing your hair color or style, do not tell your loved ones until the change has been accomplished. Otherwise they may try to talk you out of it.

11. MONDAY. Buoyant. You have even more drive and determination than usual. Your creativity is at a peak, and you are likely to be inspired to tackle new projects and develop fresh interests. Family members may not be too happy about this if doing so excludes them. While as a Scorpio you enjoy frequent change, not everyone around you feels the same. Discuss your plans in the context of developing individual interests. In this way your actions should not seem in any way threatening to the relationship. Put more of yourself into all of the day's activities.

12. TUESDAY. Manageable. Scorpio people interested in moving or purchasing real estate should begin or renew a property search today. You may be lucky enough to discover the place of your dreams. Your financial situation is improving and stabilizing. A good work or investment offer is likely to come your way. Think about the long-term future when making your decision. Relations with your loved one should improve now. The injection of more romance into your relationship, whether this comes from you or your partner, is sure to enhance the partnership and bring you even closer to one another.

13. WEDNESDAY. Slow. You may have to put your plans on hold until you have sorted out a financial difficulty. It is unwise to agree to participate in an expensive event or to make a major purchase if you are not sure how you are going to be able to pay for it. An earning opportunity which comes up may look good from a financial point of view. However, there is a strong chance that the responsibilities and time involved will impinge on other areas of your life more than you really can afford. Weigh what is truly worthwhile, particularly if you value your social time. The ideal compromise may be a part-time job which contains a social element.

14. THURSDAY. Successful. Your financial and work prospects look much more healthy today than yesterday. A money-making opportunity which you hear about could be ideal, fitting easily into your overall plans. Discussions with colleagues are likely to be helpful if you are trying to resolve money difficulties or all looking for extra work or a new position. Contacts are likely to do you favors and supply valuable information that you cannot get from anyone else. Make the most of an opportunity to glean vital information from those willing to share it with you, but guard against revealing your source.

15. FRIDAY. Sensitive. Be careful what you say to others at work. Disputes can easily arise with colleagues because everyone is nervous about a situation that is developing or a new system which has recently been implemented. If you are looking for work at the moment, rely on your own initiatives more than usual. Seeking help through old contacts may not be very productive. This is because other people have a lot on their mind at the moment and not much time to think about anything or anyone else. At another time they may be much more helpful, so do nothing that could alienate them.

16. SATURDAY. Misleading. Conditions favors getting out to see other people or to do something special that you enjoy with a group. If you have children, a visit to a zoo or amusement park is a good choice. For single Scorpios, social engagements can lead you to meeting somebody new who immediately attracts your interest. It is worth going to local events and to gatherings hosted by neighbors or relatives, even though you imagine they may be dull. Any opportunity to mix with new people is worthwhile, whether or not you are already attached. Expanding your social circle can open new doors for you.

17. SUNDAY. Variable. This is a favorable day for making plans for the future, especially in relation to property moves and financial investments. If your finances are not on an even keel, work out a new, more realistic budget. Strive to pay off current bills. Home and family life are congenial at the moment. A gathering which brings both close and distant family together ought to go well. You could receive a surprise visit from someone you have not seen in a long time. Try to make this person feel welcome, even though they may be interfering with your time and plans. You never know when you may need to call on them.

18. MONDAY. Mixed. You should find it easy to conclude discussions and agreements, particularly in relation to work and business matters. If you have been hoping to pull off an important deal, this is likely to be your day of success. Be quite careful when dealing with other people, however. It is important to show that you are giving full consideration to their interests, even if your own interests are foremost in your mind. Somebody you have to deal with may be unnecessarily combative. Try not to rise to this person's bait, since they are probably just itching for an argument. You can disarm them by finding at least one point to agree with completely.

19. TUESDAY. Fair. Avoid investing too much emotional energy in events and situations which are fleeting and of no lasting value. The same applies to relationships. If you have recently become involved with somebody new, you probably do not know at this stage how interested or committed the other person really is. Try to find out more in this respect before you begin to make plans for a joint future. A passing fancy may be a great escape from boring responsibility, but you may kick yourself later for having squandered your time and money on a relationship that was not worth such a great investment. Unless you have a long-time working partnership, you should be more productive on your own.

20. WEDNESDAY. Pleasant. This is a better day for enjoying yourself than yesterday. If you are interested in beginning a new hobby, or picking up on an old one, do not hesitate any longer. Your creative talents could lead to beginning a new business enterprise. It is well worth your while to follow an instinctive urge. New plans and ideas brewing now could be truly significant in shaping your future. Speculation is, by nature, a risky business. Today, however, you can afford to take more risks than usual providing they are well calculated and carefully timed. Be generous with loved ones, both with your time and your money.

21. THURSDAY. Good. Clear out some of the deadwood in your life. This should be especially helpful at work, where clearing away unnecessary paperwork, old files, and useless supplies should help you feel more organized. Scorpio people are generally happiest when life is under control. Being a little ruthless about how you organize your work environment can instill a greater sense of this control for you. Aim to finish up tasks or projects which have been neglected. Take the same approach with ideas. Either do something positive to get them off the drawing board or consign them to the reject pile.

22. FRIDAY. Useful. Work colleagues are likely to be helpful and supportive if you are struggling to finish a number of tasks. Ask for a little help if carrying out all of your routine duties is too much to cope with. It is due to extra work burdens that you are pushed for time. Associates tend to understand and probably will not mind giving you a little help. Having a colleague screen your calls while you concentrate on detailed work can prevent you from being constantly interrupted. Call on a knowledgeable friend for some specific advice regarding a personal situation. Do not get drawn into a romantic intrigue tonight.

23. SATURDAY. Happy. This is an excellent day for making long-term mutual plans with your loved one. If you seldom have the time to do such planning, do not put it off any longer. Discuss and clarify what you intend to do both individually and together. What you talk about should help clear up any doubts or concerns that you have had about each other or about your relationship. Joint financial arrangements can be agreed on now. If there is someone with whom you need to discuss property or other matters, do not hesitate to call. You can solve a problem quite easily if you avoid making it a formal discussion and keep the conversation personal and pleasant.

24. SUNDAY. Excellent. This is another highly favorable day for partnerships. Single Scorpio people have a good opportunity to meet someone new or to consolidate a connection with someone met earlier in the year. Luck is on your side, especially when it comes to matters of romance and entertainment. If there is someone special you want to get to know better, this is the right time to extend an invitation. Try to make it something that most people would have a hard time refusing. If there is an entertaining outside focus for you both to concentrate on, you will have plenty to talk about afterward.

25. MONDAY. Sensitive. Scorpios are at the beginning of an important new phase. It is a time for tossing out the old and welcoming in the new. If you have not already gotten rid of some of the deadwood in your life, this is the right time for doing so and then moving on. For enterprising Scorpio people, conditions are favorable for beginning a new business venture, particularly one which involves sharing financial responsibilities with another person. You should be able to draw up and agree on a contract without too many hitches. Discussions about money should be open and aboveboard, with no information hidden or held back. Check that you have sufficient insurance coverage.

26. TUESDAY. Fair. Try to make light of a stressful situation at work or in your personal life, without giving the wrong message. This is a time when other people can be flippant about matters which you think should be treated much more seriously. Not everybody shares your intensity or commitment, however, and it is wrong to try to impose your views on them. If you step back from the situation that is troubling you, you may realize that you are being a little too extreme. Do not gamble where business and financial matters are concerned. There is a strong risk that you will come out on the losing side. Be very conservative in all of your actions.

27. WEDNESDAY. Disquieting. Try to get colleagues at work more involved in your tasks if possible. Any opportunity to share responsibilities tends to ease your own burden. Exchanging tasks can also be useful, particularly if you each have something to do which you consider unpleasant, but which the other person feels indifferent about or even enjoys. This is a propitious day for working out a business situation which has been getting you down. It is unlikely that you will walk away regretting your actions. Be guarded about making rash moves where a lot of money is at stake. Joint decisions are favored in order to share the risk.

28. THURSDAY. Stressful. Background hassles and worries which have been brewing are likely to come to a head. There is a tendency for you to take too much responsibility on your own shoulders now, then sorely regret not sharing the burden. It is unlikely that you can charm your way out of a situation where a strong commitment has been made in the past. The most you can do is try your best, without breaking your word. Plan a change of scene for later in the day, or earlier even if it will clear your mind and help you get motivated. Be careful that any changes you make to your plans are not simply an attempt to avoid irksome responsibilities by passing them on to someone less competent.

29. FRIDAY. Manageable. As with yesterday, it is not a good idea to try to shirk responsibilities by doing something entirely different. It is true that a change of environment tends to make you feel better. However, a change of pace in whatever you are doing could also improve the situation. If you are having trouble completing some work which needs to be finished to meet today's deadline, find ways of speeding up by being a little less nit-picking. Once you bring your Scorpio determination to bear on the situation, little can stop you from achieving your goals. You have a great store of past experience to fall back on and should use it now.

30. SATURDAY. Mixed. Having managed to get a problem or burdensome task out of the way, you should be raring to go on to a new and more personally interesting project. Older and more experienced individuals can be a great help in this regard. Make more of an effort to cultivate good relations with people you think can help you in some special way. Also go out of your way to fulfill a responsibility which was neglected while you were concentrating on finishing other tasks. The more you get out of the way, the happier you are likely to feel. Joint enterprises are favored where a person of more experience is involved.

31. SUNDAY. Deceptive. Although you have a strong desire to fulfill a long-held dream or ambition, be a little careful about who get you involved with along the way. Somebody appealing to this burning ambition within you may not actually be working in your best interests. If you are starting out on a new joint enterprise, you are likely to have more success with someone who is a fast but thorough worker rather than a plodder. In your personal life, there may be discussions and debates with your partner or family. Make an effort to understand each other's views and to be as accommodating as possible.

JUNE

1. MONDAY. Disquieting. You are likely to have a difficult time dealing with a new acquaintance or even a long-term friend. The problem affecting your relationship is likely to be money. This is not a favorable time for trying to sort out the balance due on a loan. Whether you want to borrow from someone, lend them money, or work out a new repayment schedule for a loan which has gone wrong, state your position but do not expect others to agree right away. If your self-esteem takes a dip it is probably because you have lost a battle you feel you could have won. Try to be a little less hard on yourself; it is a good lesson learned.

2. TUESDAY. Difficult. You may be finding it difficult to cope with an individual who refuses to see your point of view or respect your wishes. Anyone who has taken you for granted in some way is probably about to regret it. However, avoid doing or saying anything which you might regret later on. It is in the Scorpio nature to seek vengeance on anyone who richly deserves it. However, experience has taught you that this is not always the wisest move, primarily because you tend to go to extremes and burn too many bridges behind you. Try to avoid acting for dramatic effect in the heat of the moment. Let your sense of power come through in more subtle ways.

3. WEDNESDAY. Manageable. Look after private and family interests above all else. Some of your more intimate thoughts need not be shared with other people. It is time for the rest of the world to leave you alone for a while. If you do want to confide in anyone, choose a friend or someone else who is close, not a co-worker or the boss. Behind-the-scenes negotiations could bring a joint financial matter to a satisfying conclusion. Your money position is generally good, allowing you to splurge on a gift for someone special in your life whom you wish to thank or acknowledge. And you can also afford to buy a present for yourself.

4. THURSDAY. Variable. This is a favorable day for finalizing an agreement which has only been tentative until now. You are likely to be quite lucky where real estate matters are concerned. If you decide to proceed with a purchase, this is the right time to do so. It is vital, however, to be sure that you have financing arranged beforehand. If you need a mortgage, thoroughly investigate a number of companies. Hearsay is not enough to go on. Shop for the best interest rate. A member of the family who is hospitalized or confined at home deserves a visit. Even if it means going out of your way or missing something else you would like to do, make time to visit.

5. FRIDAY. Difficult. You could find it difficult to concentrate on any single matter, since there are so many unresolved issues on your mind. Home could be the perfect refuge for confused and restless Scorpios looking for a little peace of mind. Family members and private pleasures can provide padding which the wide world cannot. If you are tempted to invest in a brand-new invention for the home or office, think again. What is advertised as a piece of wizardry may not actually help you much in the long run. Only invest in items proven over time to really work as they claim. If going out with friends tonight, be sure to pay your own way.

6. SATURDAY. Demanding. Personal progress is important. Put yourself first, and put the needs of others second. This is not going to make you very popular with a loved one but is vital right now. Be prepared for some aggravation if you insist on going ahead with a personal plan that you know upsets or irritates your partner. Try talking matters through to explain your reasons. A loved one may feel threatened by your outside activities. Reassurance from you could go a long way to alleviate the situation. If you want peace and quiet, it is important to try to be understanding at home without giving in or giving up.

7. SUNDAY. Exciting. A lot can be accomplished if you put your mind to it. Once again, you need to give precedence to your own considerations. Little should hinder or delay you once you have a firm plan and start putting it into action. Where finances are concerned, backers are likely to be more solidly behind you than you expect. It is easier to attain a loan now than earlier in the year. Make an effort to advance your interests while so much is going your way. Permission to proceed with an important part of a key plan is likely to speed up the process of achieving the end which you are working to achieve. Keep in mind that some rules are made to be broken.

8. MONDAY. Mixed. It is not a good idea to mix business with pleasure if you do not already know the people that well. If choosing a gathering spot for people you are more familiar with, stick with a place that you all have been to before. Putting people in unusual surroundings can make them nervous. Do not be afraid to negotiate for rewards which you feel are due you. However, it is unwise to expect the past to repeat itself. Change is swirling all around you, and you need to be more flexible. A new decorative item for the home can be a good buy so long as you can afford to splurge. Invest in lasting, quality goods rather than cheap bargains. Aim for quality, not quantity.

9. TUESDAY. Stressful. If you are in search of a new place to live, this could be your lucky day. Be careful about the financial negotiations, however. If you are considering renting or buying a home that is already furnished, be sure you can live with another person's tastes. Worn out equipment may not necessarily look old. Take a good look at what is being offered. Partners may not agree on how to spend joint money. Sit down and talk these matters through before you go shopping. Discuss what you intend to look for, rather than have an argument about basics in the middle of a store.

10. WEDNESDAY. Uncertain. Financial problems may seem a lot worse than they really are at the moment. Nevertheless, be cautious with your spending. Do not purchase anything on credit. Try not to be too heavy-handed with a loved one who has been charging what you consider much too much. It is possible that the extra expense was justified or even necessary. Your bank may not approve your request for a loan or overdraft protection. Try another financial institution, showing your responsibility in handling your finances. Someone who recently moved away may be in touch with you for advice. Help them make a major decision.

11. THURSDAY. Fortunate. This is a very promising day. A recent break from routine has perked you up and given you a more positive outlook. This is a fine time for shopping with a loved one. Together you can search out some bargains in furniture, carpeting, or appliances. A drive is also likely to be enjoyable, or drop in to visit a neighbor whose company you enjoy. For single Scorpios this is a key time for meeting a prospective new partner by getting out and about more. A new relationship is likely to progress more quickly than you expect. Joint finances should go smoothly now that you have reached a new understanding with your mate or partner.

12. FRIDAY. Good. Spend more time with those you love. Being alone is unlikely to be particularly enjoyable. As a Scorpio you shine when you are in company. Your enthusiasm may be ignited by a project which involves your mate or partner. Two heads are better than one when it comes to hatching creative ideas. A local attraction should be appealing if you are looking for a bit of fun after dark. You do not need to travel far in order to find pleasure. For single Scorpio men and women, this is another promising day for meeting someone special. Entertainment activities could put you in the company of someone who will soon be a steady date.

13. SATURDAY. Rewarding. This is a very favorable day for family involvement, particularly if costs are shared. Your parents or in-laws could treat you to something special. Enjoy home comforts and entertaining. If you are in the mood for shopping, some bargains can be picked up at an unadvertised sale. Because you are feeling in such good form, you can offer more support and affection to your loved ones. Be kind to old and young alike. Your kindness and caring mean a lot to them. Do not get involved in any type of gambling or risky speculation. Others can encourage you to invest in one scheme or another, but do not be easily persuaded.

14. SUNDAY. Fair. Your home is the center of your universe. Keep loved ones informed of your intentions in order to maintain peace and harmony. Do not make a social commitment without checking with them first. Conditions favor discussing joint plans relating to future finances. Providing for both your own old age and for the future security of younger family members deserves some thought. Your energy is likely to peak early in the day, when you are most single-minded and purposeful. Later on your personal motivation can wane due to loved ones demanding more of your attention. It is important to divide your time equally between individual and family concerns.

15. MONDAY. Useful. It is vital to fulfill key responsibilities without taking life too seriously. Colleagues are more than usually cooperative, as are family members and friends. If you have something special to do, someone close to you is likely to take on a few extra responsibilities in order to give you more free time. Travel related to your work is sure to be pleasurable as well as rewarding. You can successfully mix business with pleasure. Keep a close watch on accounts and budgets. Overspending, either on a business expense account or from your own pocket, is not a good idea without advance approval.

16. TUESDAY. Changeable. Unlike yesterday, this is not a good day for mixing business with pleasure. If you are discussing matters of a financial nature, maintain a strictly businesslike approach. Loved ones understand your need to do your own thing. This is a favorable time, nevertheless, for enjoying entertainment and leisure activities together. For single Scorpios, this evening favors getting to know an interesting newcomer better. It is also a good time for meeting people considerably older or younger than you. Accept an invitation to a party even if you have to go alone and know only the host or hostess..

17. WEDNESDAY. Tricky. Follow the same basic businesslike principles that you practiced yesterday. An entertainment bill could seem inordinately high, even if you end up with a new contract or contact as a result. You will gain more by keeping business separate from pleasure. Aim to get detailed paperwork out of the way early in the day. A need to travel may keep you on the move later on. Key opportunities coming your way after lunch must not be missed. Your focus is likely to broaden, robbing you of the patience to attend to petty details or to deal with petty people. Family members can help by taking on more household tasks.

18. THURSDAY. Good. It is surprising just how much you can get done when you really put your mind to it. This is a propitious day for completing tasks which have been on hold for some time. A lucky change in your routine is likely to be a great help. Business contracts and agreements need careful attention. Read any small print before signing a document. There is no point agreeing to something that is not crystal clear to you. You need no encouragement to push ahead with essentials. The routine work that you get out of the way is likely to make you feel a lot more organized. If you are self-employed, spend some time catching up with accounts and filing.

19. FRIDAY. Fair. More cooperation than usual, especially at work, should make your day go with a flourish. Routine tasks can be successfully completed. Once again, you do not need much encouragement to handle tasks you normally view as burdensome or trivial. If you are self-employed, this is a favorable time for plotting out a fresh routine which you can put into practice more fully next week. Attend to business matters early in the day. Later on, more personal concerns are likely. There could be an argument with a loved one about weekend plans. Try to see their point of view even if you do not understand or agree with their ideas.

20. SATURDAY. Unsettling. The same friction with a loved one that you experienced yesterday is likely to remain today. With patience, you can clear it up this morning and get back on speaking terms at least. A trip away from home is likely to do everyone a world of good. Discussing summer vacation plans should also help ease any remaining tension by diverting attention to something pleasant. The key to your happiness is to avoid being stuck in a rut. Do all that you can to make this weekend exciting, refreshing, and different from usual. The same old routine tends to get everyone down.

21. SUNDAY. Excellent. Surprise romantic gestures can make a close relationship even more loving and fulfilling. Put any disagreements behind you and concentrate on having fun. Getting together with friends or family members tends to spark off your creativity. Make both current and long-term plans together. Enjoy your closeness when it comes to domestic matters; work together on a project around the house. If you are shopping for items for the home, you should be able to pick up a bargain or two. This is a particularly favorable day for activities involving all of the family working together. The combination of everyone's energy and enthusiasm tends to make any task lighter.

22. MONDAY. Productive. Do not put off work connected with your home. Family members are likely to be surprisingly enterprising and helpful. It is worth listening to their opinions and any advice regarding repairs or redecoration. This is a favorable time for buying electrical appliances; you are likely to get a good deal at a local store. Getting away with a loved one should be a welcome change to routine. If you cannot take any time off during the day, consider going out together this evening to somewhere you have not been before. A change of scene promises to be refreshing and the perfect setting for talking about the future.

23. TUESDAY. Fair. Avoid speculation, especially in the world of business. Despite encouragement from others to take a risk with money, it is not a good idea to do so. A partner's enthusiasm is likely to be contagious, but hedge your bets. Working away from your usual environment should be very productive. If you are involved in training, the work is apt to be very intense and even stressful, but you should come away feeling you have learned a great deal. Travel for business purposes can expand your horizons. You are moving into a new phase in which a broader mode of thinking is sure to benefit you personally and professionally.

24. WEDNESDAY. Calm. Be grateful for today's change of your usual routine. If you have time off from work, it is a good idea to get away for a break. Quiet time gives you an opportunity to mull over what really matters to you. If you have been out of work, this is a key day for planning a new job-hunting strategy. Look at life from a wider perspective. Contact large corporations with a view to future employment. Check the newspaper for help-wanted advertisements from new companies. This is a favorable day for self-publicity and for going on a job interview. Promote yourself as positively as possible.

25. THURSDAY. Deceptive. A trip purely for pleasure purposes is favored. Being in a different environment is likely to fill you with creative inspiration. The middle part of the day is good for completing a business deal or at least a tentative agreement. Any contract signed now should be carefully read; do not make the mistake of assuming too much. What is written down may not agree overall with what has been discussed. A loved one is likely to have very specific ideas for home improvements, but you may not agree. Instead of arguing about plans, put forward a very sound case for what you want, but be willing to compromise on some specifics.

26. FRIDAY. Variable. If you are interested in trying to win a pay raise, approach your employer early in the day before other matters interfere with a discussion. If you are looking for new work or want to find out how you did in an interview, the earlier part of the day is again likely to be most profitable. Changes to routine later in the day can delay your progress. Try to deal with the most important matters first thing this morning. Domestic and personal issues may conflict with professional interests. Strive to keep disruptions to your schedule to a minimum. A quiet evening with one or two people is favored over going out with a crowd.

27. SATURDAY. Good. This is a highly favorable day for attending to business and joint financial matters. You may not be actually at work, but you can achieve a lot by focusing on future career planning. If you are on the job, your employer is likely to be willing to discuss a pay increase or future promotion. Improved conditions can also be negotiated and implemented with relative ease. Duties should seem less stressful if you share some responsibilities with other people. Joint effort tends to bring the most satisfying results. Take part in activities tonight rather than being an onlooker.

28. SUNDAY. Changeable. If you are doing any financial planning, do it alone. Group effort is only likely to confuse the situation. A friend who is in some kind of trouble at the moment is sure to appreciate your offer of advice and practical help. Approach this person with kindness and understanding, especially if money is the issue. Their pride could be hurt if you seem to be taking over. A change of scene is favored for restless Scorpio people. Light socializing is favored this evening after an emotionally taxing day. Neither charm nor manipulation helps where money matters are concerned; a sense of responsibility carries much more weight.

29. MONDAY. Mixed. Give yourself space to maneuver as today develops in unexpected directions. Ups and downs where business and money are concerned are likely to be upsetting. There is little point getting involved in a heated debate. Distance yourself for a while in order to collect your thoughts. In fact, a change of scene could do much to ignite your creative inspiration. The solution to a problem tends to come later in the day, when you are more relaxed. Friends and acquaintances will be helpful and supportive if you need to lean on them. You can rely on their good judgment when you have an important choice to make.

30. TUESDAY. Fair. A friend's attitudes could worry you. Someone who has not been an especially close acquaintance may try to get closer to you at a time when their presence is unwelcome. Your best policy is to do all you can to maintain some distance. If you have recently moved into a new neighborhood, the over-enthusiasm of a neighbor in welcoming you may seem suspect. Do not accept any invitation which does not appeal to you. In time you can get to know this person better, when you feel more settled and at ease. Making yourself unavailable by staying away from the local social scene is probably a good idea while you consider the direction you want to take in the future.

JULY

1. WEDNESDAY. Misleading. Behind-the-scenes activities are likely to be productive, especially in the business world. You need a greater degree of privacy in your life in order to consider all of your options. Take advantage of an unusual opportunity to relax at home. Avoid traveling far if at all. You could feel out of your depth and vulnerable if you stray away from your usual environment. An employer who appears to be working in your interests may actually have something else in mind. Do not believe all that you are told, even less of what you hear in the rumor mill. People are not out to mislead you intentionally but could do so just the same.

2. THURSDAY. Manageable. If you are at all worried about your health, this is a good time to schedule a checkup. You probably simply need more rest and relaxation. If there is a physical problem, however, it is better to know about it sooner rather than later. Even if there is nothing really wrong, it will put your mind at rest to get a clean bill of health. Also do not neglect your dental health. Your efforts to get on in the professional world may be pleasing you, but your partner could have different ideas. Increased time spent at work that is keeping you apart can create conflict in your relationship. Do what you can to right the balance, at least by bringing work home to do.

3. FRIDAY. Deceptive. Pursuing your own interests is likely to be rewarding. However, do not expect those near you to understand your need for more personal space. If anything, your increased self-absorption could seem like a threat. It is not a good idea to neglect or put off responsibilities at home, nor to expect your partner or other household members to carry the burden alone. Doing at least your share should make you much more appreciated. Your partner may lay down the law but try not to take it too personally. Keep in mind that loved ones are under more stress than usual and need more support and understanding from you.

4. SATURDAY. Easygoing. You can breathe a sigh of relief since you are freer to do as you please today. Household tasks and family responsibilities should be gotten out of the way early in the day, giving you the opportunity to take off somewhere interesting. This is a favorable day for broadening your horizons, both mentally and physically. Travel to a distant place promises to be especially enjoyable. Buy something new for the home that you have had your eye on. There is a good chance that it is reduced in price now or is available with a favorable payment option. A person of influence is worth trying to get to know better in a social atmosphere.

5. SUNDAY. Good. Scorpios are on a creative high at the moment. Inspiration is coming your way from all directions. This is the perfect time to begin a new hobby or learn a new technique. Do some personal planning involving your social life and leisure time. Increased self-esteem allows you to embark on a new project with greater confidence. Try to find some time to pay your bills and perhaps work out a more realistic budget. An effort to get debts out of the way is likely to remove a mental stumbling block and ease your mind. At home, reorganize the kitchen cupboards or refrigerator and replenish the basics.

6. MONDAY. Mixed. News of a pay increase or a bank mistake which works in your favor is likely. Generally, however, this is a tricky day where finances are concerned. You can also end up out of pocket due to other people's errors or their failure to keep an agreement. Charm and diplomacy should be replaced with a firm stand taken if others are taking advantage of your generous Scorpio nature or are declining to deliver as promised. The advice of an expert is likely to be helpful. Money spent on the home probably will not go to waste. However, figure out what you can afford before going on a spending spree. Guard against saddling yourself with long-term debt.

7. TUESDAY. Frustrating. Do not be frivolous in your attitude toward your own money or business funds. This is not a good time for taking unnecessary risks. You are likely to feel disappointed with any purchase. Where romance is concerned, putting forth a big effort to impress someone new may not be well received. Significant financial gestures tend to impress some people but turn off others. The same goes for romantic overtures. If the person whose attention you want is not responding to you, either they want something different or are not right for you. Decide what you are willing to do, and make your choice. Backing off can sometimes be more productive than coming on strong.

8. WEDNESDAY. Disconcerting. Neighbors are likely to be rather disagreeable. If they think you are being excessive, for example by making too much noise or using up too many parking spaces, you will probably hear from them about it. Do not make too much of an issue of their complaint unless you feel very strongly about the matter. An effort to meet others halfway can do much to ease the situation. If you are traveling, be prepared for a major detour or rerouting which can delay your journey. Work superiors will not have much patience with slow progress. Do all that you can to speed up your efforts in order to meet a deadline.

9. THURSDAY. Challenging. Scorpios need to strike a fine balance. Keep one eye on current paperwork while your attention remains on long-term plans you are about to launch. Local shopping and routine trips can turn into lengthy outings if you end up meeting someone you have not seen in a while. If you do not have the time to spare, curb the gossip. Any long-distance trip or change of scene shared with a loved one is likely to be enjoyable. Do some future planning together. If you are thinking of getting back in touch with an old friend, this is not the best time to do so. Wait until you have less on your schedule and can be more flexible.

10. FRIDAY. Variable. This is the perfect day for putting out feelers both in your professional and personal life. For single Scorpio people, opportunities abound to meet a prospective new partner. Treat all invitations as possible opportunities. For those currently involved in a long-term relationship, this is a key time for making plans together. Figure out how to spend more leisure time in each other's company. If a kitchen appliance suddenly begins to groan or grind, this is an indication that it might be on its way out. However, do not replace it right away; the problem could be repairable. If this has been a long-term problem go bargain hunting for a new model.

11. SATURDAY. Changeable. A day of unexpected developments awaits you. Family-centered plans could be disrupted by a visit or telephone call from someone you have not seen in a long time. It is best to leave plans as flexible as possible. If you rent your home, expect a conversation with the landlord if the rent has not been paid or upkeep which is your responsibility has not been done. Charm and diplomacy are your way out, coupled with a firm commitment to keep your side of the bargain. Any new agreement should be put in writing. Enjoy an evening on the town as part of a group of friends.

12. SUNDAY. Fair. Involve family members in leisure and entertainment activities and you are bound to have a pleasurable time. Given the choice between work with due rewards and a plan for fun or self-indulgence, you may have a hard time choosing. Play life according to your own desires. You may not necessarily take life easy but play as hard as you usually work. Guard against a tendency to overspend. It does not have to cost a lot to have fun. For single Scorpio people, events out of town could be the key to meeting someone new whose interests compliment your own.

13. MONDAY. Quiet. You have the opportunity to set your own schedule. If you are self-employed, work is likely to be more of a pleasure than a burden. This is one of those days when Scorpio creativity comes alive. Without other people disturbing you or making demands on your time, you have the freedom to do anything you want. An artistic project should be especially satisfying. If you are trying to get more involved in the art world or in another creative field, this is a good time to put together a portfolio of your work. The attentions of an admirer are likely to be welcomed by single Scorpio people.

14. TUESDAY. Mixed. Try not to berate a loved one for overspending. Although you may be watching every penny, there is a good reason for a recent costly purchase. Expenses related to children now may be higher than budgeted. Do not ask them to miss out on a leisure trip or other treat. Do what you can to cover the unexpected expense by cutting back in another area. Forgoing some personal luxuries for a short while is unlikely to seem such a hardship when you realize how much pleasure you are giving to others. This is a key day for finishing up routine tasks so that you can begin a new project.

15. WEDNESDAY. Manageable. Your priority at the moment should be to focus on overall plans and long-term developments. However, guard against a tendency to get caught up in petty details. Try not to worry about little particulars which will sooner or later sort themselves out. Even if you have to cut a few financial corners at the moment, this should not necessarily cramp your style. Make an effort to get routine matters cleared out of the way as quickly as possible. There are far more important tasks awaiting your attention which will have a great impact in the long run. Family members should be a help with practical endeavors providing you give them clear directions.

16. THURSDAY. Tricky. You are likely to repeat the same inner battle as you did yesterday. Once again, you benefit by making an effort to clear work out of the way and not dwell on trivial matters too much. New business developments look promising. If you need to hire staff, this is a key time for selecting the right people. Your partner is unlikely to be too happy about a decision in relation to your home. You could have a hard time convincing anyone that you are on the right track. It is probably best to save your energy until some time has passed and your loved one has a chance to think things through from all angles.

17. FRIDAY. Uncertain. If you are planning a trip out of town for the weekend, try to leave early in the day. Do not depart, however, without checking around your home to be sure the windows and doors are locked and small appliances are unplugged. You do not want to have to worry about such things when you are halfway along your journey. Work-based Scorpio people should not attempt to mix business with pleasure. A costly entertainment bill could come as a shock; if you have no limit in mind before going out, you only have yourself to blame. This is a better day for selling than for buying.

18. SATURDAY. Fair. Your closest personal relationship may be under some strain. The main problem is likely to be a partner's tendency to be dictatorial. Try to find out what is the actual problem; it is likely to be personal. Getting away to different surroundings can be good for you both. For single Scorpios, new activities are most likely to lead to meeting an attractive prospective partner. Stick to general conversation rather than business and all should be well. Completion of a job around the house is now in sight, but continue to be thorough. Where major investments are concerned, be sure to obtain sufficient information before making a decision.

19. SUNDAY. Variable. Efforts to rework the family budget should not go to waste. If you are worried about a deficit that cannot be easily explained, casual discussions with family members could pinpoint the problem. You may run into a stumbling block if you are trying to buy or sell property. Disagreement about the right price could result in one party backing out. If you are the one selling, do not give in if you receive an unfair offer. Surprisingly enough, the next person who comes along to view your property could be willing to pay the asking price. Do not stay up too late tonight.

20. MONDAY. Mixed. Property and financial affairs may be aided by someone of considerable influence in or out of government. If you are doing any kind of fund-raising, whether for work or voluntary purposes, it can be valuable to obtain a celebrity sponsor. Luck is not on your side where speculation is concerned, however. It is best to play by the rules just now. If you have made an agreement, stick to it. There are times when you can rely on life to bail you out with a lucky break, but this is not one of them. If you owe money, make every effort to repay it in full. Spend the evening doing something pleasurable which you ordinarily cannot do.

21. TUESDAY. Fair. You should be more fortunate today where joint arrangements are concerned than you were yesterday. Someone who owes you a favor can be called upon to help you out of a difficult situation. Cultural activity shared with a loved one is likely to be rewarding. If you have high aims for the future, now is the time to start the ball rolling. This promises to be a profitable day when it comes to researching subjects of special interest to you. A new diet is likely to require considerable reading so that you understand the principles. Eliminating excess sugar and caffeine from your diet may be the answer to a skin complaint as well as a weight problem.

22. WEDNESDAY. Uncertain. Traveling is likely to keep you out of circulation for most of the day. A change of environment should do you a lot of good, particularly if you have stimulating company. Any problem that is hindering a close relationship is more likely to be solved when you are off home ground. Your partner could come up with appealing plans for leisure activities. Make the most of an opportunity to develop your ideas and broaden your horizons. One of your acquaintances is likely to have sound, professional advice to offer. Consider it carefully as this person probably has your best interests at heart.

23. THURSDAY. Deceptive. You are starting a new phase in your working life. The time is ripe for making a major change. Do not be deceived, however, by an offer which seems too good to be true. It is quite possible that the details of the job have not been made entirely clear. Try to get on better terms with coworkers, the boss, clients, and suppliers early in the day if you mean to do business. A deal or opportunity with the right figures involved is likely to come up before long if you are patient. Insecurities relating to your long-range professional life may be present for some time. You need to play the waiting game.

24. FRIDAY. Calm. The worries of the past few days should lessen today. Put on hold a decision you need to make regarding a professional or family matter. Whatever is out of balance needs to be gradually straightened out. If you have devoted too much time to career and not enough to family, or vice versa, figure out how you can restore some equilibrium. Use your spare time for future planning. As pressures in your career lift, make more of an effort to put your home life on an even keel. Try to make up for recent times when you were moody or argumentative. Be big enough to apologize even if you were provoked.

25. SATURDAY. Good. Focus on long-term career planning. This is a favorable day for contacting influential individuals who might be able to open doors for you in landing a new job. It is in your interest to respond quickly to fresh opportunities and offers. The veil of deception which was a worry to you last week has now disappeared, at least temporarily. The way is clear to plan for the future and move forward with confidence. Friends and loved ones are there for you if you need them. This evening favors a friendly social gathering. Even guests who have never met one another before are likely to get along well. You could also be successful as a matchmaker.

26. SUNDAY. Difficult. Pursue your outside interests. A journey made with friends or for a specific personal purpose is likely to be both enjoyable and productive. Try to broaden your vision when making future plans. You have more options than sticking to what has worked in the past. This is not a time for limiting yourself too much. Partners may try to impose their own limits in an attempt to demonstrate who is boss, but you do not have to fall prey to this. When dealing with older people, be sure to pay them respect. Any attempt to talk down to them, whether or not this is justified, is unlikely to be well received. An elder may also be able to help in resolving a partnership dispute.

27. MONDAY. Unsettling. Friends are likely to ask you to take part in activities which do not appeal to you or are too expensive. You need to put your foot down, since their encouragement can quickly turn to strong persuasion and even to manipulation. Light socializing will probably be welcome. You can become quite bored if your mind is not sufficiently stimulated or occupied. The key to success and happiness is not to go to extremes. If you are about to launch an important plan or project, take it one step at a time. Aim to achieve small, realistic goals. Driving requires extra attention to the road, especially at high speeds.

28. TUESDAY. Starred. Quiet time spent alone is likely to be more productive than you expect. If you have a problem to solve, you can do so more easily alone rather than seeking the advice or guidance of others. Involvement in behind-the-scenes activities at work is likely to be profitable. Leave the hard bargaining and negotiation to those who have more energy and staying power than you do at the moment. A medical checkup is likely to bring reassuring results. An examination and tests may be costly or uncomfortable but are probably worth it for your peace of mind. An expert opinion on a matter you have struggled with for most of this year should put it to rest once and for all.

29. WEDNESDAY. Disconcerting. Do not undertake a long-distance journey if you are not feeling too well. This is especially important if a lot of driving is involved. A tendency to want to escape from problems by going out of town is the equivalent of sticking your head in the sand like the proverbial stork. A short break can renew your energy, and taking a back seat for a while can give you a clearer perspective. Do not, however, try to run away from difficult situations altogether. Distancing yourself is likely to be productive only if you are willing to let other people find a solution to the problem.

30. THURSDAY. Tricky. Listen to the advice of an older, more experienced person. The struggle you have been having with a problem which seems overwhelming is likely to diminish with the help of this individual. Encouragement to take more responsibility for your actions is sound advice. Your self-confidence may be wavering, which makes it difficult to recognize the right choice and then to act on it. Those closest to you are not necessarily working in your best interests, even though they think they are. A loved one may be appealing to your conscience in such a way that you will only act out of guilt. You must follow your own judgment.

31. FRIDAY. Disquieting. Conditions today are quiet dissimilar from yesterday. Older and more experienced people are apt to disagree with you. Some of their advice has been helpful, but you do not see eye-to-eye on all matters. It is very important not to turn your authority over to others at this time, when your personal confidence is increasing. Trust your good intuition not to let you down. An unexpected visit early in the day from somebody connected with your past could throw you off course temporarily. Later on you should be able to take a step back and view the whole situation with a great deal more clarity. Even if you owe this person a favor, you do not have to repay it right now.

AUGUST

1. SATURDAY. Mixed. After this rather grueling workweek in some respects, today's opportunity to indulge in lighthearted activities should be most welcome. This is an especially promising day where creative enterprises are concerned. Get started on new projects and hobbies. You are likely to feel inspired by artistic and cultural excursions close to home. The only real trouble at the moment may be lack of approval or acceptance from an authority figure whose opinion you value. Do not allow this to spoil your day. You have to prove that your ideas can be translated into something practical. If others want to pick fights, you do not have to rise to the bait. Hold your tongue if tempted to reveal a secret.

2. SUNDAY. Uncertain. This should be a positive day where financial matters are concerned. Spend some time balancing your accounts and the family budget. If you have had many bills to pay recently, it could be difficult to make ends meet for a while. You are probably not completely out of the woods yet; expert advice could give you a lot of useful guidance. Delay making a decision where property matters are concerned. If property you want to buy is quite old, have a full survey done and await the results before you decide. There could be structural problems or a lien that would cause you many headaches in the future.

3. MONDAY. Manageable. Any financial troubles you may be having calm down today. If you have not balanced your checkbook in a while, this is a good time to do so. A business or property deal may not be settled as quickly as you want, even if you have all the resources you need, because other people are apt to change their minds. You cannot control what they do. However, if you have signed any kind of contract, you at least have some legal remedies to fall back on if you choose to do so. You would expect older and more experienced people to know best, but today this is not necessarily the case. Trust your own good Scorpio judgment.

4. TUESDAY. Variable. Yesterday older persons tended to be more of a hindrance than a help, but the reverse is likely to be true today. If you are hoping to borrow money, investigate all of your options. It is not in your best interests to rely on someone's charity or to go to a meeting with your bank manager without having done some homework beforehand. The greater the effort you make to demonstrate that you are responsible, the greater chance you have of getting what you want. Keep pleasure separate and distinct from business. The problem with entertaining is that your clients, or others that you are negotiating with, could end up making false promises after a few drinks.

5. WEDNESDAY. Quiet. Hardly anyone is likely to interrupt you, giving you a golden opportunity to get on with urgent matters. It is a favorable day for contacting people to discuss your new ideas. Also catch up on any outstanding correspondence which needs a reply. If you have received an interesting special offer but have not had time to pursue it, act now. You are apt to be bored if you do not have much to occupy your mind at the moment. If work is quiet and no one is around to notice what you do, exercise your brain by doing a crossword puzzle. Skip any social offers this evening and get to bed early.

6. THURSDAY. Buoyant. This promises to be a day of exciting developments in both your business and social life. Enticing invitations are likely to come your way. If it is your turn to do the entertaining or contacting, put together some alternative ideas and ask friends or family members which ones appeal to them. Greater involvement in sports activities is a good way to get more friendly and expand your social circle. For single Scorpio people, a business liaison could have romantic connotations. If someone is obviously interested in you, respond from the heart. There is no need to play hard to get. Avoid thinking too far ahead; enjoy what is happening now.

7. FRIDAY. Disconcerting. Squabbles at home are quite possible because a family member is losing patience. You may see this simply as nagging, but there could be more to the situation. If you are not spending as much time at home as your partner or family would like, they may not feel able to mention anything about it directly. Instead you could be greeted with sarcasm, hotheadedness or total lack of cooperation. Something needs to change. Sit down and discuss the matter openly and calmly. Be willing to see views other than your own, even though you feel that what you are doing is for the benefit of the person who is complaining the loudest.

8. SATURDAY. Unsettling. You are unlikely to be firing on all engines. Part of the problem may be that you feel unsettled. There is much to achieve today, but little time to do it; for problems at home such as a leak or broken window it is best to call in an expert. Spending a lot of time trying to fix the difficulty yourself could end up being wasted and fruitless. Family members are likely to be difficult to please. Your patience is apt to be put to the test due to their inability to accept your plans or offer any of their own. Tact and diplomacy are required. Practice self-control and listen to other people's objections; you could benefit.

9. SUNDAY. Disquieting. Avoid anything speculative. The danger of loss is larger than the promise of gain. Scorpio people who have recently become involved in a new romance may be feeling the pinch financially. If it has come to the point where you are spending more than you can comfortably afford to entertain your partner, find a way to balance the situation. Lack of available funds could mean that you have to cancel out of a social event you were looking forward to. See if there is some kind of compromise that could be made, perhaps borrowing appropriate attire or sharing the cost of a gift. Be careful to eat a well-balanced diet. Too much sugar may make you feel unwell.

10. MONDAY. Excellent. This is a starred day where personal projects and hobbies are concerned. Use your creative talents to make your interests more rewarding. This is one of the few opportunities this month to take a risk without having to worry about the outcome. A speculative venture is apt to bring worthwhile rewards, although it is unwise to risk more than you can afford to lose. Enter a competition even if you have never won anything before. Send off for samples or free goods. Business negotiated with someone at a distance is likely to be profitable. Traveling for pleasure is highlighted. If you are on vacation this week, you should have a memorable time. Just be wary of overdoing physically and of staying in the sun too long.

11. TUESDAY. Pleasant. Pushing ahead with routine matters is sure to bring satisfying results. You may be surprised at how promptly and efficiently a matter can be concluded once you put your mind to it. Increased cooperation at work allows you to confidently press on and tackle tricky matters that you have been putting off. Scorpio people temporarily out of work are likely to be in for a few pleasant surprises. If somebody offers you work, it is likely to turn out better than you expect. Efforts to make your resume fit advertised job requirements are likely to pay off. Go all out to impress those in positions of power and authority.

12. WEDNESDAY. Fair. Guard against a tendency to worry needlessly about your health. A problem with your digestion is not likely to be serious, so do not allow your imagination to run riot. If you cannot put a problem aside and let it rest, seek the opinion of an expert. The boss is likely to reward you for your efforts on the job. Whether this is financial recognition or just a pat on the back, it should do your self-esteem a world of good. A project which has been delayed may now receive the go-ahead signal. If you are looking for a promotion, extra effort now could go a long way toward achieving this. If you have been temporarily out of work, things are looking up; make a few phone calls to companies which have your resume on file.

13. THURSDAY. Deceptive. Some rough seas are likely where your relationship with your partner is concerned, especially if one of you is not playing strictly by the rules. Now is the time to forgive and forget, as well as to establish a new agreement. Apologies are also in order if either one of you imagines that an injustice has occurred. The opportunity to advance your career is very strong. A discussion with your employer could help you find out more about your future prospects, but do not expect much to be settled today in relation to a promotion or job transfer. Move forward one small step at a time, building a solid foundation as you go up the ladder of success.

14. FRIDAY. Rewarding. A partner or loved one may be taking too much of the lead in your relationship at the moment. Rather than allow this to continue to irritate you, talk about it. Where work matters are concerned, you could be at a disadvantage due to lack of formal training. A colleague competing for the same promotion, or an outsider applying for the same job, could beat you out based on academic or professional qualifications. This does not have to always be the case; it may give you encouragement to return to school. Time spent in a location far from your usual environment should lift your spirits.

15. SATURDAY. Successful. Pooling resources can be your key to success. This is an excellent time for financial or property investments if you can afford to do so. However, if money is tight, do not make the situation worse even though an opportunity or offer appears to be too good to pass by. It is wiser to clear debts out of the way and build up your savings. Other similar opportunities are sure to crop up in the future. A trip for pleasure is likely to be highly stimulating and could lead to a new romance for Scorpio singles interested in marriage.

16. SUNDAY. Slow. This is another day when a golden investment opportunity is likely to come your way. If you are about to
sign a property deal, your timing should be perfect. With any long-
term plans, it is vital to take the wishes of your partner or those
closest to you into account, especially where professional matters
are concerned. You may need to hold back from making a commitment or agreement until you have discussed matters further
with your nearest and dearest. Although you may be tempted to
rush into a new project head-first, it is better to look before you
leap. Whatever is worthwhile will wait; exercise patience as well
as good judgment.

17. MONDAY. Good. Prepare for a journey in relation to work
or for pleasure purposes only. Either way, you are lucky if you
have a loved one close by. Getting away from your usual environment is likely to be exhilarating and refreshing. Business con-
ducted at a distance is bound to go according to your highest
expectations. Make an extra effort to guard your own good reputation. Career-minded Scorpio people may actually be carving
out a reputation which will greatly enhance earnings in the future.
People in key positions are taking note of you and judging you
closely but favorably. Prove that you are capable of handling whoever and whatever comes your way.

18. TUESDAY. Calm. This is a good time for broadening your
horizons both in business and personally. There is opportunity to
develop overseas contacts to a greater extent. Be sure to practice
tact and diplomacy in all situations. If you are looking for ways
to enhance your career options, further education or on-the-job
training is the answer. It might be well worthwhile signing up for
an evening class in a subject which interests you. Learning a language, in particular, could be the vital step for your next career
move. More time on your hands means that you have the opportunity to plan for the future. A flash of intuition about the future
makes it clear what must be done.

19. WEDNESDAY. Misleading. This is another excellent day for
long-distance travel, especially for a vacation. If you have a chance
to take time off from work, or have some time on your hands,
give yourself and a loved one a special treat, perhaps going to a
theme park or to the zoo. Expanding entertainment options for
yourself include trying out a new restaurant or club this evening.
Someone in a position of authority may be misleading in relation
to promises being made. Take what you are told with a pinch of
salt until you see some positive action stemming from the promises. What seems too good to be true probably is just that.

20. THURSDAY. Deceptive. Today's schedule is likely to be disrupted due to unexpected developments where other people are concerned. As with yesterday, you cannot trust all that anyone tells you. Even friends or family members are likely to change their mind without much warning. Concentrate on continuing to make a good impression. In the long term your efforts will not go to waste, but do not expect great recognition or acknowledgment at the moment. In both personal and business matters, this is a better day for buying than for selling. A personal relationship that is important to you could be threatened by a new person on the scene.

21. FRIDAY. Unsettling. You may feel that you cannot do anything right or manage to please others at the moment. Try to be patient with yourself as well as with them. As a Scorpio you are going through a process of change now. The environment around you is probably also changing. You cannot depend on other people to stick to their plans or ideas since they are feeling as unsure as you are. If the rug is pulled out from under your feet, try hard to react calmly. Getting angry is not going to solve anything. Focus on what you want to achieve for the future. Give yourself plenty of options, providing room to maneuver or change your mind.

22. SATURDAY. Happy. This promises to be a particularly happy day if you are getting together with various friends and acquaintances. With you in the role of social leader and organizer, everyone is bound to get along well at a social occasion. It is a favorable time for hosting a party. However, money needs to be budgeted carefully. There is a tendency for you to get carried away with spending in an attempt to cater to everyone's individual needs. Try to trim down your plans to make them more affordable. You might want to encourage your guests to bring food to share at a potluck meal, or to bring video tapes for entertainment.

23. SUNDAY. Disquieting. There is risk that a friendship which you desire to remain just that may turn into a more personal encounter which you do not want. The problem lies more with the other person, who appears to have romantic designs on you. If their overtures are unwelcome, it is best to say so loud and clear as soon as you realize what is going on. Social activities should be easygoing on the whole, although one of your group may make life difficult for everyone by refusing to go along with the crowd. As a Scorpio you have a special gift for resolving problems to everyone's satisfaction. However, only get deeply involved if you really want to; otherwise trust that their good judgment will see them through over time.

24. MONDAY. Excellent. This should be a much better day for friendships and social contacts. If there is someone you have been out of touch with for a while, make an effort to reconnect via mail or telephone. You are likely to receive a warm response. Quiet time is vital later in the day. You can get a lot more done if you are left to your own devices in peaceful surroundings. Make the most of an opportunity to move ahead without being disturbed or distracted. Concentrate on background work and on redeveloping old ideas. What has worked for you in the past is a good guide to follow into the future.

25. TUESDAY. Good. Behind-the-scenes activities are favored both in your professional and personal life. The boss is likely to notice your efforts and be quite impressed with your ability to solve a problem that no one else has managed to sort out. For Scorpios who have been out of work, the local library might be a good source of fresh leads. This is also a useful resource if you are doing some long-term career planning. If an older relative is hospitalized, make an effort to visit this evening. This person may be feeling lonely and is bound to appreciate your company. Be willing to listen more than you talk, and do not offer any medical advice.

26. WEDNESDAY. Mixed. This is another favorable day for working behind the scenes and for tying up loose ends. If you have a pile of neglected paperwork and bills stacked on your desk, attend to it now. You can make a better start on a new project once older work has been cleared away. Friendships should be on a pleasant, even keel. Your partner is likely to be extra supportive, doing more to help you as a friend than some of the people you have leaned on in the past. Where new friendships are concerned, however, you have to proceed slowly and warily. Someone may be hoping to use you solely to advance themselves socially or in business.

27. THURSDAY. Cautious. Although your impulse is to take more initiative in all matters tread carefully. The boss or another person who ranks higher than you may not agree with your ideas. Try not to make moves that could jeopardize your future. Even though superiors may break the rules, they probably will not allow you to do the same. Play by the book, even if it means having to stifle a strong urge to do your own thing. It should not be too long before you have more opportunity to act on your own initiative. You could be misled by someone's appearance; watch out for the proverbial wolf in sheep's clothing.

28. FRIDAY. Challenging. You are likely to be up against the same issues that dogged your life yesterday. People in authority may appear to be playing games, but you should not take this too personally. Reasons for their actions should become clear before too long. You may receive some kind of a reward for your efforts if you manage to succeed within the limitations that have been set down by others. Where more personal plans are concerned, you are unlikely to receive financial assistance or any other specific help. Do not even expect your mate or parents to condone what you have in mind. They probably think they know better, and this time they may be right.

29. SATURDAY. Excellent. At long last you have the freedom to act more on your own initiative without worrying about offending anyone or jeopardizing your future. This is a highly favorable day for making new contacts, both in business and personal circles. It is also a good idea to initiate correspondence and make preliminary or introductory telephone calls. Review budgets and accounts. If you are seeking a loan, you have a good chance of approval for an application filled out now. An older individual can be especially helpful in finding the solution to your long-term financial needs. If you need quick cash, consider selling or pawning an item of jewelry you never wear.

30. SUNDAY. Promising. This is another particularly productive day where money matters are concerned. Financial agreements can be completed, even if you expected them to drag on for a while. If you have the urge to spend, concentrate on a practical item for the home. You have a good chance of discovering a bargain or two. On a more personal note, your self-esteem is on the increase. Rewards or at least a pat on the back for the efforts you have put in during the past are likely to give you an emotional boost. This is a key time if you are interested in moving or are looking for investment or retirement property. It is never too soon to plan for your future.

31. MONDAY. Changeable. Some say money is the root of all evil, but as a Scorpio you tend to view it more as a potent power. What comes your way today in relation to your working life is likely to convince you that financial and material rewards are definitely worth the stress. The status and clout accompanying an increase in pay or a promotion are also to be prized. Your only problem at the moment is the tendency to want to splurge. Celebrate by all means, but try to be a little restrained with your general spending. This is a starred day to offer your services to a volunteer group whose goals you admire.

SEPTEMBER

1. TUESDAY. Buoyant. This promises to be a lively and sociable start to the month. It is an especially favorable time for making new contacts and for catching up with the news from old friends. If you need a favor or other help, you should not have to go very far. Words are your ally in the workplace; you can talk yourself into or out of anything. This is also true for Scorpios looking for new work. Your various contacts are likely to be a great help. They may be able to put you in touch with the hiring officer of a company you are interested in working for. Sharing views and opinions with friends this evening can help you gain fresh perspectives. Do not hesitate to branch out in a new direction.

2. WEDNESDAY. Positive. Easygoing relationships mark this day. You should also have more opportunity to enjoy your leisure time, doing what you really like rather than what you must do. For single Scorpio people, sports and games is a good way to meet a new partner or simply make some new friends. Share your ideas at work. Colleagues and higher-ups are in a lighthearted frame of mind, and your ideas and suggestions should be well received. Local travel, even routine trips, ought to be quite enjoyable, giving you a chance to chat with people you see all too infrequently. There is a strong element of happy coincidence that is definitely to your advantage.

3. THURSDAY. Stressful. Although you are apt to have that stay-at-home feeling, duty calls. It is likely that you have no choice but to rise and shine and get on with the day's tasks. If you are out of work, concentrate on new job options rather than following up old leads; you are likely to have success this way. Do not expect to have an easygoing time with loved ones. Your partner could be annoyed if you are not doing your fair share around the home. Find time to help with chores which are too much for one person to handle alone, such as painting or washing windows. Instead of asking if your help is needed, pitch right in.

4. FRIDAY. Difficult. As was true yesterday, you may not be in the mood for work. It is important, however, to maintain a professional image. Avoid being late for work or for an interview; tardiness tends to put you in a bad light. This is one of those days when people are taking note of everything you do and do not do. You need to be on your best behavior in order to create a good and lasting impression. A legal problem concerning a property matter is unlikely to be resolved through discussion alone. A price or a contract offered today could be annoying or disappointing. Keep in mind that the deal may take a long time to finalize but will be worth the wait and effort.

5. SATURDAY. Enjoyable. Scorpio people can look forward to a romantic and enjoyable weekend. Your relationship with your loved one is likely to be especially cozy. Consider going out for a candlelight dinner together this evening. Single Scorpios are likely to benefit from getting out and meeting new people. Accept an invitation to a party where it is likely you will make new friends. Handle money with care. Because you are enjoying yourself more and spending more on leisure activities, you need to cut back in another area. Organize your plans so that your budget still balances. Enjoy your advantages without taking advantage of anyone else.

6. SUNDAY. Mixed. You are apt to be in the mood to go on a spree. It is a good time for buying new clothes, but beware of becoming too trendy. It could be difficult to decide among the various design labels. Guard against buying every single thing you like if you cannot really afford to do so. Somebody you like in a romantic way wants to keep your relationship a just-friends affair. This could be disappointing, but there is little point chasing after them. Playing hard to get could actually turn the tide in your favor. As a Scorpio you often get a sense of grim determination. However, you are doing yourself no favor if, recognizing the truth, you do not simply back off for a while.

7. MONDAY. Fortunate. This is a wonderful day for both friendship and romance. If you are single you can look forward to receiving a love letter or romantic telephone call. A social invitation is likely to be too enticing to turn down. There is no reason you should miss out on either a little fun or a romantic opportunity. If you have been out of touch with a certain friend or former schoolmate for a while, this is the time to get back in touch. You can count on a warm reception if you drop by to visit a friend without calling ahead. Be spontaneous; follow your instincts and impulses and you will not go wrong.

8. TUESDAY. Quiet. It may be hard getting back into the world. Try to get up a little earlier than usual so that you do not have to rush. This is an excellent time for getting to grips with filing and paperwork. Reply to outstanding correspondence and generally get your desk in order. Paying more attention to planning and organization is likely to pay off. Come up with a list of goals for the remainder of the year. It is not often you have the peace and space to get things done according to your own schedule; today you have both so take advantage. Colleagues should be cooperative if you need their help or input. Teamwork is favored providing everyone pulls their own weight.

9. WEDNESDAY. Fair. Good progress can be made on the work front. Concentrate on detailed work and routine matters. Do not get too caught up in vast visions or grand plans just now. The most planning you should do is from a purely logistical point of view. A strongly philosophical outlook can wait for another day. For Scorpio people who are temporarily out of work, this is a favorable time for dealing with employment centers and personnel offices. An interview is apt to go better if you make every attempt to be coolly professional despite wanting the job so much. Family members are likely to be a great source of support and encouragement.

10. THURSDAY. Unsettling. An argument with your mate or partner is possible. This is one of those times when important people in your life are apt to get on their high horse and try to boss you around. Strive not to get too worked up about this. Problems discussed calmly and logically are more likely to be resolved than if you are both hotheaded. Do not worry about minor disagreements early in the day; they should soon blow over. Your love relationship is likely to become much more romantic later on. In work, relationships with colleagues ought to ease and become more congenial by the end of the day. You can take a more light-hearted approach to all that is said.

11. FRIDAY. Variable. Take advantage of an opportunity to talk in depth with a loved one about a problem that needs to be discussed or about basic plans. Share your dreams and long-term schemes. It is likely that you can offer each other good advice or come up with specific ideas for executing a plan. Discussions in relation to joint finances or property are likely to be tricky. The deeper you dig into a situation, the worse it may appear to be. However, there is little point running from the truth. The more you know, the more choices you have. Try to avoid getting involved in any type of financial dealing with friends. Do not count on someone doing what you should actually be doing yourself.

12. SATURDAY. Tricky. This is another day when joint finances are tricky to handle. It is not a good idea to listen to the advice of too many other people; you could find it confusing and counterproductive. Instead, heed the advice of an expert. If you are involved in a property deal at the moment, another interested party could complicate ongoing negotiations. A neutral third party can help straighten out the situation, and it is likely that a firm price can be agreed on before the day is through. Make a point of having any contract or agreement put in writing; a handshake is not enough to seal a deal under current conditions.

13. SUNDAY. Easygoing. More time on your hands today means that you can take off for a break and a change of scene. If you do not feel like going out, or if the weather is not good, travels of the mind could be appealing. Enjoy looking at some vacation brochures or talking to a knowledgeable travel agent. You might also want to brush up on a second language or start to learn a new one. Time spent with your partner or another family member should be inspiring. For single Scorpios, travel and education are the best means of meeting someone new. Do not allow a large age difference to stand in the way of new love or friendship.

14. MONDAY. Successful. This is a key day for promoting yourself both in and out of work. If you are applying for a promotion or a new job, go all out to shine in an interview. You are likely to make a good impression if you act naturally and rely on your Scorpio talent to charm and impress. Do not be daunted by people who are judging you. An invitation from a friend could end up taking you on a long journey that is likely to be most enjoyable. If you deal with people overseas, put more focus on improving communications. Relations can be greatly improved if you make the first move. Scorpios who are in school should find it useful to get together with other students to share ideas. Strive to understand basic principles, not just to memorize facts.

15. TUESDAY. Happy. Friends can bring you out of yourself. Accept an invitation to do something a little unusual. This is a very good time to return to school, particularly to study a subject that has intrigued you for a long time. If you are trying to lose weight, take a sensible approach. Avoid any fad diet. A group is likely to be more supportive than trying to slim down on your own. You can pick up a lot of useful tips through discussing dieting with others who have the same goals. Romantic yearnings could spur you to go on a long journey or make a long-distance phone call. It is likely that you will meet with a warm reception.

16. WEDNESDAY. Sensitive. Scorpios are apt to be rewarded for efforts put in at work. The boss is likely to give you a pat on the back, if not a bonus, for a recent breakthrough that you engineered. It is a good idea to gingerly break news of a career change or transfer to loved ones. This is especially important if you are going to be working longer hours or if a job change will mean selling your current home. A loved one's irritation or restlessness may stem from their sense of insecurity. Take the time to find out exactly what they are thinking. Knowing what to expect is always preferable to vague promises.

17. THURSDAY. Calm. You should be able to move along with work projects. If you are thinking of changing your career, this is an excellent day for planning how you want to proceed. You have space and time to use as you wish now. Fewer interruptions give you the chance to concentrate on the most crucial matters. If you work for yourself, focus more on marketing and building your reputation. Think of ways to give your enterprise a higher profile and thus increase business revenue. If your work is very specialized, decide how to target the clients you want to attract. Advertisements that are too general are apt to be a waste of money.

18. FRIDAY. Variable. Friendships should be a source of great pleasure. There is an opportunity to get to know one particular person a lot better. Make an effort to remember people's birthdays and to acknowledge their achievements. Someone who has just passed a test or has just adopted a new pet would appreciate a congratulatory card. It is not a good idea to get involved in financial dealings with friends and acquaintances. Putting such money matters on a businesslike basis could strain the friendship now or in the future. Pay some attention to your overall health. Make an appointment with your doctor or dentist for a checkup.

19. SATURDAY. Rewarding. Plan to get together with good friends this weekend; you are likely to have a very enjoyable time.

A group get-together is favored. If you want to learn a second language or study some other academic subject, consider signing up for a course without delay. More general and informal seminars and lectures should also be stimulating. If doing the chores does not appeal, you should have no trouble finding something more interesting. Consider focusing again on a pastime that used to bring you a lot of pleasure. Shopping could be worthwhile, particularly if you have a special purchase in mind. Shop around for the best price; take advantage of an unadvertised sale.

20. SUNDAY. Sensitive. A social event is sure to be stimulating and rewarding. Single Scorpios could become annoyed, however, with a friend who gets in the way of a romantic opportunity. Diplomacy is the key to getting what you want. If someone is annoying you, take the person aside and explain tactfully. Most likely you will be left in peace afterward. Becoming involved in a group is likely to be enjoyable. However, there could be one particular person who seems intent on spoiling everyone else's fun by being selfish. Find a way to tactfully point this out without making the person seem totally out of step with the crowd. Opposition to your ideas is likely to be only temporary; keep plugging away.

21. MONDAY. Tranquil. Quiet time alone is just what you need. You can make good progress with a work project if you have few distractions. There is apt to be one disruption, but it should be a pleasant one. You may receive a phone call from somebody you have not seen in a long time; make a date to get together in person soon. This is a good day for quiet reading and study. If you cannot find any peace and quiet, a trip to the local library might solve the problem. Try to catch up with neglected paperwork and correspondence. In the process you could find something important that you have forgotten about.

22. TUESDAY. Productive. This is another good day for focusing on professional matters without too many distractions. Behind-the-scenes activities are favored. If you are waiting to hear the results of an interview, a call to the individual with whom you talked could be helpful. This is a favorable day for a reunion with someone you have not seen for a while. Air your views today to get some feedback on your plans and ideas. Scorpio people are often good at scheming but not necessarily at putting plans into action. Bring your natural determination to bear on a secret wish you want to fulfill. There is no time like the present to take action.

23. WEDNESDAY. Confusing. It is unlikely that you will have the opportunity to hide yourself away as you wish to do. While you may not be feeling in top form, people may be determined to obtain your advice and opinion. Try to keep conversations brief; use a few excuses or delaying tactics if necessary. It is best if you can avoid stress. You are likely to feel quite sensitive and vulnerable. Be sure not to pay much attention to rumors that are floating around the workplace or among friends. It is said that there is no smoke without fire, but it is also true that rumors are most often unreliable or totally inaccurate sources of information.

24. THURSDAY. Manageable. You should be able to make a good start on a personal plan. People tend to leave you more to your own devices if you have your head down and are obviously deep in thought. Focus on what you want to achieve for the future. The most important aspect of your life is not necessarily your career at the moment; concentrate on what is interesting you the most. A friend is likely to get in your way where a romantic interest is concerned. If there is rivalry between you, keep in mind that it will not disappear overnight. If your friend's behavior seems out of line, have a few quiet words in order to reach an understanding.

25. FRIDAY. Fortunate. This is a highly favorable time for publicizing yourself both socially and in connection with your career. Do not hesitate to blow your own horn. First impressions count for a lot at the moment. If you are meeting someone important for the first time, be sure to dress well and act politely. There is no reason why you should clam up in a business meeting or interview; speak your views honestly and with tact. If you have special plans for your savings, keep them to yourself for now. You are under no obligation to reveal your intentions to anyone outside your family circle, and even a loved one does not need to know right now.

26. SATURDAY. Exciting. Everything may seem to be happening all at once. You can rely on there not being a dull moment during the day. Your self-esteem is likely to get a boost due to contact from an old friend or acquaintance. Compliments could come your way also from an elected official. If you have made extra efforts to look good this week, you are sure to have been noticed. A change of diet can do much to improve your general sense of well-being at the moment. Try cutting out sugar if you want to lose weight or improve a skin or digestive condition. Money and property matters may hold a nice surprise for you.

27. SUNDAY. Sensitive. Friends are likely to want to either borrow or loan money or an item of value. If the latter they probably think they are helping. If the former, they may be expecting you to repay a favor. It is not in your best interests to get involved in financial exchanges either way, unless you are willing to draw up an official document. This may seem rather formal but could save a lot of heartache in the long run. Private discussions about investment strategies and goals are likely to be useful. Someone who is older and wiser has some good advice to impart if you are willing to listen. Postpone a major decision until later in the week.

28. MONDAY. Useful. Discussions with your mate or partner are likely to be reassuring. It is a good idea to talk about individual and mutual plans rather than simply assume that you both know each other's intentions and arrangements. This can prevent confusion and double booking now and in the future. Secrecy in the workplace could be a worry. Try not to pay too much attention to current rumors, even if you suspect there may be more than a grain of truth involved. When higher-ups want you to know what is going on they will tell you. If you are worried about your finances, consider a part-time job where you can earn tips.

29. TUESDAY. Challenging. This is a good day for strengthening your relationships. Both old and new contacts are worth pursuing. For single Scorpios there is a strong likelihood of a romantic invitation disguised as a group outing. Sports and social pleasures are likely to be very stimulating. Strive to achieve a balance between getting out and spending time on solitary pursuits such as a hobby or exercising. It is a good idea to rest as conscientiously as you work and play. Surprises stemming from your past are a theme at the moment. You are also in for a pleasant surprise where job or property negotiations are concerned. Hold out for what you know you deserve.

30. WEDNESDAY. Fair. Joint and group enterprises should be developing nicely. A legal complication is likely, but a good lawyer can settle it out of court. Putting your head together with others is your key to success. It is not smart simply to dwell on matters and worry. Do not rely on somebody influential being able to pull strings on your behalf. It is likely that the matter has gone too far for them to be of much assistance. Try to avoid getting stuck in a rut where your relationship with a partner is concerned. Mixing socially is likely to lessen any strain that exists between you. If you stay in you are apt to get on each other's nerves. Even a walk together can be a cure-all.

OCTOBER

1. THURSDAY. Variable. You are likely to make more progress if you stick to behind-the-scenes involvement. Discussions which have been going on without you recently probably are open to you now. If you are involved in property negotiations of any type, much could happen in a hurry. Expect the unexpected, and be prepared to make a quick decision. No matter what this might be, developments are working in your favor. If a family member is upset, encourage sharing the problem with you. Being able to confide the difficulty should help diminish it if not solve it. Attend to practical domestic problems sooner rather than later, particularly household repairs.

2. FRIDAY. Challenging. Try hard to be more inventive and innovative. This is not a time for being stuck in a rut. You may meet with opposition from a work superior, but this does not have to thwart your progress. You can talk your way out of anything. The more forward-thinking your approach, the farther you are likely to get. For Scorpio singles there is good opportunity for deepening a potential love connection. A romantic gesture on your part could cement a relationship and turn it into a long-term proposition. In general it is a good day for ironing out problems in close relationships and reaching mutual understanding. Give a little and you will get a lot in return.

3. SATURDAY. Easygoing. Put your feet up and rest today. There should not be anything pressing to do. If you happen to feel restless, get outside and play a sport or take a bike ride. If you have time on your hands, this is the perfect day to take loved ones out for a treat. Single Scorpios are apt to be feeling more romantic than usual. If you want to make a good impression on someone special start hatching some plans and ideas. Home entertaining should be enjoyable this evening. Whether you are hosting or attending a party, you are likely to have a wonderful time and meet some interesting new people. Mingle rather than talking only to the usual crowd.

4. SUNDAY. Calm. Do not hesitate to contact those closest to you. If it is the birthday of a relative, call to congratulate them. Creative ideas are likely to be bubbling through your mind at the moment. This is more of a day for planning and discussion than for testing a new scheme. However, you could be inspired if you put your mind to creative writing of any kind. Write a letter to someone special, or a short story if you are feeling more ambitious. You could end up discovering a hidden talent. Fade into the background if you are with a group, but keep your eyes and ears open.

5. MONDAY. Pleasant. It is a case of back to work today, whether or not you are employed for pay. This is the right time to do something about a situation that has been bothering you. If you are temporarily out of work, make a point of following up past contacts. It is possible that a company that did not have any vacancies last time you called may now have something for you. You should be able to make excellent progress with ongoing work. Although you want to reach the end of one particular project, try to avoid overdoing. You are apt to make careless errors if you try to rush. Keep an eye on your health, and get extra rest when you feel tired.

6. TUESDAY. Deceptive. Mixed messages are the order of the day for Scorpio people. It is a good idea to double-check information passed on to you second or third hand. If you are dealing with a lot of paperwork or figures, take extra care. In trying to skim through a document, you could overlook some important details. Also be very cautious if you are writing a detailed report or list of any kind. A higher-up is likely to be taking more notice of your efforts at the moment, making it useful to put in that little extra in order to create a good impression. Conditions are changing rapidly, and you have to step smartly to keep up with them.

7. WEDNESDAY. Challenging. A relationship that has not been going particularly well is about to take a turn in a new direction. You are reaching the make or break point. If you truly feel that the relationship is not right for you, there is little point in trying to continue. However, if you sense there is a chance for growth and improvement, keep working at it. Although a loved one or business partner may reveal plans which seem rather sudden to you, it is quite possible that these have been brewing for some time. There is food for thought in what is being proposed, and probably a choice to be made within a day or two.

8. THURSDAY. Variable. You should be feeling a little more comfortable with the ideas that a love or business partner has come up with recently. There is a tendency to see your relationship through rose-colored glasses, but this is not necessarily a bad thing. Now and again every partnership benefits from a change. This is likely to come about as both of you discuss future plans with a particular goal in mind. A romantic element in the relationship could be the prelude to a greater commitment between you in the not so distant future. A joint financial situation is apt to be less complicated if the other person involved is not a close friend and can be treated in businesslike fashion.

9. FRIDAY. Good. You should be able to put a joint financial situation or property deal on firmer footing. This is a favorable time for reaching final conclusions and agreements and for drawing up a formal contract. You may be surprised how quickly things move along, especially if you have been waiting some time for the situation to develop. When discussing money and real estate matters, it is best to do so behind closed doors. Do not involve other people in your affairs if you do not really need their input. The fewer people involved, the less complicated the situation will be and the quicker the matter can be processed. Keep mum about a secret even if a friend pumps you for information.

10. SATURDAY. Useful. An issue which you have neglected or overlooked in relation to finance or property negotiations is likely to become obvious. The discovery made now can turn the situation much more in your favor. As a Scorpio, secrecy is one of your great trademarks. For today and the next few days it is imperative that you play your cards close to your chest. Continue not to get outsiders or anyone new involved in your ongoing affairs. Where a close personal relationship is concerned, strive to broaden your perspective. Consider the future and where you hope to be a year or a decade from now. Travel to a distant place ought to be eye-opening.

11. SUNDAY. Misleading. A trip may have to be canceled because either yourself or a family member is not feeling well. Do not let this worry you. It is quite likely that the postponement will lead to something more successfully at a later time. What you are told and what you read are likely to be misleading. It is not that others are trying to lead you astray as that they probably do not have all the facts. If you think that a story sounds unlikely, do not believe a word of it. If you are planning to visit someone who is hospitalized, check visiting times beforehand. It could be quite inconvenient to turn up at the wrong time and have to wait around.

12. MONDAY. Difficult. A dream or scheme you have been working on for some time may crash, but do not get too down in the dumps. Something even better is likely to fire your imagination. For single Scorpio people, romance is connected with both travel and educational interests. For those who are more settled, opposition from a loved one is likely, although probably just a difference of approach is the problem. As a Scorpio you tend to be very fixed about your point of view, but now you are the one who needs to back down. Consider all alternatives with an open mind. Resist an urge to buy an item just because it is on sale.

13. TUESDAY. Mixed. Professional conduct on the work scene and in any group situation is of paramount importance today. If you are meeting with someone influential, be sure to look your best in order to create a good first impression. You may not agree with an employer's or elected official's viewpoint, but it is in your interests to be deferential just now. Being too outspoken could jeopardize your long-term prospects. With anyone and everyone, being a little humble is likely to pay off before too long. Changes of plan are likely, upsetting your routine. It is a good idea to prioritize early in the day so that key matters are dealt with first, prior to any major interruption.

14. WEDNESDAY. Successful. Business and professional interests can be advanced to a greater degree. Your contacts behind the scenes are likely to be unusually helpful, particularly if you are self-employed. If you work as an employee, it is likely that the boss is working in your interests although this may not be obvious. A new scheme should be kept secret for the time being. Personal aims and ambitions are also highlighted. Move quickly to take advantage of a golden opportunity. You can benefit by contacting friends and getting together to share ideas. Air your view and see what response you get. The optimism of other people can inspire you to aim higher.

15. THURSDAY. Changeable. It is not always advisable to get involved in financial dealings with friends. If someone is low on cash you may think that there is no harm in helping out. And if you need to borrow money, you may assume that it is safe to do so. However, either lending or borrowing can have a negative effect on your relationship in the future. Be wary of such transactions. An agreement made in haste could be one you live to regret. A special partnership should be moving onto a more even keel. Your partner has definite goals and points of view, which should keep you from getting off track. It is a time to be a follower, not the leader.

16. FRIDAY. Quiet. Work on developing some of your most prized, private plans. It is rare when you have plenty of time on your hands to do as you please. Now, however, you have the opportunity to schedule your own time. Sharing the workload with others tends to be helpful in this respect. Group activities are favored at the moment. If recent evenings seem a little boring, consider joining a group of people who share your hobby or other interest and who meet regularly. Or join a club where you have the privilege of using the facilities on a regular basis, such as a gym or golf course. Find a way to get some pleasurable exercise.

17. SATURDAY. Pleasant. Make plans to go somewhere special this weekend. The company of relatives, neighbors, or friends is likely to be very pleasant. If you have not seen certain family members for some time, pay them a visit. Being around water is especially favored. If you have friends who own a boat, do not turn down their invitation to go sailing or fishing. Try not to be too insular this weekend. By being too inward-looking you are apt to miss out on a lot of fun. Continue to shy away from financial involvement with a friend. Save up for a major purchase rather than buying on credit.

18. SUNDAY. Tranquil. This should be a fairly quiet day, a favorable time for relaxing and resting. Take the opportunity to recharge your batteries. If you have not balanced the household accounts for some time, do so now. If you feel restless, concentrate on tying up loose ends. It is best to finish up old jobs and get problems out of the way before starting anything new. Scorpio people who have been busy all week may feel quite weary. Treat yourself to a relaxing long hot bath or an afternoon nap in front of the TV. Try to avoid too much contact with the outer world. Maintaining good health should be today's priority.

19. MONDAY. Easygoing. Although this is likely to be another quiet day, this does not mean that it is going to be uneventful.

People should leave you alone to get on with your tasks. Behind-the-scenes activities are especially promising. Single Scorpios interested in beginning a new relationship could get involved in a romantic intrigue which, for one reason or another, needs to be kept secret for a while. If you feel at all vulnerable at the moment, maintain a low profile both at work and socially. It is best to avoid stress and strain and keep yourself fairly unavailable except on your own terms.

20. TUESDAY. Sensitive. You are entering a new phase when it becomes increasingly important to take better care of yourself. If you have been feeling unusually tired lately, take time to rest and recuperate. If you are worried about your health, do not jump to conclusions. Information passed on by friends or that you read in a medical book may not be accurate. Be especially wary of advice offered by anyone except your doctor. Do not take any medicine not specifically prescribed for you. Concentrate on resting when you are tired and eating a healthy, well-balanced diet. Opposition does not necessarily mean that you have to abandon personal plans, but you may want to postpone them for a while or do some rethinking.

21. WEDNESDAY. Productive. This is a more lively day than yesterday. You should have more energy and also more confidence to pursue your goals. Personal initiatives are particularly valuable. People will give you space to do your own thing simply because you appear to need it. A comment about your appearance may provide the incentive to make a positive change. Something as simple as a haircut or shoe shine can make you feel quite different about yourself. A new outfit could also boost your morale. If you are in the process of changing jobs, this is the right time to alter your image to suit the new position. Take to heart advice you have been giving another person.

22. THURSDAY. Tricky. Believe only half of what you hear or are told. Seeing is believing is very apt for you now, although you cannot even trust the written word in all cases. Other people's promises are especially unreliable. You should be able to make a good impression on someone important. If you are going on an interview, your appearance is likely to speak volumes; first impressions count a great deal. Allow your true Scorpio nature to shine in an interview situation. If an unexpected question is fired at you, do not get rattled. Take a minute to think it through, then speak your mind. Honesty is definitely the best policy, although you need to be tactful at the same time. As the Scorpio birthday period starts, make firm new resolutions.

23. FRIDAY. Cautious. An opportunity is likely to clinch a property or financial deal. It is important, however, that you do sufficient research before making a major commitment. If you know that you have reached that point, now is the time to act. Developments can move forward much quicker than you expect, but do not feel that you have to hurry. Individuals putting pressure on you to get moving may not be working in your best interests. Personal initiatives are unlikely to be agreeable to your partner, at least not right away. It may be fear of the unknown or another worry; try to find out. You have to read between the lines in order to come up with any sound answers for behavior that takes you by surprise.

24. SATURDAY. Confusing. Overindulgence can strain your finances. It is up to you to watch that you do not get carried away, despite the efforts of friends or family members to tempt you. Do not waste time or energy on somebody who may be taking advantage of your generosity. Scorpio people are noted for being quite careful with resources. To discover that you are wasting them can make you angry. Look at your role in any dispute or misunderstanding. As soon as you realize your mistake, you can move on. Strive to forgive and forget. News from a distance is likely to be misleading; wait until you know more before making any key decisions. Avoid carrying much cash in your wallet.

25. SUNDAY. Mixed. Family members are likely to be a lot more supportive of your ideas and plans early in the day. A trip together should be stimulating and is likely to get you thinking about the future. This is an excellent day for focusing on your long-term goals and making contact with people who are part of those plans. You should be able to expand your social circle if you wish to do so. As the day progresses, you may wonder if you have done something to upset a loved one. Be considerate and try to find out what the problem is. However, if you are given the silent treatment despite your best effort, it is not worth probing any deeper at this time.

26. MONDAY. Good. Group endeavors are likely to be helpful in the business world. News from an old friend should make you happy. This is an excellent time for networking and getting to know more people. If you have recently moved into a new neighborhood and are feeling a little lonesome, an invitation which comes your way ought to mark a change in this respect. For single Scorpio people, this is an ideal time to make new contacts. If you get out and about this evening, it is quite likely that you will meet someone of the opposite sex with whom there is a strong, mutual attraction. Mental compatibility promises a longer lasting relationship than mere physical attraction.

27. TUESDAY. Disconcerting. New contacts made in the business world cannot be relied upon totally. Fall back on people you have been allied with for a long period of time. If you are awaiting news regarding your current job or a career move, it could be slow in coming. Try not to become overly anxious if you do not hear anything today; it could well be the case that no news is good news. Despite any setbacks, your confidence is unlikely to falter. Late in the day is the best time for self-promotion. Pressure to get work completed should lighten as the boss and your colleagues get involved projects of their own and leave you to proceed at your own pace.

28. WEDNESDAY. Variable. This is a day full of surprises. Keep your plans fairly flexible. You may wish to take advantage of a new opportunity that comes up and change your schedule to incorporate a special meeting. Home life is likely to be up and down. It is likely that you feel hemmed in at the moment and need more personal space. Try not to take your irritability out on loved ones. A money matter can be resolved late in the day. Developments that take place earlier are likely to temporarily change your view of a certain situation for the worse, but overall for the better. Do not postpone writing or calling a friend at a distance. Plan a birthday party for another Scorpio.

29. THURSDAY. Changeable. Today may not start off quite the way you planned. News you receive in person or through the media could feed a growing sense of insecurity. Do not be too quick to lose belief in yourself, however. You have many talents to offer and should not really doubt your own capabilities. The good news is that, later today, an event is likely to boost your ego. If you are meeting somebody new, you should make a very favorable impression. Even if a boss does not congratulate you on your work efforts, you should feel a sense of pride in relation to your recent achievements. Paying attention to your grooming also makes you feel better about yourself and more self-confident.

30. FRIDAY. Rewarding. Loved ones, especially children, are likely to be a source of inspiration to you. If you work in a creative field, this should be a day of considerable progress. Scorpio people interested in developing a new hobby can get to work on it now. This is a time when you are full of creative expression, which needs to come out somehow. If you are single, there is a strong possibility of meeting your match this evening. The type of person you are attracted to is likely to be more like yourself than the opposite of your nature. Together you may be able to fulfill a cherished personal dream. Volunteer your time or give a donation to a cause you believe in strongly.

31. SATURDAY. Fortunate. Luck is very much on your side. While it is not always a good idea to get involved in risky ventures, if you are going to do so you may as well jump in when fortune is smiling on you. If you work today, conversations with colleagues are apt to be confusing. Double-check anything that is not clear to you. The same is true if you are making social arrangements. It is best to appear foolish for five minutes but ensure that you have the facts right early in the day. If you do not do so, later on you may be left to wonder if you are in the right place at the right time and are dressed appropriately for the occasion. Scorpio parents will enjoy celebrating Halloween with the children.

NOVEMBER

1. SUNDAY. Mixed. There is a lot going on today, most of which should be good for you. A creative project can be enhanced through discussions with your talented friends. Do not hesitate to ask them for advice or constructive criticism. There is a strong likelihood of a financial or property deal reaching a conclusion. You may not be able to tie up all the loose ends but should be able to complete most of the necessary paperwork. As a Scorpio you sometimes give way to doubts and uncertainties about your own abilities. Fortunately this is just a passing phase. Do not allow a temporary setback or negative reaction to spoil an otherwise fruitful day.

2. MONDAY. Quiet. You should be able to press ahead with routine tasks and ongoing projects without too much distraction. This is a particularly productive day if you focus on detailed work. Scorpios who have been temporarily out of work should have the time, energy, and self-confidence to renew efforts to find another job. You may not have boundless enthusiasm in this respect, but it is worth sending resumes and setting up interviews in response to weekend employment ads. If you have no job possibilities right now, at least you can be making some plans for future action. This is also a helpful day for beginning a new exercise program or diet.

3. TUESDAY. Uncertain. A work matter which you thought was completed could appear to be unraveling at the seams. This is probably due to a mix-up in communications more than anything else. Do not be too hasty to jump to conclusions. Once you are in full possession of the facts, you will be in a stronger position to gauge the situation accurately. Unexpected opposition from your mate or another loved one is likely to center around domestic issues. It is quite possible that you will be chastised for not doing your fair share of household responsibilities. This matter is better negotiated at another time when both of you can talk calmly and work out a mutually agreeable division of labor.

4. WEDNESDAY. Good. Relations with loved ones should improve. You can help the situation by aiming to be both a friend and a lover to your partner. This is the ideal and is also achievable. For single Scorpios, this is a key day for meeting new people of the opposite sex. A friendly social gathering is worth attending even if you have to go by yourself; you are unlikely to be ignored. A legal situation can be amicably settled without going to court. General business matters are helped through contacts who are willing to share significant information which is not yet public knowledge. Be sure not to reveal these sources.

5. THURSDAY. Disquieting. There may be opposition from your mate or partner where joint finances are concerned. Discussion should help clarify the situation. If you are considering making a new investment, take your time in choosing who to use as a broker or middleman. You are bound to benefit from exploring alternative options. This is a good time for exploring and discussing future business plans. If funding is a stumbling block, pooling of resources could be the answer. Assess your ongoing financial commitments to ensure that you are getting a good rate of interest. Try to pay off credit cards to avoid high finance charges.

6. FRIDAY. Disconcerting. Joint investments with a colleague or partner need careful scrutiny to ensure that your own interests are being adequately addressed and protected. This is not a time for making compromises that you do not really want, merely in order to maintain harmony with others. While you may not want to rock the boat, there is little point going ahead with an agreement which makes you personally uncomfortable. In fact, your happiness is what you should really be investing in most of all at the moment. If the cutthroat approach of the business world is getting you down, at least find a way to escape during the upcoming weekend.

7. SATURDAY. Cautious. Taking a break from normal routine gives you the opportunity to reassess key areas of your life. Concentrate in particular on any area which has been causing you sleeplessness or anxiety. This is a time to seek ways to expand your personal horizons. Both educational and travel interests could inspire you. If you have the opportunity to spend the weekend away from your usual environment, do not hesitate. Getting back to nature is likely to be particularly rejuvenating. If you are staying home and have time on your hands, today is favorable for reassessing your financial situation and working out a new personal budget.

8. SUNDAY. Excellent. This is another day for exploring greater personal horizons. Friends are likely to be an inspiration. Share your dreams with each other. It is likely that you can learn a lot from one another. For single Scorpios, a friendship which has been showing signs of turning into something a little more romantic may now do so. Relationships that have a basis of friendship can turn out to be the strongest. This is a favorable day for enjoying sports or an indoor hobby. If you intend to enter a competition, there is every chance of coming away with a prize. Just be sure to follow the rules to the letter.

9. MONDAY. Lucky. If you are traveling a long distance, plan some extra time to allow for possible delays. It is also a good idea to check your car if you are driving. It will be very annoying to be held up by what turns out to be a minor problem which could easily have been repaired. Career-minded Scorpios can now push for a pay increase if deserved. Superiors are likely to be quite receptive. This is a propitious time for bonding more closely with someone you want to get to know better. Do not hesitate to issue a romantic invitation, especially if you have been playing a little hard to get.

10. TUESDAY. Sensitive. Get up a little earlier than usual so that you do not have to rush this morning. Avoid taking your personal problems to work with you. This is one of those times when higher-ups are not particularly understanding or sympathetic. A better alternative is to take some time out for yourself in order to collect your thoughts and plan your next moves. Socializing can be a great tonic if you could do with a little less seriousness in your life. Romance is a particularly healthy escape route from the stresses and strains of the working day. If your loved one does not have plans this evening, going to a romantic movie can bring you closer together.

11. WEDNESDAY. Rewarding. You should be able to make significant progress where professional matters are concerned. This is likely to be an easier day than yesterday in the business world because you are less troubled by personal issues. It should be possible to clear away once and for all a project which has dragged on and been a burden for some time. Your boss is sure to notice your efforts. Although you may not receive much acknowledgment at the moment for what you are doing, in the long term there are rewards in store for you. Steady progress can be made with career development provided your personal goals are clearly defined and your determination does not waver.

12. THURSDAY. Stressful. It is not advisable to combine business with pleasure. Avoid being overly generous with business acquaintances and clients; you could end up having to personally pay an exorbitant bill. It is not a good idea to either borrow from a close friend or lend money to anyone you know socially. In the long term it could end up putting a strain on the relationship or even on another one which you will develop in the future, such as a romance. A new romantic partner could feel threatened by your close connections and financial obligations to someone of the opposite sex. Avoid trying to keep a secret by telling a series of little lies.

13. FRIDAY. Fair. Conditions favor meeting new people and making new friends and contacts. Keep in mind that your first impression counts. If you are invited to a formal occasion, dress accordingly. It can be helpful to discuss your ideas and future plans with friends and associates. They are apt to have some good advice based on their own personal experience. Although you want to get a personal project off the ground, there is a risk of merely dreaming about it and not doing enough on a practical level. Enlist the support of your more ambitious acquaintances. Just telling them about your goal can serve to prompt you to take action. Scorpios celebrating birthdays today are in luck.

14. SATURDAY. Manageable. This is a useful day for paying household bills. Spend some time working out a new budget. Check the kitchen cupboards to see what food supplies are in short supply. If you have run low on essentials, now is the time to replenish your stock. This should be a relaxing day; you have time to simply rest or to mull over your thoughts and dreams. Daydreaming is sometimes considered a mindless activity, but not so for you at the moment. Fleeting visions and ideas from the past few days can be developed into more concrete plans if you allow your mind to wander a little. Clearing out a closet or bureau drawer is likely to help clear your mind of trivial worries and anxiety.

15. SUNDAY. Good. Taking a step back from the hurly-burly of everyday life can do you a lot of good today. If you have the opportunity to join a health club, it is likely to be well worth the investment. Any temporary retreat will help you renew your energy. For Scorpio people with restless urges, a social gathering is sure to be stimulating. Get together with friends whose company you always enjoy. This is also a favorable day for extending your network of contacts. Whatever you normally do on Sundays, break the mood and try something a little different and off the beaten track. New experiences are bound to energize you.

16. MONDAY. Deceptive. It is unwise to pay too much attention to rumors circulating at work at the moment. Somebody who is worried about the future could get carried away and simply spread their fears around, without these being based on concrete facts. Make an effort to deal with neglected paperwork, especially if it is holding up your progress in other related areas. Someone who promised to write an important letter on your behalf may not keep their word. Do not hesitate to remind them tactfully. This might be your accountant failing to write a tax letter or a former employer or school not sending a recommendation.

17. TUESDAY. Suspenseful. Unexpected developments and changes of plan are likely to throw you off schedule. You can handle surprises better if you maintain a flexible approach overall. It is the nature of Scorpios to fixate on certain ideas and not budge. This does not serve you well, however, when change is in the air. Be willing to alter your arrangements at the drop of a hat, since it is in your best interests to do so. Otherwise you may miss out on a good opportunity. The reason for worrying early in the day may be hard to pinpoint. Fortunately, your spirits and self-esteem are likely to rise later on, giving you the courage to try something new.

18. WEDNESDAY. Happy. You should feel a lot happier about life as a fresh surge of confidence allays your concerns. This is an excellent day to focus on important personal goals. You may want to lose weight, get more physically fit, improve your image, or deepen your understanding of yourself. Whatever your aim, make them central to all that you are doing. Come up with a concrete plan. Other people are likely to give you the space you need to pursue your own interests once they realize you are serious about achieving specific goals. Friends, in particular, are a great source of support. For single Scorpios, new romantic involvement should chase away any self-doubts.

19. THURSDAY. Productive. This is a good day for developing and consolidating financial interests. Write up your expense report if you recently took a work-related trip, and settle your accounts. Today is also favorable for making purchases for the home and for buying special gifts for others. Stores and mail order companies with an innovative approach are likely to be a good source of unusual as well as useful items. If a family get-together is overdue, be the one to do the organizing. Older members of the family are sure to appreciate you taking charge, especially if they are short on the time required to make arrangements.

20. FRIDAY. Sensitive. A partner may try to persuade you to spend money on something you do not really want. It is probably not so much that the item is undesirable as that you feel the price is excessive. Do not allow yourself to be influenced by any manipulative comments if you can help it. As a Scorpio you are shrewd and incisive by nature. It is up to you to cut through attempts at emotional blackmail and speak your mind about the matter. Business and pleasure do not blend well today. If you must entertain clients at lunch or dinner, choose a restaurant to avoid overspending while getting the service you want.

21. SATURDAY. Changeable. Although this is a day of rest for many, it is a working day for some Scorpio people. The offer of a substantial reward for a little extra work put in now is great incentive to be industrious. Try to avoid getting involved in financial transactions with a friend. It could end up complicating both your lives in the future. There could be a disagreement with a certain individual who persistently fails to pick up their part of a joint bill. You have every right to be angry, but consider the best way to turn that anger into a positive response.

22. SUNDAY. Excellent. Hearing from an old friend is likely to warm your heart. This is an excellent time for getting involved in local activities. If you wish to take a larger role in your local community, consider volunteering to be on a committee and taking a greater part in school and charity functions. A gathering hosted by a relative is likely to go very well; you will probably enjoy it more than you expect. A special personal wish or dream has a good chance of being fulfilled. It is up to you to think on your feet and seize a golden opportunity. A new contact made now could become a lifelong friend. Be sure to honor a promise that you have made to yourself.

23. MONDAY. Disquieting. Work problems may weigh more heavily on your mind than they usually do. There could be an argument with a colleague who you feel has let you down in some way. Be wary of denying your feelings even to yourself. You may not agree about working methods, but it is quite likely that two alternative approaches both have something valuable to offer. A recent romantic connection is likely to be followed up today. This is a good time for showing your true colors. Do not be afraid to reveal your positive feelings toward someone you hope to get to know better. Developments in relation to your finances could be unsettling. Stick to your budget despite temptation.

24. TUESDAY. Fair. This is a profitable day for networking and making new contacts. In the business world, go out of your way to promote yourself; what you say and do is likely to be well received. Write letters and telephone people with whom you want to develop better relationships both in your personal and business life. If you have been thinking of running for elective office, this is a favorable time to do so. A financial or property arrangement can finally be concluded despite initial ups and downs. Time spent with your family is apt to be profitable in some unexpected way. Try to maintain harmony and balance in all of your activities.

25. WEDNESDAY. Good. This is another useful day in relation to family concerns. A family member who is struggling with a problem is likely to be grateful for the opportunity to talk it over with you. If you are having problems with money at the moment, it is most likely that a family member will come to the rescue. A needed purchase for the home can be made today, probably at a reasonable price. If you enjoy antiques, this is a good day for either buying or selling an item of value. Exchanges of goods, without money being involved, can be worthwhile for everyone. If traveling today, get an early start or leave late in the evening to avoid the crowds.

26. THURSDAY. Mixed. If there is work to do, volunteer to do a little more than your fair share. Your efforts are unlikely to go unnoticed. You may not necessarily receive the thanks you desire right at the moment, but be patient; long-term rewards are truly worth waiting for and are often the best. If you are trying to launch a new creative venture, it is likely to be a case of try and try again. While you may not receive the response you desire first time around, this is not an omen of continuing failure. It is probably just a case of finding the right market and being in the right place at the right time.

27. FRIDAY. Tricky. As with yesterday, do not expect too much initial success with a creative venture. This is especially true if you are learning a new technique. If artistic skills are involved, keep in mind that talent and flair are only part of the equation. Making items that you can later sell also involves a degree of business acumen, which has to be learned by trial and error. Behind-the-scenes work should be profitable. At home, keep a low profile, particularly if you have private matters you want to handle in peace and quiet. Opt for a low-key evening so that you can rest and relax. A dream may give you a clue to future action.

28. SATURDAY. Fair. A personal project should be moving along just as you envisioned. At home or at work, it is likely that you will be satisfied with your efforts. You should be able to relax knowing that things are now under control. It is a good idea to make an effort to also keep your domestic life as settled as possible. If there are chores to do, get them out of the way early in the day. The only matter that is likely to make you a little anxious is a concern about your financial position. If your future is uncertain in this respect, keep in mind that new developments will be taking place soon. Avoid any type of gambling.

29. SUNDAY. Exciting. Expect the unexpected. You are in for a few pleasant surprises. Money problems that have been on your mind could be resolved a lot quicker than you think. The opportunity to take on extra part-time work may be just the solution. For Scorpio people who have been temporarily out of work, this is a key day of opportunities. An old contact from your prior employment or a lead which you pursued a while ago is likely to finally bear fruit. This is a starred day for buying a major item for your home if you have the cash on hand or can get interest-free financing until the new year.

30. MONDAY. Demanding. This is a day for getting down to hard work. Responsibilities must not be neglected. The greater the effort you make to get organized, the easier your life will be in both the near and long term. If you are worried about the security of your job, now is the time to discuss it with your boss or another superior. Establish what your promotion prospects may be and what future benefits might be due you. It is possible that a partner has not been entirely straight with you. Discussing advance mutual plans should clear up any confusion. If an invitation does not appeal to your mate or partner, you can still go alone and have a good time.

DECEMBER

1. TUESDAY. Unsettling. Home life is likely to be topsy-turvy at the moment, probably because your partner is feeling out of sorts or worried. Do what you can to be supportive; if you are given the cold shoulder, still persist. Some warmth should seep through sooner or later. Money matters can be put on a more even keel. Concentrate on finding new ways to increase your income. If you have a major debt to clear, assess how long it will take if you make regular, fixed payments. If this is still longer than you want, consider increasing the amount if possible to free yourself of the debt as soon as possible.

2. WEDNESDAY. Rewarding. This promises to be a particularly productive day where property deals are concerned. A joint financial arrangement can be concluded. If you have been carrying a personal burden for some time, there is a good chance that it will lift now. Nevertheless, it is important to be careful with your spending. Try to organize social arrangements ahead of time so that you can buy needed supplies on sale. If you are booking theater tickets or making restaurant reservations, choose what you can personally afford. If you go out this evening, keep a close watch on your coat, wallet, and any other valuable.

3. THURSDAY. Variable. An unexpected variation to your plans is likely to be helpful. If you are applying for a mortgage or other loan, shop around. There may be new deals available, providing more advantages than when you last looked at what was being offered. Once again, be careful with money. If you believe that you have been overcharged for goods or services, it is worth putting up a fight for a fairer deal. Do not expect that getting a refund will be easy, however. A love relationship could be draining your energy. If this has been a long-term problem, consider if it is worth all the effort and anguish.

4. FRIDAY. Slow. Joint working arrangements are a big help when it comes to handling difficult, lengthy projects. If you are planning to make a major investment soon, it is important to get relevant details today. Scorpio people entering into a new partnership need to formulate the ground rules now; start as you mean to go on. Long-distance travel is likely. If you are going to be doing the driving and your route is not a familiar one, plot it out on a road map before leaving home. If you are taking a companion along with you, do not expect much peace and quiet along the way. A backseat driver is sure to get on your nerves.

5. SATURDAY. Good. This is a much better day than yesterday for making a long-distance journey, especially for pleasure. If you have children, consider taking them on a trip somewhere unusual. Even if you have to do all the driving, you should have plenty of energy and patience. Sport-minded Scorpio people are likely to have an enjoyable time dancing tonight; this is a great way of releasing pent-up energy. If you are single, dancing could also lead to meeting a new companion, particularly if you take part in partnered dancing.

6. SUNDAY. Stressful. Cultural studies and activities can be a source of much needed mental stimulus. If you want a change of scene, you may be able to combine a pleasurable trip with business interests. If you are staying home, be careful not to overdo with the household chores. There is a tendency to get bogged down in details at the moment and end up taking on more than you really want. When you get tired, call it a day. Lack of support for your new plans may make you wonder if you are proceeding along the right lines. Have faith; some of your efforts should be rewarded before the day is done, others during the coming week.

7. MONDAY. Fair. Influential people that you make an effort to contact may not be able to help you as much as you hope. This is only a temporary problem, however. If you can be patient, the situation is likely to turn in your favor before too long. Your career prospects look promising overall. This is a key time for developing plans to increase your income and status. A discussion with an older individual is likely to be useful. Obtaining an advanced degree could ensure your future success. Despite initial opposition to your ideas and plans, you are likely to emerge the winner when the dust finally settles.

8. TUESDAY. Fortunate. Opportunities to increase your income and your career prospects are likely to come your way. If you want to move into a new career field, do not hesitate to start at the bottom of the ladder. If your prospects for the long-term future are good, there is little to worry about. Besides, you are apt to advance faster than you think. A new business plan is likely to meet with the approval that you need to go ahead. If you are looking for funding, this is a starred day to go in search of it. People in high places can do much to help you. People are anxious to work with you because of your past successes.

9. WEDNESDAY. Mixed. Friendship and money are unlikely to combine easily. It is best to avoid getting too involved in business and financial matters with close personal associates. Similarly, try not to mix business with pleasure. For Scorpios who have been temporarily out of work, this should be a rewarding day. Concentrate on finding employment at the pay rate you want. There is a good chance that a solid offer will come your way. It is important to establish exactly what a new job encompasses before you agree to take it; also inquire about benefits and whether there is a profit-sharing plan.

10. THURSDAY. Disquieting. It may seem that a friend or associate is taking liberties or is taking you for granted. Selfishness in relationships should only be tolerated to a certain degree. If the balance is not there, this is the time to openly discuss the situation. Not everyone sees the world from the same serious viewpoint that you do. Nonetheless, it is only fair that your views be equally respected. Someone you think of as merely a friend may have other ideas about your relationship. Be prepared to be asked a question that you find embarrassing or at least too personal. If this does not appeal to you, temporary distancing yourself should ease the situation for a while. Guard against being talked into anything.

11. FRIDAY. Stressful. This is another day when your relationships with friends are likely to be stressful. Be prepared for a showdown over money matters or differing values. Peace and quiet is most likely to be found at home. As a Scorpio you tend to be secretive by nature, but you also need to reveal what is on your mind from time to time. Talking to a family member can help resolve any problem with which you have been struggling. Consider whether a romantic relationship which is causing you a lot of grief is really worth continuing. Do not make any ultimatums, however, unless you are prepared to carry them out.

12. SATURDAY. Successful. You need to rest and relax more than usual. Give yourself a chance to recharge your batteries. Emotional problems can use up a lot of energy. You now need to wind down due to recent emotional and mental stress. Quiet, relaxing pastimes are favored, such as reading or listening to music. If you have the chance to get completely away from routine this weekend, so much the better. Time spent in a retreat or at a health spa is likely to do you a world of good. Keeping a low profile socially gives you a chance to check out the character of someone who may figure in your future.

13. SUNDAY. Mixed. Solitary tasks are likely to be especially profitable, but do not give yourself too much to do at a practical level. Detailed mental or physical work can take too much of a toll on your energy. Concentrate on doing what you sense is good for you. The more rest and relaxation you get now, the better you are likely to feel. Contact from somebody from your past could be quite disturbing. If you do not wish to get involved in a lengthy discussion, come up with a good excuse for cutting the conversation short. The solution to a financial problem is most likely to come from a family member. Friends care but probably cannot loan you any money.

14. MONDAY. Changeable. You should be feeling in top form if you managed to relax and wind down over the weekend. Take advantage of your renewed energies. Doubts that have dogged you for a few days should start to disappear. Your increased self-confidence is likely to encourage you to reach out to others to offer them ideas or a helping hand. Useful contacts can be made in the business world and in your personal life. Avoid relying too much on any one person to provide the support you need for a new enterprise. You are likely to get better results if you discuss your plans with a variety of people. Relatives and neighbors are good company if you keep the conversation general.

15. TUESDAY. Exciting. So much that is good is likely today. Your creativity is reaching a peak. This is the ideal time to begin a new project, venture, or hobby. Scorpio people ready to make any type of long-term commitment are approaching a potent and fruitful time. Being around young people is likely to lift your spirits and inspire you. It is also important to put aside some time just for yourself. Behind-the-scenes activities should be productive. If you are hoping to conclude a property deal, let the other party make the next move. If you seem to be losing interest they are almost sure to sweeten the deal.

16. WEDNESDAY. Satisfactory. This is an excellent day for getting together with both old and new contacts. For single Scorpios there is a good chance of putting a relationship on firmer footing. A reunion is especially favored. If the flicker of an old flame is still there, consider getting in touch with the person who is on your mind. A financial investment made now is likely to bring good returns in the future. You could also profit from investments made a while ago. A compliment given to you is sure to boost your self-esteem. A purchase for the home should not be put off if you can get it on sale. Do not wait any longer to put up holiday decorations.

17. THURSDAY. Fair. Be very careful with your possessions. If you are going out in public, keep a close watch on your valuables. Keep important papers locked away somewhere safe, even if you have to pay a fee. If you are experiencing personal financial problems at the moment, it is possible that your family will come to your rescue. Associates from long ago could come back into your life, which is likely to turn out to be quite fortunate for you. They may turn out to be of particular help if you are looking for new work or ways to increase your income. Strive to keep financial negotiations private until the deal is signed, sealed, and delivered.

18. FRIDAY. Rewarding. You are entering a new period where financial matters are concerned. Scorpios hoping to obtain part-time work are likely to come upon a golden opportunity. The same applies for those who have been temporarily out of work. It is not often that opportunity comes out of the blue just when you need it most, but luck is with you today. Jump at this one before it is offered to the general public. Your self-confidence is likely to improve immensely as the result of your recent personal efforts. Give yourself a well-deserved pat on the back, and a special treat as well.

19. SATURDAY. Calm. At long last, this is a weekend when you can take life easy without the least pang of guilt. You could actually begin to feel quite restless now that the pressure is off. This is a good time for getting in touch with friends or family members at a distance. Pick up the telephone and catch up on their latest news. Do not neglect to send a thank-you note for a gift or a favor. That special person in your life is tuned in to your needs and eager to please you in every way. Be open and honest in communicating what you want or need. Even if you attend a large party tonight, you are likely to be happiest close to your mate or partner.

20. SUNDAY. Variable. This is not as good a time as yesterday for getting in touch with people who live far away. You could end up having to listen to someone's problems and troubles for hours if you get in touch by telephone. If you need to get an irritation out of your system, consider writing a letter to the person involved; do not necessarily send it, however. Reread it in a day or two. Just writing down your feelings can give you some relief. A comment from someone you thought had your best interests at heart could be quite upsetting because you are more sensitive and vulnerable than usual. It is best not to take such comments to heart. Go out of your way to avoid nosy neighbors.

21. MONDAY. Confusing. There are likely to be mixed messages in the workplace. If you are giving directions to colleagues, take the time to make them crystal clear. Double-check the details of an important document before signing it. Much as you may wish to save time, cutting corners now could cause you a headache in the long term. Focus on future plans. This is the time for taking a concrete step to fulfill an important personal dream. Relatives or neighbors may try to get you to take on some burdensome tasks. If you can bear to do so, it might just keep the peace. Otherwise say no firmly without feeling compelled to give a reason.

22. TUESDAY. Uncertain. Settlement of a financial or inheritance arrangement is likely. While matters may still be up in the air during the day, developments this evening should help to put your mind at ease. Guard against giving too much information to the wrong people. If you meet someone entirely new to you and not known to your friends, maintain a healthy, suspicious distance. It is possible that there is a meddler in your midst. A tale of bad luck may be quite genuine, but check it out for yourself. Better to be safe than sorry if you are considering giving money or other help. You do not want to waste your generosity on an undeserving person or charity.

23. WEDNESDAY. Good. If you are looking for new business, you have to put in a lot of work to get a good idea of what is in demand. Your labor is likely to be worthwhile, bearing fruit in the new year. Scorpio people planning to purchase property should see some progress being made today. If you are presented with a contract, be sure to read it in detail. The fine print could mean that you do not have quite so many rights as you imagine. It is better to find this out now rather than after you have signed it. Keep this evening open for friends who may drop by or invite you to visit.

24. THURSDAY. Fair. This should be a sociable, lively day. An invitation to go out for lunch or after work should not be turned down. Last-minute shopping can solve the problem of what to buy for one person in particular. If you are going out to a restaurant or club, be sure to keep an eye on your valuables. Do not carry too much cash in your wallet. If you are spending some time with relatives, relax and enjoy reminiscing about the past. This evening is a perfect opportunity to spread goodwill in your neighborhood, perhaps by caroling door-to-door or bringing a home-cooked gift to friends.

25. FRIDAY. Merry Christmas! Scorpios are in for a wonderful time of celebration this Christmas. It is likely to be the young ones in the family who make the day so special. For Scorpio singles, romance should add a special aura. Whether you are giving or going to a party, it ought to be memorable. If you are not with loved ones this Christmas, get in touch by telephone. A chat with friends or family members who are far away is likely to fill everyone's day with joy. If you are not with them because of a dispute that has alienated you, an apology now can be the best gift of all.

26. SATURDAY. Mixed. This is apt to be a back-to-work day, although the work involved is mostly around the home. You are likely to be especially appreciated if you do at least your fair share of household chores. Cleaning up after a party is sure to be less of a hassle if everyone pitches in. An interesting offer is likely to come your way. Money troubles that have been worrying you could be solved through the help of a family member. If you are visiting relatives you normally find a little boring, do not be surprised if nothing has changed. Going out together could add some spice to your visit.

27. SUNDAY. Manageable. You are likely to make good progress whether you are at home or on the road, but try not to exhaust yourself. Rest and relaxation are important later in the day. Try not to schedule anything hectic this evening. If relatives have been staying in your home, you may be feeling weary of their company. It is a good idea to motivate everyone to get out for a break. A nice long walk could be just the tonic to relieve tension and perk up everyone. Drop by to visit a friend or neighbor who may be lonely. If you have to return to work tomorrow, get to bed early.

28. MONDAY. Demanding. Scorpios who are back on the job after a brief holiday should be prepared to get right back into the swing of work. It is likely that new responsibilities await you as well as leftover jobs. Prioritize your tasks at the start of the day, and delegate excess work which someone else has the time and capability to handle. Squabbles with a loved one are likely to center on disagreements concerning your home life. You may feel that you are expected to do too much after a busy day at work. Gentle discussion can calm the situation before it erupts into a full-fledged argument. Recognize that there is more to do than you can possibly handle in one day.

29. TUESDAY. Pleasant. Relations with your loved one are likely to improve if you make a greater effort to be thoughtful. A weekday treat, such as going out together for dinner this evening, could do a lot to lift your spirits. Look for ways to get your relationship out of a rut; have fun together and take your differences a lot less seriously. This is an excellent day for you and your loved one to discuss your thoughts and views openly. Single Scorpios are likely to meet someone interesting at a club or group this evening. Do not be shy about introducing yourself or asking for someone's home phone number.

30. WEDNESDAY. Sensitive. This is a starred time for making new financial investments if you have money to spare. If you have debts to clear, however, work on getting those out of the way first. Be careful to guard your possessions in a public place. Scorpios in the process of purchasing property should be able to move one step nearer to finalizing the deal. Contracts are likely to be exchanged soon. Take no risks where joint finances are concerned. Thoroughly investigate any new proposition before making a commitment. Taking care of details may be delegated to you even though someone else was supposed to be doing so. At least this way you know it will be done.

31. THURSDAY. Promising. This is another helpful day where a major purchase is concerned. If you are buying with another person, be sure that you are both clear about what you can afford. The agreement does not have to be fifty-fifty if it does not suit you both. For Scorpio people settling into a new home, it is important to agree on the ground rules right away. Do not waste time talking about trivial matters. Partying can be fun tonight, but a quiet time at home with your loved one may be just as enjoyable. Greet 1999 with enthusiasm and the confidence that whatever comes, you can handle it.

SCORPIO
NOVEMBER–DECEMBER 1997

November 1997

1. SATURDAY. Easygoing. You should be able to make plenty of progress with personal plans. It is a good time for attempting to further your own aims. Conferring with relatives may be quite helpful; they are apt to have worthwhile ideas or suggestions based on their experience. You should get along well with people at a neighborhood event and could make some useful contacts there, too. If you are considering altering your image in a significant way, talk with a professional consultant. Discussing the look you want is vital if you intend to change your hair color or have any elective surgery done to improve your appearance.

2. SUNDAY. Variable. This is a day for creating a more secure financial future for yourself and your loved ones. Think about taking on extra work, which could be lucrative. You have many skills and talents that are in demand, including some which have not been fully developed; it could be exciting to work on developing these. Investment in a formal training course to help hone those skills should pay off at a future date. Home life should be quite stimulating. If housemates or family members want to borrow things from you, make sure that you do not mind what happens to them. Certain people are naturally careless even with other people's possessions.

3. MONDAY. Calm. Whatever you initiate today, you should get fairly positive results. It is a good time to reply to advertisements in the newspaper, particularly if you are looking for work. Also send application forms and proposals. If you recently applied for a grant, loan, or other funding, do not worry if you do not hear any news just yet. The administrative aspect could take some time. Check that any financial paperwork you are dealing with is in order. It is important to get figures right. Your mind is more on

230

the immediate future than on long-term plans. It is not too soon for creative Scorpios to begin making holiday gifts and cards.

4. TUESDAY. Lucky. This is one of those days when you can count on being lucky. Most of your undertakings should seem effortless. If you are short of cash at the moment, do not worry. Money should be coming your way without your having to do anything in addition to what was required last month. This is a good day to consider how to make the best use of your talents and your time in general. Happiness and contentment characterize your outlook. There should be little happening to ruffle your feathers or worry you. Bask in this time or relaxation and comfort and do not analyze it too much.

5. WEDNESDAY. Mixed. Time spent with people connected with your hobbies and interests should be rewarding. However, you can find work somewhat taxing. Colleagues may take a long time understanding basic information. Or you may have problems pinning people down or motivating them. If those around you seem to be rather slow, try to be patient. Not everyone is able to think or work at the same fast rate as you. Avoid contacting your parents, in-laws, or other older relatives. You will probably not catch them at a good time, for one reason or another. Try to postpone any prearranged socializing until a future date.

6. THURSDAY. Fair. There is a dreamy quality to all that you are doing today. It may be hard to concentrate on matters at hand because your mind is on other things. Do not forget to make important telephone calls or mail out checks which are due. There is a tendency to overlook urgent matters unless they relate to you in a personal way. Your nerves may be on edge. It is a good idea to avoid exacerbating this by avoiding beverages which contain caffeine. This is a good day for consolidating financial arrangements or negotiating a new business deal providing you do not ignore the vital details or any information contained in the fine print.

7. FRIDAY. Useful. Use traditional methods in attempting to resolve problems both in and out of work. You should meet with more success if you do not deviate from established rules. You should be able to finish up one particularly laborious task and put it behind you. If you are ready to sign a financial contract, make sure that you first read the small print. It is in your interest to be familiar with all of the details. If you have been suffering with a health problem lately, it should start to clear up today. Continue to follow doctor's orders even if you feel better. The only way to tackle a long-winded task is to plod along consistently. Do not expect shortcuts to be effective.

8. SATURDAY. Changeable. If you are fighting to get financial funding you need sound reason as the basis of your argument. Be prepared with written facts and figures to back up your argument. Time spent with your family this morning ought to be comfortable. Later today you should feel more energetic and may want to go out with friends. Try to make it easy on your wallet. Elaborate social arrangements are apt to be too expensive for you. Speculative risks in hopes of making a quick profit are not a good idea. Stick to the tried and tested. Children can get on your nerves, but it is important that you do not give in to their demands even if they make you feel guilty.

9. SUNDAY. Good. This is an excellent day for beginning a new creative venture and also for making progress with an ongoing project. Your relationships with younger people in your life should be much improved. Romance is in the air. A loved one could give you a special gift or a sincere compliment. If you are single you could meet your match at a party. There may be a lot of flirting going on between you and someone with whom there is obviously a strong attraction. You will not have any problem charming new partners. Much of this has to do with looking good because you feel confident and self-assured.

10. MONDAY. Cautious. Socially, activities today should be fun. You can make good new contacts in the business world and also in your social life. Do not turn down an invitation to a party organized by a neighbor. Work could become increasingly tense as you rush around trying to cover a lot of ground. When you are expected to juggle several projects at once it is not easy to keep everything together. Do not be surprised if you start to run low on energy by this evening. You will particularly notice this if you attend an event where you have to be on your best behavior. There is a devil-may-care quality about you, and you are tending to live by your wits.

11. TUESDAY. Fair. Work responsibilities are likely to be heavy going. You need to plod along with certain tasks in order to complete them. Becoming preoccupied with details will probably mean that you fall behind. If you are temporarily out of work, you need to again get down to job hunting. You could meet with success close to home. It is important to complete whatever you start, particularly application processes. Take time to fill out applications thoroughly, and also make an effort to get them in the mail on time. Money matters are promising. A savings scheme could start to pay off, and you should be able to hold down your spending. If you are planning a major purchase, do some comparison shopping for quality as well as price.

12. WEDNESDAY. Deceptive. It could be difficult to make any real progress with work matters, largely because you are waiting to receive vital information. There is little point trying to move forward if facts are not yet sufficiently clear. If you or your partner is going for a medical test, first results may be inaccurate; do not jump to conclusions. Schedule a follow-up test on another day. Scorpios involved in drawing up a contract should make sure that every possibility is covered. It is easy to overlook or ignore details of important consequence. Take good care of your health. It is not wise to skip meals or try to exist on junk food and little sleep.

13. THURSDAY. Changeable. Overall, your relationship with a partner should be close and satisfying. However, you may argue about basic matters such as spending or saving, moving or staying put. You need to search for some form of compromise. Try not to let a disagreement escalate into a full-fledged argument. If you are single you could meet someone very special, but be careful. The relationship may be based only on physical attraction, not on anything lasting. You need more than just a surface attraction to create a long-term relationship. However, if you take a light-hearted approach to love, a romantic fling could be fun.

14. FRIDAY. Good. You may feel that the whole world is against you. Although you know that this is a misconception, a lot of little things can get you down. You may have to battle for anything that you really want. Try to meet partners halfway. It is not helpful being too single-minded or too fixed in your ideas. A partner's hopes and dreams are very important; try to understand even if you disagree for some reason. Scorpios who are newly attracted to a special person may be up on cloud nine. While this is enjoyable from a romantic point of view, you may be overlooking vital factors such as your basic compatibility and the baggage that this person is bringing into your relationship.

15. SATURDAY. Variable. There may be a lot of talk about money-making schemes. It is important to distinguish between solid plans and get-rich-quick ideas. The latter could result in large losses, particularly if you are expected to invest a significant amount from the start. Trust your good Scorpio intuition. While you may have a lot of faith and hope in one particular scheme, be guided by your basic instincts as to possible long-term success. Look realistically at the quantity of work that may be involved in any plan for making money. Do not be overly optimistic about the amount of time that you can spare, given your regular ongoing commitments.

16. SUNDAY. Quiet. You may be thinking about the past and what is now ancient history. It is your Scorpio nature to discard what does not work in your life, sometimes leaving hurt feelings in your wake. You may feel tempted to go back and try to pick up the pieces of a failed relationship or business venture. This is justified if you feel you were too hasty or if you simply have changed your mind about something or someone. Nevertheless, consider that you may have burned some of your bridges and now have no choice but to forget those elements of your past. You are in a position to gain through a partner's good fortune if you have both come to an agreement about sharing it.

17. MONDAY. Fair. There could be a misunderstanding over joint financial matters. Try not to jump to conclusions. You are inclined to speak before you think now. It is best to negotiate your way through a tricky situation. Extra effort at work is likely to be well rewarded, if not immediately then in the not too distant future. Home and family life should be comfortable. If you have put up with a lot of hassle during the daytime, stay in and relax this evening. It is good for you to unwind and let go of the day's problems. Actually, you may not really feel up to doing much else. Get to bed early.

18. TUESDAY. Easygoing. You are likely to take a more philosophical attitude than usual to problems and difficulties, which helps to make light of them. Scorpios sometimes suffer from tunnel vision, becoming too fixated on one problem area. Ignoring it for today gives you a chance to recharge your mental batteries. You may have quite an interest in foreign peoples and lands and perhaps be thinking of taking a winter vacation or of spending the holidays abroad this year. Or it could be a sign that you need a change of scene. Getting away from routine matters is healthy. Getting together or telephoning a good friend this evening should be rejuvenating.

19. WEDNESDAY. Mixed. Recognition for your recent efforts at work could be coming your way today. This may include a bonus or extra time off which is due you. Nonetheless, it is a time when you may feel uneasy about being in the spotlight. At some level you could be doubting yourself. Try to overcome whatever reservations you have and enjoy the acknowledgement which you deserve. This is an excellent day for contacting people with whom you have a close personal bond. If you are trying to finalize a business deal, you may encounter problems. Try to be patient; other people need time to make up their minds.

20. THURSDAY. Manageable. Concentrate on matters at hand rather than planning far into the future. Thoughts of the past are apt to flood your mind and may end up being a distraction. Try to focus on the moment. Once again you may be doubting your own capabilities. Take a good look at the results you are getting and you will see that there is no real reason for underestimating your abilities. You may find it difficult to get along with authority figures who refuse to deal with you as a person. In business matters you have to respect the fact that some people only pay attention to the bottom line and can be ruthless.

21. FRIDAY. Disquieting. You may find yourself battling with authority figures once again, but today you have more ammunition than you did yesterday. However, it is not in your best interest to try to prove a point merely to satisfy your ego. By doing so you could end up only hurting your own chance for success. Do not do anything that could jeopardize your position in the long term unless you firmly believe it is going to be worth it from the point of view of personal satisfaction. Being dominated by anyone else is not in accord with your basic Scorpio nature, so you may take drastic measure.

22. SATURDAY. Variable. Putting the needs of friends before your own may mean that you end up draining your personal resources. It is important to draw the line and stick with what feels comfortable. Because you are naturally loyal to those you like, you may find yourself torn in two different directions. Light-hearted contact with various people in your life should be uplifting. This is a good day for getting out to visit, but not for spending too much time with any one person. Group activities can be pleasurable, but again, aim for light and stimulating company. You need an emotional boost.

23. SUNDAY. Confusing. Quarrels with friends and acquaintances are possible, probably due to basic misunderstandings. Once you have your teeth into a project it can be hard for you to let go. However, it is wise today to give up where someone else's problems are concerned. You are in no position to be forcing others to do anything, especially to impart information. If money matters are worrying you, sit down and work out a new budget. It may help to have figures clearly in front of you. When it comes to who owes who in a relationship, it is not worth counting. If you do not really want to do something, opt out.

24. MONDAY. Good. Quiet time to yourself can be profitable in a number of ways. On the job you are likely to get more done if you work in seclusion. You may be required to work more behind the scenes than usual. If you are feeling at all run-down, a night spent relaxing at home should help to recharge your batters. A family member needs your support at the moment at an emotional level, and you should be well equipped to help them cope. This is a favorable day for making progress with work that has been previously neglected. You may come to realize today that someone or something that hurt you in the past no longer matters.

25. TUESDAY. Unsettling. You should have plenty of time to yourself this morning and can get on with sorting out a backlog of work or other tasks. You need the opportunity also to focus on private matters. Later in the day, however, you have to cope with frequent distractions. The telephone may not stop ringing, or you could be deluged with questions from colleagues or staff members. Unless you can put yourself in an environment more conducive to head-down type of working, you are not apt to get much done. An opportunity to work from home could be the perfect solution. Any commitment made today should be put in writing for future reference.

26. WEDNESDAY. Frustrating. You are likely to have similar problems in making progress that you had yesterday. Visits from neighbors if you are at home, or from colleagues if you are at work, can distract you from what you are trying to get accomplished. You may just have to grin and bear it. This can also be a frustrating day if you are trying to carry out research and obtain specific information. Other people are likely to be cagey or evasive; in certain cases it is obvious that they are just unsure. You will benefit from being patient. What is hard to get is probably worth waiting for.

27. THURSDAY. Sensitive. You are likely to feel unsettled this Thanksgiving. It can be hard to choose any one course of action, partly because you keep changing your own mind. It may be growing increasingly clear that you need to change a long-term situation in which you find yourself. Trust your Scorpio instincts by all means. However, do not be surprised if you wind up creating a lot of upheaval in your life; perhaps it is necessary. Your urge to make your money grow is strong. Savings and investments should be your main concern, particularly as they are relatively effortless. Any form of gambling will not appeal to you very much; avoid it.

28. FRIDAY. Buoyant. The admiration and respect of your associates is likely to be quite apparent in your life. There is no doubt that you are popular at the moment. In the business world you should find it easy to persuade other people to accept your ideas or your urgings. Much of this is due to the force of your own personality. Focus on what you personally want; you have every chance of being able to get it. You may feel a desire to update your appearance or wardrobe. The advice of a professional image consultant could be useful if you do not quite know how to make the most of your assets.

29. SATURDAY. Variable. You could spend a lot of money, especially if you are doing some early Christmas shopping. You should be able to find a few unique and perfect gifts for the family. This is a good day for reassessing your overall financial situation. Some changes may be in order, particularly in the percentage between what you save and what you spend. If you have a number of various ongoing debts, such as credit card bills or school tuition, consider a bank loan to cover them all. This could help you reduce interest payments. If you find it hard either to give to people or receive from them, try to change your pattern.

30. SUNDAY. Useful. An interesting and lucrative opportunity could come your way. If you have turned your talents to a particular hobby, try to find a way to convert it into a profitable venture. You should be able to complete one particular financial action and get it out of the way. At an emotional level you may feel quite protective toward family or friends. Your care and concern are likely to be both needed and very appreciated. Scorpios working in a temporary job could soon be offered a more long-term position, which should be more suitable. You could also begin to receive the payoff for work recently completed.

December 1997

1. MONDAY. Rewarding. This promises to be a busy but pleasant day. You are apt to be on your feet much of the time. A morning meeting with business associates or clients ought to be especially productive. Make an effort to contact people at a distance in order to find out how their affairs are progressing, particularly if these have a bearing on your own. New contacts that you make today may be able to supply you with valuable information in the future. You could receive a lot of mail; make sure that you reply promptly to the most important letters. Scorpios deeply involved with a romantic partner may receive a long-awaited positive answer.

2. TUESDAY. Productive. Today is just as active as yesterday, but you may be running around a lot more rather than actually spending time with people. Be careful about what you do say to others. There is a tendency to speak before you think, and you may regret that shortly afterward. There is an impatience in all of your actions at the moment. This is of little use when it comes to routine matters, which require basic plodding. Try to balance the way you utilize your energies. Avoid trying to hurry along staff members or colleagues who clearly cannot work at a faster pace. If you are pushy they may respond by going even slower.

3. WEDNESDAY. Sensitive. There is no getting away from socializing both in and out of the business world. It is important to communicate in depth with a number of people. You will not be able to get away with sitting back and waiting for them to come to you. You need to be a major player yourself, and in doing so you have to live by your wits. Affectionate feelings are likely to be aroused with somebody special in your work life. If you are getting involved in a love relationship, the atmosphere should be very romantic today. Scorpios who have been involved with someone for a long time should also feel emotionally close and more aggressive romantically.

4. THURSDAY. Fair. There are likely to be upheavals in your domestic life. Although this is part of an ongoing situation, it could affect you more than usual. You need plenty of space and may become irritable if you feel boxed in. Nevertheless, you are apt to be considerate and understanding with the people around you. This is a favorable time for putting property on the market, with a good chance of attaining the price you are asking. If you have placed ads to sell real estate or merchandise, you may receive an excellent offer. It is important, however, to be sure that the other person's financial credentials are sound.

5. FRIDAY. Good. Home and family life are smooth and comfortable. At an emotional level you are on a more even keel. Money matters look promising, particularly in terms of achieving greater long-term security. Work efforts you put in now should bring excellent rewards. Scorpios looking for new work could be offered a lucrative proposition. Transactions which have been dragging on for a long time can be brought to a speedy close now. It is important for you to touch base with old friends and even old places. You have some unfinished business to sort out, perhaps even going back to childhood days.

6. SATURDAY. Disquieting. While you may be resourceful in creative terms, you may not have the same initiative when it comes to your financial situation. One particular social event could be costly due to having to buy a new outfit or a special gift. This does not mean you have to forgo the occasion, but it would be helpful to try to find less expensive alternatives. When it comes to romance, some Scorpios may take the view that it is not worth the effort that has to put into it, but this is probably a temporary attitude. Sports activities could be fun although exhausting; try not to overdo it.

7. SUNDAY. Pleasant. Scorpios should be feeling unusually sociable. Impromptu visits ought to be pleasant. This is a time when spontaneous arrangements suit you better than those that have been carefully worked out in advance. Accept an invitation to a cocktail-type party, particularly if it is being given by a neighbor or friend. You are likely to be introduced to some interesting new people. If you are single, going out could lead to romance. Scorpios already involved in a love relationship can look forward to a very romantic time this evening. There is magic in the air. There could be talk about becoming engaged, married, or expanding your family.

8. MONDAY. Deceptive. Be careful dealing with staff members, colleagues, and clients. Although not at a conscious level, there is likely to be some degree of deception. You could also start out on a project that looks quite simple, only to find that it is a much more complicated than it initially appears to be. It is important not to take anyone or anything at face value. Follow the maxim that warns not to judge a book by its cover. Although there may be more work to do than you expect, your efforts should produce worthwhile rewards. At an emotional level, it should be a welcome relief to get one particular task out of the way once and for all.

9. TUESDAY. Fair. Scorpio people who have been temporarily out of work could find that a well-paying opportunity comes along today. Your efforts to find new work should be very successful. If you are already employed, it is worth plugging away at routine chore even if they seem dull. The people who matter in terms of advancing your career are taking note of your efficiency and your willingness to give that little bit more. One telephone conversation today could irritate you, but try to stay calm, cool, and collected. It can be a waste of energy to lose your temper. An angry outburst could turn out to be quite detrimental.

10. WEDNESDAY. Variable. Discussions with partners ought to be useful. Where romance is concerned, a heart-to-heart talk could bring you a lot closer. Your willingness to discuss intimate feelings works to your benefit. If you have some time off this week it might be fun to take a field trip. Variety is the spice of life just now. However, if you scrap your schedule altogether you could be creating major problems. Try to keep everything in perspective. Relations with older people, especially in-laws, may be strained. This is not likely to be solely your fault; you may disagree on basic issues and not be able to find common ground.

11. THURSDAY. Mixed. The basis of your relationship with your romantic or business partner may be in question. There could be some jealousy on your part if you feel that this person is spending too much time away from you. While it is a basic part of your Scorpio nature to be jealous at times, this negative aspect of your sign needs to be controlled. Figure out for yourself what drives your jealousy. In doing so you will find a way to free yourself of it. Getting away from a constricting or stifling environment is good for you. If you are single, go out and be sociable if you want to meet a new partner. You are unlikely to be alone for long tonight.

12. FRIDAY. Changeable. You are likely to begin the day worrying about money matters, particularly if unexpected expenses have cropped up. Fortunately, your situation should improve as the day goes on. There is a chance to make your financial future more secure through new investment or new work. If you are owed money at the moment, chase up payments with true Scorpio determination. If you are doing holiday shopping and know what you want to buy, shop around for the best price. Otherwise you may be irritated to see the items you have just bought being sold for less in another store. There are bargains to be had if you take the time to comparison shop.

13. SATURDAY. Cautious. Today is somewhat the reverse of yesterday in that you start out well and then conditions can go downhill. Once again, money is apt to be the main issue. A delayed payment should turn up now, making you feel more financially secure. Write checks to cover bills that have not been paid because you did not have sufficient funds in the bank. However, you cannot yet relax about money or spend freely. Keep in mind that your income has to stretch over the entire holiday period. You can cut your gift buying expenses by making some presents instead of purchasing them.

14. SUNDAY. Frustrating. If money issues could be sorted out, you would have few problems at the moment. Discussions regarding joint finances could end up with you not getting what you want. This is not likely to be due to any lack of diplomacy or pleading on your part. Certain ongoing expenses have to be met even in this high-expense month. Your real concern is that more money seems to be going out than coming in. You cannot afford to be let down by anyone who owes you money. Try to find alternative ways of coping with this situation, perhaps by eating out less often or making do with last year's holiday outfit. The less pressure you put on your romantic partner, the more congenial a time you should have.

15. MONDAY. Slow. Try as you may, this is one of those days when you find it hard to make progress with work matters. Despite wanting to get routine tasks out of the way so that you can move on to more interesting projects, you are going to have to plod along. Completely finish the matters at hand before starting anything new. If you take time for a leisurely breakfast or lunch you will probably get behind. However, it might be better to be in this position than to exhaust yourself. Be willing to delegate part of a major assignment. Do not overdo physical activities; unusual exercise can make you feel drained.

16. TUESDAY. Misleading. You need to keep one eye on the present and one on the future in order to make life run smoothly. Information regarding travel arrangements may be misleading. It is a good idea to double-check details before you pay for tickets. If you are driving today and not sure of a route, look it up on a map rather than risk getting lost. It is also wise to consider alternatives in case certain roads are clogged or closed. It may be possible to combine business with pleasure, but do not expect that combination to be without problems. If you can keep the two apart, do so. Be wary of acting on information that comes from an anonymous source.

17. WEDNESDAY. Changeable. You and people in authority may rub each other the wrong way. If you have to confront a store manager or other in-charge person, be genuinely assertive but do not go in with an aggressive attitude. Put more effort into keeping routine matters on track. You can make a good impression on a boss by doing your job without having to be prodded, especially if he or she has to be away for any length of time. Scorpios looking for a career break should consider taking a job which involves basic work in a new field that you want to enter. You could be planting the roots of better future opportunity.

18. THURSDAY. Variable. Arguments with family members are likely. If these are about the holidays, the question of who hosts the main celebration may be the subject of more dissension than you expect. Although it is in your nature to want to be in control, slacken your hold a little where loved ones are involved. One person in particular may feel that their integrity is at stake at the moment, so tread carefully. You may actually be able to get what you want if you negotiate in a diplomatic way. Try to keep private matters separate from your working life. Otherwise you could be creating a bad impression.

19. FRIDAY. Disquieting. Some of your more important aims cannot be achieved at the moment due to lack of resources. Try not to be too disheartened. The situation should change to a more positive one before too long. If you are hoping to buy impressive holiday gifts, look at your finances from a realistic angle. As much as you may love others and want to demonstrate this in material ways, you may not be able to afford to purchase exactly the perfect gift. Try to find a compromise even though this is not easy for your Scorpio nature. An evening out with friends could be costly. Opt out of the arrangement if it means that you may later regret this expense.

20. SATURDAY. Challenging. It may seem important to attend a function organized by members of a club or other organization to which you belong. However, if the affair is going to be too costly, skip it. If you think this action could lose you friends consider whether you are having to buy those friendships. If so, they may not be really worth your while. You have the ability to overcome a major obstacle to your happiness. It comes down to pinpointing what you like and what you want. Once you are sure of this you should have little problem making major decisions. Go out of your way to please a younger family member.

21. SUNDAY. Fair. Accept an invitation to a social function. You are in the mood to get out and see other people. Also, the individuals you are likely to be in contact with can become valuable allies in the future. Also give yourself some time to be alone. This is important to your Scorpio nature. You often need time just to switch off or to mull things over. Too much time spent with other people can be exhausting. Create a balance between privacy and social interaction. You should be feeling more secure about finances now and also more confident about your personal capabilities.

22. MONDAY. Demanding. Work matters may take a toll on you. Try to find some time simply to clear your mind. If you do not give yourself a chance to recharge your batteries you could make a regrettable error. There is the possibility as well of putting your health at risk by failing to acknowledge signals that tell you to slow down or stop for a while. Family relations are apt to be a little up and down. Although there should be a lot of mutual affection, too much familiarity can breed a degree of contempt. Because you are tired you are more likely to feel irritable. Rather than take out your feelings on those you love, get some extra rest.

23. TUESDAY. Excellent. This is an excellent day for completing tasks that have either been neglected or hanging over you for a long time. Your relationships with family members should be improving. They will understand if you need some time alone. Your current sensitivity includes picking up other people's emotional signals. Because you understand what is going on, you may be able to offer support to someone who needs it but is not making a specific request. The season is a time for giving, and there is no doubt about your ability to give of yourself at the moment. Your self-confidence should soar because something you recently did is being received positively.

24. WEDNESDAY. Variable. You should be feeling festive and sociable. It is a time when you can shine at party gatherings. You are in command of any situation in which you find yourself, unless it reminds you of the past or involves a former friend. In these matters you can be caught off guard. Another problem with the past is that you may start to miss someone whom there is no opportunity of seeing again. If you start to feel very sentimental, it is important to get this out of your system in as positive a way as possible. Strive to appreciate the company of the people who are around you now. Today's Scorpio Moon creates magic for youngsters celebrating Hanukkah and Christmas Eve.

25. THURSDAY. MERRY CHRISTMAS! You will especially enjoy if you can be the center of attention or at least share the limelight. This may not be too easy, however, if you are part of a large gathering. It is important to give as well as take when it comes to socializing as well as gift giving. When important occasions arise you sometimes cannot help but feel outside the crowd. Rather than becoming irritable because you are not getting your own way, aim to make this a fun time not only for yourself but for everyone around you. Keep in mind the true spirit of the season, and practice goodwill toward all. Your self-confidence can grow from proving to yourself that you are accepted and loved.

26. FRIDAY. Fair. Your efforts to be kind and considerate toward other people are likely to pay off as you are awarded center stage. Do not hesitate to get involved in intimate conversations. Looking back to the past may have upset you recently, but today it should make you feel happy and secure. You are coming to terms with a situation you cannot change; only you can change. There is excitement in the air based on the sense that you are moving forward and are in control. Relationships with a certain family member may be electrically charged, but it is positive energy running between you.

27. SATURDAY. Positive. Whether you are working today or not, it is relaxing to be able to return to some form of routine.

This is a day for taking extra care of yourself. Indulging your sweet tooth can be almost irresistible. And, against usual conceptions, it should not be unhealthy for you to do so. One positive factor is that you are able to recognize where to draw the line. Older relatives and friends can be good company at the moment, particularly if you do not often get the chance to see them. Discuss an idea that you have been hatching in your mind. Their input can inspire you not to give up on it.

28. SUNDAY. Good. You are likely to be in the mood to please family members in order to show how much you love them. You should feel particularly happy and secure in your home environment. If you decide to go out shopping you could spot some bargains, especially in some advertised sales. Past experience is likely to be useful to you in one way or another. Do not be surprised if you have a sense of having done something or seen something before. You may hear from an old friend; there will be lots of news to catch up on. This is a good time for organizing a reunion. If you are considering a move, focus on what lies ahead and not on what you may be leaving behind.

29. MONDAY. Stressful. For Scorpios who are back at work there is likely to be a lot of catching up to do. It is one of those days when you can spend almost all of your time opening mail and on the telephone. You have the advantage of being able to work at great speed at the moment. However, one or two matters cannot be solved quickly because you have to wait for more information or special permission. Neither can colleagues who generally work at a slow pace be hurried along. Try not to worry too much about lack of organization; everything will fall into place soon. If you are able to keep track of essential details you can consider yourself ahead of the game.

30. TUESDAY. Deceptive. It could be difficult to get to the bottom of a mystery or puzzle. Information which comes your way may be quite confusing or misleading, even purposely deceptive. If you try to delve further you could still come up empty-handed. Try to take a relaxed attitude. You have no choice but to be patient for a while. A mistake that you made on a previous work assignment may come back to haunt you now. Do what you can to rectify it. If you are making social arrangements, double-check them at the last moment. It is possible that the details of a message have been incorrectly passed on to you.

31. WEDNESDAY. Exciting. A reunion with an old friend and possibly an old flame should be exciting. Some people have moved on, others have stayed much the same. Most likely the people who interest you most are the go-getters. It is possible that you will meet someone with whom you strike up immediate rapport. You may be able to get together in the future and launch an intense relationship. Where romance is concerned, Scorpios in a long-term relationship may feel that love is being reborn. If you are single you could meet somebody tonight with whom you can make your dreams come true. As you think about the year ahead, do not limit yourself in any way.

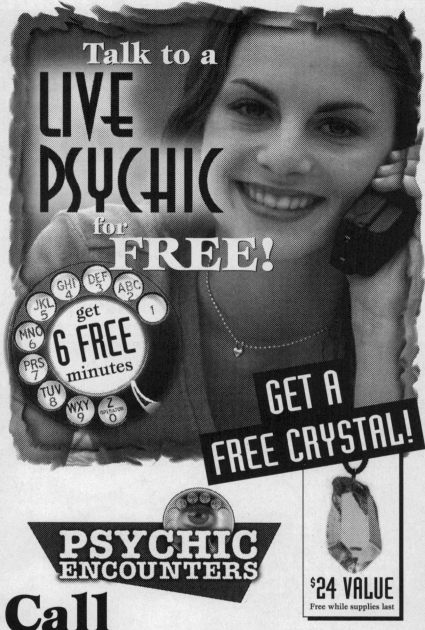